INKSTAINED

JOHN URBANCIK

ALSO BY JOHN URBANCIK

NOVELS
Sins of Blood and Stone
Breath of the Moon
Once Upon a Time in Midnight
Stale Reality
The Corpse and the Girl from Miami
DarkWalker 1: Hunting Grounds
DarkWalker 2: Inferno
DarkWalker 3: The Deep City
DarkWalker 4: Armageddon

NOVELLAS
A Game of Colors
The Rise and Fall of Babylon (with Brian Keene)
Wings of the Butterfly
House of Shadow and Ash
Necropolis
Quicksilver
Beneath Midnight
Zombies vs. Aliens vs. Robots vs. Cowboys vs. Ninja vs. Investment
Bankers vs. Green Berets
Colette and the Tiger

COLLECTIONS
Shadows, Legends & Secrets
Sound and Vision
Tales of the Fantastic and the Phantasmagoric

INKSTAINS
Multiple volumes

In Memory of
Mary Lescher

My Sabine, My Rose Fairy,
and My Inspiration.

TABLE OF CONTENTS

PART TWO
WRITING

PART THREE
EVERYTHING ELSE

CONCLUSIONS

ACKNOWLEDGEMENTS

INKSTAINED

JOHN URBANCIK

INTRODUCTIONS

INKSTAINS

What are InkStains?

They're what you get on your fingers when you use a fountain pen. That, really and truly, was the source of the name; but I'm also staining the pages with violent slashes of ink. That was the whole point.

InkStains became an annual project, a challenge to myself, wherein I wrote a complete story every day for a year. I had very few rules. Primarily, I gave myself one mandatory day off every month to be used as a sick day, vacation day, relaxation day, whatever I needed. But only one.

Another rule: the story had to be complete. It did not have to be long. It could be experimental, fiction or nonfiction, on any topic or theme or subject or thing. In the second and third years, I had monthly themes and touchstones. But the original InkStains project had and needed none of that.

Another rule: it was still today until I went to bed. If I stayed up till 3am Saturday night and then wrote my story, even though it was Sunday morning, it was still my Saturday story. Furthermore, I couldn't write a story at 11p and then, after midnight, start the next day's.

There was no writing ahead. There was no catching up. What would I do if I missed a day for any reason? I don't know. I did this project three times and never missed a day.

Essentially, it was a crazy stupid project I did as a reaction to a heart attack that failed to kill me. I realized I wasn't writing as much or as often as I should. Before anything else, I'm a writer. This felt like a natural project to take on.

I had done other, smaller projects in the past, 7-in-7s (seven stories in seven days) and the like, even the month-long challenge I called 30 Days of April. This time, I needed for it to be a year. Maybe you need less time, or need it for different reasons. My rules are not your rules. You carry forward however you want.

The Podcast

After writing two years of InkStains, and knowing I was about to start a third, I got together with the Project Entertainment Network to launch the InkStains podcast. Was it good? Technologically, there were rough patches: too much hiss, too many pops, too much noise. Though I had help behind the scenes, the audio never really became as clear or professional as I wanted.

Closing in on two years of weekly podcasts, I spoke with Armand at Project Entertainment about concluding the show with its 100th episode.

In this book are some of the best, most important, most useful stuff I talked about during that time. It's an accumulation of almost two years of advice and stories regarding creativity, writing, and I don't know what else. Some topics came easily. Some did not. I've compiled, collated, redistributed, edited (because I definitely meander when I speak, and you don't want to read that), and finally put together this collection of essays from the show.

I call them essays now. They were originally segments of the show. What you're missing are things like my Summer of Movies (I took a part time job at a theater and reviewed films I saw) and other things that don't directly tie into improving your creativity and writing skills. Not all of those things were wastes of time. But they don't matter here and now, not stacked against what I have included. In all, the transcriptions of those shows broke 175,000 words, and that's too many.

Hopefully, I've chosen the right ones to present to you here.

WHERE WAS I?

The podcast started while I lived in Tallahassee and ran for 100 weeks. During that time, I moved to a Richmond, Virginia apartment for six months before moving into a friend's house owned. A couple months after that, I moved to Madrid, Spain. This book is not in chronological order, so at any point I can be in any of these places.

WHAT TO EXPECT

The essays that follow are all transcriptions or scripts direct from the podcast divided into three sections: Creativity, Writing, and Everything Else. Theoretically, the writing section should be applicable to other arts, but I can't always promise that. The final section is a catch-all for things I thought important but didn't fit the first two sections.

Occasionally, as the author, I interject. I include some of the InkStains Challenges, designed to get your creative juices flowing and exercise your artistic muscles. I break some pieces out as little asides. I take information from multiple shows and smash them together in a single entity.

I do my best to shed what I think nobody needs.

My hope is that you can take from these essays, both the general and the detailed topics, and apply them to your own creative life. Become a better dancer, director, painter, musician, chef, martial artist, poet, artist, and writer.

IS THE ADVICE I'M GETTING ANY GOOD?

Let me just say, straight up and honest, you don't know if any advice is good. Typically, everybody follows their own path, and people often give advice based on the paths they have followed. Not all paths are necessarily helpful to you. Their goals and backgrounds may be different, they may be going to and from different places; the things they have done may be interesting, may be helpful to know, may even give you guidance for specific decisions on your own path, but none of that means they are the definitive way to do a thing. There is no one way. When somebody says *this* is what you must do, what I hear is, "I believe I know better what you think you want to do, I know better what you're doing with your path and your goals, I know better your background and skills, and my way is the only way you can do something, because any other way obviously leads to failure." Which is absurd.

There's no golden ticket to propel you to whatever you define as success. We might not even share the same definition. For one person, success isn't achieved until they've topped the *New York Times* Bestseller list for an entire summer. The best person to give them advice would be, I suppose, people who have achieved the *New York Times* Bestseller list. Go talk to one of them. Their background, their methods to get where they are currently, and where they were compared to where you are now, will be different – so not even their advice will be 100% applicable.

Other people define success as, "I would like to write a poem every day." The path to writing a daily poem, and the level of success, is necessarily judged on a different scale than in the first example.

Find what you want to do. Listen to the advice of all sorts of other people. Find out what worked and didn't work for them, then apply what might work for you.

Bruce Lee said you should learn multiple styles of martial arts so you can take what works for you and ignore what doesn't. The same is true for everything. It doesn't matter if it's how to find success as a musician, illustrator, mom, or business analyst. You learn not just from the experiences of other people, but your own goals, background, and direction. It's never the same path. There is plenty to gain from listening to other people. There's a lot of good information out there. But the best advice is that which you tailor to yourself.

I am never going to suggest that anything I say is gospel and you should follow me exactly. I'm merely trying to offer guidance, not lead you. I just want to help you on your way. I'd rather encourage than dictate what you should do.

If at any point you feel I am dictating, either you're not listening right or I'm not saying it right. I may say the wrong things in the wrong way – but at no point do I ever intend to define what is right and what is wrong. I will tell you the paths I have taken, the paths I've seen work for other people, and the paths I've seen fail. Combined with all the other people you listen to and read about and watch on TV, all the interviews and biographies, all the successes and failure of people who have tried to do the same thing you're trying to do – I hope you find what's best for you.

Ultimately, how do you know if the advice you're getting is good? Most advice is at least well-intentioned. You can follow some of it verbatim, you can be aware there's something to look at, or you can ignore it entirely because it may simply not be part of your path.

There's a lot of conflicting advice out there. There's a lot of advice that means well but is misguided. There's advice that's plain wrong. And sometimes, I fear, some of it is malicious.

The truth, or as close as we'll get to the truth, is that there's more than one definition of success. Is it a success to make art? To sell it? To rise to the stratosphere and become a household name? Is it a success to live off your art, or just to find an hour a week where you can play? There are no wrong answers. You define your own success. You define what you're aiming for. You define your intentions.

How can every available bit of advice be aligned with your intentions? Even contradictory recommendations might be wrong for you for entirely different reasons.

Further, there's no one path to your success. Look at the people who have achieved what you hope to achieve. Read their biographies and interviews, and you'll realize one thing: no two people arrived where they are by the same path.

The world is a maze. A big, huge complicated thing. There are obstacles, traps, aids, and advisors. There are things unknown, unique to your experience, and there's no map. None. Nothing that will navigate you from where you are to the end.

And yet, it's a straight line. We all move forward through time.

In writing, people will tell you how to best use adverbs, and how many stories there really are – it's a different number every other week – and how often you should use *said*. All of this is based on something – none of it on the model of your success.

We start in different places, have different allies, different talents, and different intentions. We may find our paths crossing, and we may find comfort in the advice of strangers, but the only way to know how to reach your success is to reach it.

Maybe that means fighting. Struggling and arguing and wrestling with the demons in your head. Maybe you haven't got demons, but fairies and muses. Maybe you're struggling with an emptiness inside and you don't know how to portray substance when you feel like you have none.

The people giving you advice are neither inherently wrong nor evil. They are not gurus on the tops of mountains; nor are they shining a light on the one true path. Most advice is well-meaning and even helpful, and there'll be times in your life, your artistic life and your regular life – which are really one and the same – when the advice is precisely what you need to hear.

It's up to you to discern what is good, positive advice you can use, what's good advice you can't use, and what's genuinely bad. The best way to do that is to be open to all of it, to listen to everything, to read how everyone you admire travelled along their paths, how they got to where they are, how they're moving forward from there. There's a saying that those who cannot do, teach. I think that's fundamentally wrong. A teacher's role is to arm us with the skills and knowledge we'll need to function in the world, to give us tools we'll use in the future. Teachers are our first advisors outside of our parents. Not all of them are good. Not all are bad.

I vividly recall only one thing my sixth grade teacher said to me, one thing that was possibly meant to be flippant or even dismissive. I was just discovering music at the time, and my musical tastes ranged from the Beatles to the Beatles. And I told this teacher I wanted to be a paperback writer.

He said, "Write hardcovers. You'll make more money."

It probably wasn't meant as advice. But in the early 1980s, it may have been entirely valid. Today, however, it's probably better to say, "Don't write only paperbacks. Write hardcovers and limited editions, sell to specialty presses and publish some of your own stuff, get HBO to buy series rights, and Universal Pictures to buy film rights. Diversify, little boy who wants to be a paperback writer, because the world is changing and you'll never know when one of those outlets will simply vanish."

Maybe he wasn't a good teacher like Mr. Hogan in fourth grade, who read us things like *James and the Giant Peach* and *Tales of the Fourth Grade Nothing* – read them aloud – and got me going to the library to find other books by these same authors.

The point of this is: if you're going to be a teacher, be a good one.

And if you're going to be a student, be a good one. Learn broadly, from numerous teachers and advisors, apply what's appropriate when it's appropriate. Be discerning, understand the point and intention, reject the bad advice for actual reasons.

I don't claim to be a teacher, though I've taught. My aim isn't to tell you how to do this thing you're doing. My goal isn't to give you the path. I'm on the path myself, and I don't always know how to get where I want to be.

For a long time, I've been saying I feel it; *this* is the year, this is when everything changes. The truth is, I don't want *everything* to change. I want to get closer to my success. I want to chase my dreams further down this uncertain and unstable path. Maybe this year things aren't going to magically change, but I intend to move forward in ways I've never moved before.

That, I think, is always a good intention.

InkStains: A History

My name is John Urbancik – *Urban* as in cowboy, *sick* as in puppy. I've written dozens of books, and published at least ten novels, a number of novellas, and dozens of short stories since 1999. For 100 episodes, I hosted *InkStains*, a podcast about creativity and writing, on the Project Entertainment Network. Now that introductions are out of the way, let's get to it.

In 2013, on January 1st, I opened a notepad, broke out a fountain pen, and started writing the first InkStain – a 365 day project with a complete story every day. Taking one day off every month, that's over 350 stories. That's a lot of writing. You go through a lot of cramped fingers, a lot of ink, you a lot of paper. There was no need to connect any of the stories to each other. There was no requisite length. I just went until the story was over. Some are barely a hundred words. Others are almost three thousand. It depended on how much time I had that day and how much time it took to tell that particular story. Not all stories rush to an end.

I learned a lot about writing, and my own writing process, doing this project, and I encourage you to take on your own project. I do not, however, encourage you to start with a 365 day project.

Over twenty years earlier, an online writer's group on CompuServe, the IMPs, gave me my first extended writing project: seven stories in seven days. That sounds more possible, a smaller scale than 365 days. After doing several seven day challenges with the group, I started doing them on my own. I later wrote other types of challenges: *Six Nights of Midnight*, six stories all set in my city of Midnight; and *30 Days in April*, where I went for a whole month.

At this point, I had also done other long term projects. I'd taken on a photography challenge to do a self-portrait every day for a year. My goal was threefold. One: there were few pictures of me anywhere and I needed to be more comfortable in front of the camera. Two: I needed to be more comfortable behind the camera. And three: I wanted to have a reason to use and learn Photoshop.

Some days, the Photoshop part would be simple, and I wouldn't do much more than resize the picture. Other days, I used multiple layers to portray me emerging from a mausoleum wall. I made a lot of mistakes, but that was the idea. You learn by making mistakes.

I eventually published the first year InkStains in a series of monthly books. I made no editorial choices regarding story. Every story, failure or success, made it into the books. I edited for spelling, grammar, clarity, a few things like that, but I made no major changes, I pulled nothing out, I did not say this is a bad representation of me – because it's an art project. These were never meant to be included in collections of my best work. Some might be my *worst*. The point wasn't whether or not they were good; this was an exercise in quantity over quality. The point of quantity was to learn, play, and experiment. I wrote in first person, in third person limited and omniscient, and even second person for a number of stories. I tried to make some of those second person stories apply to anyone regardless of gender, age, orientation, religion, or physical ability. I didn't always succeed, but along the way I learned how to play with words and use them effectively.

I discovered a different thought process when you write a story by hand than when you type it. It's difficult to precisely describe – but you think differently putting it down on a paper, which somehow makes it a little bit more – final, maybe? I don't know that it made me think more or harder, just differently, and in different directions. Some stories turned out really odd because of that.

I came up with the title InkStains at my Day Job. I always kept a sticky pad at my desk, and sometimes, when bored, I'd write random words – especially during longer phone meetings. I'd write words people said, or words I thought of because of something someone said. Those were generally very dull little sticky notes.

One particular afternoon, I was playing with ideas for a title for this story-a-day project. I don't remember the other variations I tried on that scratch pad of sticky notes, but I eventually discovered I had written *InkStains*, a single word with capital I for Ink and capital S for Stains. I had found my title.

Originally, I expected to have as many as three days off monthly, but I soon realized that was overdoing it. Some of these stories required as few as 15-20 minutes of writing time and could be written during my lunch hour. There were days when I sat at my desk at 11:45pm wanting to write my day's story and had nothing – not the slightest hint or suggestion. My office was filled with a number of things that inspired me, some more inspiring some days than others. One particular night, I looked at a box of Magic the Gathering cards, a game I hadn't played in twenty-something years. On the side of the box I had written "Magic Box." One InkStains story begins with the line, "I have a magic box."

When I wrote that line, I had no idea what the second line would be, never mind how it was going to end – I didn't even know who was narrating. I, the author, am very different than I, the narrator.

Some days, even when I wasn't writing, I played with ideas in my head that gestated for hours or sometimes days.

On 31 December 2013, I wrote the final InkStains story. Forever, I thought. But on New Year's Day, my fingers itched for something to do. I had been slashing paper with fountain pens for so long, they needed the work. But they also needed time away, and I needed to focus on other, longer-form projects.

At first, it was a relief. I had set a monumental goal and met it. Sure, I had done a month of daily stories and those seven day challenges. You don't run a marathon by setting out for 26.2 miles on the first day of training. You work up to it, and I did. But as 2014 neared an end, I wanted to do it again. On 1 January 2015, I began a second set.

In 2017, I wrote a third set. And I want to share this with you. Not just my stories, but the concept. The challenge. The adventure.

Though my InkStains projects are strictly stories, there are numerous other potential 365 day projects – or one-month or one-week projects – that don't have to be *written*. They can be anything. Photography. Illustrations. Fashion sketches. Culinary explorations. Songs or compositions. Poems. Cookies. Dance routines. Films. Depending on the art form, you may not be able to do your work daily, like I can with writing. Maybe you can only do your project every other day or once a week. Maybe you need collaborators. My rules are simple: one complete story daily, one day off a month, handwritten. But those are *my* rules. Your rules can be different.

InkStains is about creating a routine in your life, a routine of art and creation. Or admiration – there's no reason you can't do an InkStains project in which you go every week to a museum or gallery to study a single piece of art. Your InkStains might be to see live music every Friday for the summer. Or explore craft beers.

I'm not here to tell you what to do, and I'm not going to prescribe the ways in which it must be done. I'm here merely to encourage you to find and explore your personal forms of expression, push past the boundaries you've inadvertently created for yourself, and help you grow. Become a better, more fulfilled version of you.

All I want is your success and happiness.

IF YOU'VE NEVER DONE ANY PROJECT LIKE THIS ON YOUR OWN, I SUGGEST STARTING SMALL, WITH MAYBE A SEVEN OR EVEN THREE DAY PROJECT. START TODAY. STARTING TODAY IS ALWAYS THE BEST THING TO DO. IF YOU'RE GOING TO START TOMORROW, YOU MIGHT AS WELL START NEXT WEEK, YOU MIGHT AS WELL START NEXT MONTH, YOU MIGHT AS WELL START NEXT YEAR, YOU MIGHT AS WELL NEVER START. SO START TODAY. WRITE THREE STORIES A DAY FOR THE NEXT THREE DAYS, ONE TODAY, ONE TOMORROW, ONE THE NEXT DAY. THERE ARE NO OTHER RULES.

PART ONE
CREATIVITY

CREATION OF CREATIVITY

Once upon a time, right here on this very earth, in a cave, one of the very first cavemen picked up a rock. He looked at it and said, "Rock." This was the very first noun. The first time anyone anywhere had used a word. It was humanity's first act of creativity.

His buddy was with him. His buddy invented a word as well. A verb. The verb he invented was *Give*. "Give Rock." The first guy, all excited, gave him the rock. His buddy then bashed him in the head and killed him. Outside of the cave, he gathered all the other cavemen around, lifted the rock above his head, and proclaimed, "Rock."

That was the creation of language. And the creation of intellectual theft.

Many centuries later we got Shakespeare, and eventually reached today.

What is Creativity?

During the course of the podcast, someone asked me to talk about "something beyond understanding." That's the whole point of this, isn't it? I'm attempting to articulate something slippery and inexact and incomprehensible. I'm seeking some sliver of understanding in the vastness of this concept we call Creativity. So many theories apply, and so many techniques, because there are so many perspectives and we all look at it from our unique vantage points. We may share the experience of being human, but we've all done that in a different way. So we attack this notion of Imagination, and the application of that Imagination, in different ways. Almost none of them are wrong. Maybe it's a bigger thing than can be conceived and retained by any single mind.

But let's try. What is creativity?

Not the easiest question to answer, it doesn't have to be the most difficult, either. You can go to dictionary.com and the first definition there is just, "The state or quality of being creative." The third definition is "the process by which one utilizes creativity ability."

I think we can go deeper.

Creativity is, basically, the creation of something out of nothing. You might think we do this as artists, writers, musicians, painters, sculptors, dancers – but we're not alone. Creativity is everywhere. Creativity is all around us and everyone uses it all the time, to lower and higher degrees depending on their circumstances. Creativity is merely getting from Point A to Point B by means that are not the obvious answer. Thinking "outside the box," if you want to use corporate speak – corporate speak, by the way, scares the hell out of me. Creativity is going outside what is normal to find a new method, a new path. It was an act of creativity when sailors departed Europe seeking a route to the Indies over the Atlantic. When a computer programmer writes code – to make not just games but spreadsheets, operating systems, anything that wasn't there before – that's creativity. Cooking – culinary arts, it's right there in the name – is an art. Gardening is a form of art. Raising children – if you have ever raised children, I'm sure you'd agree.

Creativity is available to all of us, and often we tap it in less obvious ways than art.

I usually refer to Creativity meaning creative arts of some sort, because I am a writer, I am a photographer, and I've got friends who are musicians, artists, illustrators, animators, filmmakers, dancers – I'm surrounded by artist of all types, who engage in acts of creativity on a regular basis.

InkStains, the idea that you can write a story every day for a particular length of time, is an act of creativity. Here it is, the next day, and you have to do another – in my case, another story, but it could be anything. It's a forced act of creativity. That doesn't make it any less creative. In fact, it lubricates the gears of creativity inside your mind. It makes you more creative.

The more you use it, the most you *can*. It's like anything else you practice. If you want to learn how to cook macaroni and cheese, at first you might not do a good job even following the directions on that box of Kraft. They might not be terrible, but the next time maybe you'll do something better, and the next time you'll do a little better than that, until one day you find you're grating cheese fresh and making the pasta yourself to create a macaroni and cheese completely unlike that first box.

WHERE DO YOU GET YOUR IDEAS?

One question constantly comes up for writers: Where do you get your ideas?

I think Stephen King once said he got them wholesale from a warehouse in Ithaca, which I liked. I use it often when people ask where I get mine. The truth is worse. Ideas come from art I've seen, conversations I've overheard, places I've driven past, things I've heard on the radio. It comes from music, it comes from other people – a single word in a story I'm reading (or writing) can inspire something entirely unrelated. Ideas come from everywhere. I don't think it's possible to say definitively, "I get my ideas from reading Shakespeare" – because you absolutely can, but they're never limited to just that.

The thing that makes it interesting isn't the idea, but the juxtaposition of two or more of them. I often find, in the middle of a project, another idea strikes that contributes perfectly to what I'm already working on. It weaves itself in, despite that I didn't have it when I started. Or I'll develop an idea for another project I have to hold for later. If it's a short story, maybe I'll just write it out of my system. Some ideas are bigger than others. Some require only three or four pages. Those, I channeled into my daily InkStains stories. The bigger ideas, I try to use in bigger projects. Am I always right about how big an idea is? No. Ideas don't come with a blueprint and a map and schematic diagrams. Usually, the instructions are complicated, in multiple languages I can't even read, and the illustrations are unrelated. Another truth: ideas often present themselves at the most inopportune times, and often start with the question, "What if...?"

I get ideas through my eyes, through my ears, through my fingertips. I get my ideas through my senses. From everywhere and everything. And then I throw them into the pot inside my brain and let them stew, or gestate, sometimes for years before actually using them, sometimes only the two minutes it takes to grab my pen and start writing. Some ideas take more time to reach fruition.

I read a lot about other writers, about other creative artists, about other people who have accomplished things, because I'm interested in the stories of how they became who they are to reach their level of success. I pay attention to what roads from their path might work in mine. If I have not yet reached the level of success that I want, what can

I possibly borrow or steal from somebody else?

All artists get this question at some point. It's not just boring, it's impossible to answer, and all sorts of people have developed stock answers that are, essentially, jokes. Not just Stephen King. I believe Neil Gaiman, quoting someone else but I don't know who, pointed to the Idea of the Month Club. Of course, *there really is a such thing.* You can't, as a writer, get away from all the people who have great ideas for books they will never write, but maybe they'll share their idea with you and you can write it and they'd be willing to split the money.

Having the idea isn't any part of the work. The going rate for ideas is, generally, twelve for a dime. You want good ideas? That'll cost more. You can upgrade. Send me ten bucks, I'll send you a great idea for a book. Promise. The truth is, I have more ideas than I have time. I have more ideas than I have ability. My novel *Stale Reality* existed as only a title and concept for years because I wasn't ready. I was missing one vital thing: the right setting. I couldn't write the book set in New York City, where I was born, because I just didn't know the city well enough. I couldn't set it in Orlando, where I was then living, because it wasn't exciting enough a city for the project. It wasn't until after I left Australia that I connected Sydney with the idea of *Stale Reality* and finally wrote the first draft.

I've seen this question answered a thousand times, and the answers are never really the same because there's nothing concrete. Where do we creative people get our ideas? Warehouses, or the tattered souls left on our doorstep by supplicant blue jays, or some poor innocent muse we've got locked away in a cellar or attic or shed?

Inspiration is not the same as an idea. Inspiration sparks ideas. As an example, I love Van Gogh's *Starry Night.* It's one of my favorite paintings ever. It hangs in the Museum of Modern Art in New York City. I've been there, I've seen it, I've almost touched it, I was close enough to breathe its air, and it has inspired several stories – but the idea is never to *write the story of Starry Night.* You can be inspired by the painting without having to do a story about the painting.

If you read something fantastic and it makes you think of all these marvelous things you've never seen and done and heard – the book is the inspiration, but the book itself is not the idea.

I'll use one of my own examples. Many years ago, while living in Australia, I went to the eastern beaches. Between two beaches was a waterfront cemetery on the Pacific Ocean. I was taking pictures. Looking through them at home, one looked like the cover of a book. Not any book I had written yet, but it had to be the cover of *something*. A gravestone in the foreground, a bunch of stones in the background, a raven or crow prominent on one of the stones. A perfect display of clouds. It was late in the day, sunset, so there was color in the sky.

The photograph inspired only the idea that it needed to be a cover. I didn't know what for and didn't think about it much until a year later when, while pre-reading the manuscript for *Ghoul* by Brian Keene, one word leapt out at me: *necropolis*. I immediately knew that word was the title that belonged with that photograph.

I took Friday off that week, visited a local necropolis – in Sydney, we had one – and took my camera on what I called an inspiration research expedition. I journeyed to, through, and into an enormous cemetery. It was easily the largest cemetery I've ever been in – with the possible exception of one in New York City.

Sections devoted to Anglicans and Catholics, as well as old Anglican and Old Catholic sections, were the majority of it. But there were also non-denominational sections, and areas devoted to particular other denominations, like Greek Orthodox and Russian Orthodox adjacent to the Quaker section. The Orthodox were all very ornate and richly designed, while the Quakers were basic two-inch slabs of granite without any design or ornamentation – an extraordinary juxtaposition. There was a large Asian section, and long, snakelike walls containing urns full of cremation ashes. It was a fantastic trip. I discovered a lot of things I hadn't thought about in relation to cemeteries.

That weekend, I wrote the first draft of the novella *Necropolis*. The title was inspired by a word in Brian's book, but not by the story itself. That was completely mine, though I found ideas for scenes and potential plot points while wandering the cemetery. I spent maybe six or eight hours there, and it worked because I not only wrote *Necropolis*; I sold the novella to Bad Moon Books. It was published in 2007 with my photograph, the one that inspired the story in the first place, as its cover.

I think it's safe to say our ideas come from inside ourselves, from the way we see the world and how we interpret the things we see. The trick, of course, is being able to see in that way: to walk through a garden and recognize members of the dragonfly patrol on an important mission; to touch the side of a brick wall and not just feel the rough, brittle stone, but to see into the stone's dreams and memories; and to look to the clouds and say yes, that one is certainly a tiger.

Maybe it starts there, with the clouds, with our four year old selves seeing shapes in water vapors that are actually cotton candy, fairy floss, spun sugar, ghost breath, whatever you call it. Ideas don't come to creative people because they're more creative. They come because creative people tend to put effort into nurturing those observations.

In school, we're taught at an early age to color between the lines, that grass is green and the sky is blue. But creative people sometimes make the grass blue, and sometimes redraw lines or ignore them altogether. We're often discouraged from doing so, but that's exactly the kind of play – creative play – that's necessary to instill an inquisitive nature into us at an early age. That inquisitive nature is part of the creative process. We ask questions, not just *What if?* We seek answers, and sometimes make up answers that best fit our knowledge of the situation.

At the movie theater where I worked for one summer, as we were cleaning concessions and getting ready to go home, someone said something about our Slushee machine lying. It shows four flavors – red, blue, orange, and yellow – but we only sell three – red and blue and Coca-Cola. A kid had asked why he couldn't get yellow. I told him the sign is actually a remnant from the 1970s when we had all those flavors, but now we don't have any of them. Our red and blue are cherry and blue raspberry, but back then neither flavor existed. Red was strawberry and blue was blueberry. Everyone was awed by my knowledge, which of course came with age because no one else there was alive in the 70's or even the 80's. Then I said, and this is important: "I made up every single word there. You can do the same."

The truth is, I don't care about the colors or flavors of Slushees. But he asked a question – he expressed a desire to know something unknown – and my response was to illustrate that the truth behind the sign colors didn't matter as much as the story.

Maybe it was a cruel thing to do. His friends laughed at him later because I'd played him like that, but they had all believed every word because I didn't spend time figuring out what I was going to say. I didn't pre-think the story. I looked at a cloud – the four colors of the Slushee sign – I saw a shape, and I spun the story of that shape into a creative weapon that may have encouraged a bit of make-believe in the people working at concessions – and maybe tomorrow in the next kid who asks why we don't sell yellow Slushees.

When someone later asked me how I did all that on the spot, I shrugged and said, "I'm a writer. It's what I do." We can all do it. I've just nurtured and exercised my creativity more than the average person.

When I write my InkStains stories, I'm obviously exercising my writing skills – something we can all practice and improve – but also my creative talents – something else we all can nurture. Not just when we write stories or paint pictures or sing songs, but every day when we face obstacles in real life. When we face problems, financial or romantic or other, a bit of creative thinking might help find a way through. Major corporations want to hire innovative people, and innovation is the practical application of creative thought. You don't have to be an artist to be creative, and you don't have to be an artist to cultivate your creativity.

MORE ON INSPIRATION

What I want you to notice from that *Necropolis* story is the numerous inspirational points. First the picture. Then the trigger word in another person's book – it inspired the title – but the story was inspired by my experience of that necropolis, walking around, seeing what it was like, feeling it and being immersed inside that atmosphere. I wanted it to feel like a city of the dead. I was thrilled to do it, and spent the whole weekend writing – 10, 12, 14 hours a day. I wrote until it was done. The experience of the necropolis helped inspire the actual story.

Inspirations come from music, people you know, things you do, all sorts of stuff that contributes to what you're working on. Inspirations come from everywhere. Inspiration is not something I find lacking. It's all around. But there is also a difference between inspiration motivation.

Motivation is what gets you to write, to actually put words on paper or get to that typewriter or keyboard or guitar or camera or paintbrush, to keep doing what you do. What motivates you and what inspires you are likely two different things.

You can find inspiration everywhere and in any way – in the line of a song, in a word overheard at the supermarket. Everything can offer a tiny spark of inspiration. Inspirations are not necessarily ideas. The story may be going great, you may be in the middle of a project and thinking this is fantastic, and something a stranger says inspires maybe just a little sidestep or resolves an issue with a character point in the story. The inspirations don't stop just because you're working on the main idea. Inspirations, and the ideas they spark, continue to thrive even after you've started on the bigger project.

You never know what's going to set you off. As artists, it's part of our job to find inspiration. You can't just sit in the same room surrounded by the same walls, the same pictures, the same music. You have to get outside your usual self.

You can get on a plane or bus or the Long Island Railroad, make your way into Manhattan, find 53rd Street, climb to the 5th floor, and study the thick brushstrokes on Van Gogh's *Starry Night* in person. Or notice the flash of color in a person's eyes as they buy a movie ticket from you, or a slice of pizza, or whatever other no-future day job you hold. It doesn't always have to be about big journeys and grand statements.

You can find inspiration in the people you love, even if from afar. In a place, or the memory of a place. The scent of those particular flowers. The buzz of hummingbirds dive bombing the neighbor's cat. Finding inspiration is often just a matter of looking outside yourself, shifting your focus, and seeing what's immediately around you. Listen to the rhythm of traffic, catch the scent of fresh Belgian waffles, feel the weight of the world through every footstep on the parking lot asphalt of an I-95 truck stop in South Carolina. It can come from a word in someone else's book or song, the warmth of a breath on your shoulder, or the unexpected juxtaposition of two tastes.

The smallest, slightest thing can be an inspiration. It's up to you, as an artist, not to ignore it. Like opportunities, inspiration can be neglected. Unplucked, it withers and dies on the vine, leaving the rotted corpses of wasted inspirations filling your garden.

WHERE DO ALL THE INKSTAINS IDEAS COME FROM?

A LISTENER ASKED IF I GOT IDEAS FOR INKSTAINS FROM PHOTOS, OBJECTS, ART, CONVERSATION, OR JUST LIVING LIFE. AS IF THAT LIST WAS COMPLETE. THE ANSWER IS ALL OF THIS AND EVERYTHING AND MORE. EVERYTHING ENDS UP IN A STORY. EVERY CONVERSATION. EVERY LOOK. EVERY CLOSED FIST. EVERY UNSAID WORD. EVERY PHOTO, EVERY FILM, EVERY SHOW. EVERY PIECE OF ART. EARLIER THIS YEAR, A SINGLE PIECE OF ART INSPIRED TWO ENTIRELY DIFFERENT STORIES. INSPIRATION ISN'T ALWAYS A DIRECT LINE. A FRAZETTA ILLUSTRATION OF TARZAN DOESN'T HAVE TO LEAD TO A TARZAN STORY. WORDS PEOPLE SAY BECOME FUEL FOR CHARACTERS. NEWS HEADLINES LEAD TO PLOTS. THE INKSTAINS STORIES, GENERALLY, ARE SHORT, NOT OVERLY COMPLEX, AND DEAL WITH ONLY ONE IDEA. SOMETHING LONGER, A NOVEL, REQUIRES AN INTERSECTION OF MULTIPLE IDEAS BEFORE IT BECOMES SOMETHING WORTHWHILE.

MOTIVATION AND INTENTION

I've been thinking lately about motivation. Or is it intention? They're intertwined in some weird, Kama Sutra kind of way. It started when a friend posted on Facebook that they'd completed a project and sent it to the publisher. This got me thinking about all those books contracted to publishers and written to satisfy deadlines. That led to books authors are writing purely for the fans. And that got me wondering why.

Do we write a novel because the fans demand it? Do we write it because a publisher requires it?

All writers started for the same reason. We had a story to tell and a means by which to tell it. Maybe those stories were born because we read or saw something that made us think, "I can damn well do better than that." Maybe those stories were inspired by something that made us think, "There's more here to be explored."

We have stories inside us that need to get out.

In the beginning, those first stories, the first time any of us touched pen to paper or banged on a keyboard, we had absolutely zero idea what we were doing. We thought we had the means – pen and paper, typewriter, computer. We couldn't necessarily join two sentences together. We didn't understand grammar, narrative flow, or the difference between plot and story. We had no concept of structure. There were a lot of lessons ahead of us. None of us wrote the Great American novel our first time out.

We worked on our skills. We learned what to include and what to exclude. How to build suspense and suspend disbelief and breathe life into characters. We learned to borrow from real life and write what we know, and we learned to go beyond our real world experiences to explore not just what we know intellectually but what we know emotionally.

It's not like this is a race with a ribbon at the end. The first novel we write, the first novel we publish, and our last novel will likely all be written at different levels of skill and experience.

I've been going through one of my earlier novels, one whose first draft I wrote so long ago I barely remember it, with an eye toward re-releasing it. *DarkWalker* was published by EvilEye in 2012. The second book in that series was supposed to follow the next year. Plans, however, got disrupted, the publisher never released it, and I've been sitting on it for years.

Just when I was wondering how to get out of the contract tying all those rights to that publisher, they released me – and all their other authors – because their plans and intentions had changed with their business model. I never had to ask for my rights back, and I never had to extricate myself from that contract.

But I did nothing with the book. Not right away.

Eventually, I realized it was time to release the series, the whole series, beginning to end. A lot of the heavy lifting has already been done. The first two books were written and revised and ready to go.

Except they weren't.

I wrote the first book at the very beginning of the century, and last revised it sometime around 2010. The story never went away from me; I've been wanting to get back to Jack Harlow, the DarkWalker, for a long time. But when I picked up the manuscript – just to clean it up some, remove any errant typos and the like – I discovered the 2001 and 2010 versions of me didn't have the skills of today's me.

I put it aside. Almost for good. I thought it would be too much work to make the first *DarkWalker* worthy of me today. Better to let it disappear and never speak of it again.

No publisher was waving a contract at me demanding the second book. A few readers asked about it, but not in such numbers that I felt obliged. The first book could stand on its own and be done. For a brief time, I was good with that. But something changed. Something inside started whispering in my ear. I wasn't done. The story had no intention of remaining quiet. In my first editorial pass, I excised thousands of unnecessary words. I tightened the book, streamlined it, and improved its flow. I removed things that didn't need to be there, added focus to bits that mattered, and cleaned up the language to be more in line with the way I write today (2017). I whittled it down by more than ten percent, and now I'm going through it again to make sure it's clean, readable, and that it represents me.

I'm happier with it now than when I looked at it last time. I'll finish this pass later this week, and the first two books are scheduled to come out in February 2018. [Author's note: the first four books came out in

2018, and the last two are expected in 2020.]

I've learned a lot about how to write since I first wrote *DarkWalker*. I know better what needs to be included and what can be excluded. I'm strong enough to remove everything that doesn't need to be there. And I can't ignore the fact that, though few fans and no publishers are demanding these books, the story nevertheless demands to be written.

In another ten or twenty years, I'll read it again and cringe.

A Metaphor Goes Amok

When I started prepping for the podcast every week, I didn't always know what I would talk about. Same was true with my InkStains stories. Every day, I opened my notepad, broke out my fountain pen – all those little rituals with no purpose but to bring me joy – and I wrote a story.

Often, I just started writing, inspired by something I'd seen that day. *Inspired* might be a big word here. Influenced? Set off in a direction? I found a theme, a subject, a question in my everyday life, then went after it in the InkStains story. This was my usual method. I walked from my day job to a bench under a tree during lunch break and wrote about a tree's reaction when a daily visitor stops showing up. I looked out the window of my home office at the tree line and wrote about a light in the woods. I read Ray Bradbury's *The Martian Chronicles* and wrote about shiny silver rocket ships.

Some days, I had ideas too big for quick scribblings. Most InkStains stories were done in any spare twenty minutes I carved free. But I let some ideas gestate. I pushed and prodded at them, let them grow and forced them to grow. It's difficult to define exactly how much work I did consciously and how much I allowed my subconscious to tackle. The end result was a Saturday afternoon where I wrote for hours and hours until my fingers cramped, my eyes blurred, and the story was done.

Occasionally, the blank page stared at me – and I dropped my pen to paper to write any first sentence just to see where it might lead. Sometimes, those first sentences were not born, were not consciously crafted, were not imagined and considered – they were merely written.

The subconscious contributes a lot to the artistic process. Art involves thought and deliberation and precision. But the subconscious constantly works in the background, reaching in new directions, exploring other shadows, asking questions we might not be asking.

Is all of this to say artists are weird? Maybe. The point is: today, prepping for this show, I started the same way I started some of those InkStains stories. Without knowing where I was going, I set off in a direction on an exploration. I've always called writing an act of discovery.

It's always been part of my process, to allow my subconscious to work in the background. I'm not so much cultivating a garden inside my imagination as encouraging it to grow wild. That way, when I need something, I can wander the insides of my own head and pull something out – and I don't always need to wander. The blank page is the wandering. The challenge. The mocking.

I can't say I've never suffered from something like writer's block. But it's never been because I've run out of ideas. I don't always know what to do next. The story goes in the wrong direction and I'll have to pull back to figure out how it went wrong. Usually, writer's block is something external, some gunk that gets into the imagination gears and stops up the whole works. Yeah, I know, I'm throwing metaphors randomly. That's sometimes how it works. External things – like in tax season 2018 when I suddenly realized I had a massive bill – that knowledge, that obstacle, circled my head like a tornado, destroying everything it touched. The only way to deal with the so-called block was to deal with what was doing the blocking.

Sometimes, the project just isn't ready. It needs more work, more depth, more background, more character or setting, more *something*. No amount of pushing will change that. Yet sometimes all it needs is a push, gentle or violent: a day of playing in that story's world even when I don't know what's going on or why until I break through.

How do I know the difference between a project that needs to be pushed through and one that needs to be put aside? I don't. Not always. I can say it's all about experience. I can point at things I've put aside in the past and went back to finish – things like *Once Upon a Time in Midnight* – but I've also put things down, taken my lessons (and maybe wounds), and left them undone – like the *Roses Grow* trilogy, ghost stories I never published, never sold, and never finished.

Concepts, however, may re-emerge. They're still in that wild garden of imagination behind all my gears and mechanisms. Now the metaphor breaks down completely. I mean that even the failures – the glorious failures – still wait on the right moment – which may never come – to say, "Oh, I've been here all the time." Maybe the next time I sit, or you sit, with a fountain pen and a notepad open to a blank page.

Start a 3-Day Challenge

I don't recommend starting a 365 day project if you've never done anything like this before. A three day project is the perfect place to start.

The most important thing it to start.

If you're going to start tomorrow, you might as well start next week, you might as well start next month, you might as well start next year, you might as well start when you're dead. It's never going to happen. Start today.

If you want to do a three day poetry challenge. Write a poem every day. Pick up a pen now and start. It's that simple. It doesn't have to be good – remember, the point isn't necessarily quality, but to get a first draft, a sketch of a concept. You get to improve it *later*. What you might do is write three first drafts (or take three pictures or draw three sketches), take a day off, then use the next three days to revise those stories or poems, process those pictures, ink the pencil sketches. Go on, go further, go beyond. *Quantity* is important at the start. *Quality* becomes important during the revision process.

MY MUSICAL BACKGROUND

I often I listen to music when I work. I like a wide variety – not as broad as some people, but definitely not as narrow as the 20 year old version of me, though I still listen to most of what he listened to.

I create soundtracks for particular projects. I put together a list of songs or albums I think would be appropriate. They help set a mood, establish ambiance, and put me in the right head space. Provocative and evocative, they help me get deeper into where I need to be. For some people, that's simply won't work. Some artists absolutely need silence. Some writers work best when there are talking heads; when I have voices talking behind me, I can't write. When I listened to the radio, I paused during commercials or when the DJ spoke because that noise is a distraction. If there's a television on in another room, I can't work with that chatter. It doesn't resonate with me. It doesn't align with the frequency I'm on when I'm working. But music – music becomes background. I can listen for hours without realizing it. Long ago, playing CDs while I worked, I only knew an hour had passed because the CD stopped and silence filled the room. I rarely notice particular songs, often missing my favorites, but I noticed the silence. I would press play again, and maybe take a bathroom break or get something to drink. One night, I left the CD on repeat, so it just kept playing. I wrote for some eight or ten hours straight without anything more than a bathroom break.

In one of my earlier novels – one you'll never read under any circumstance I can imagine – a character asked a ghost, "What about the roses?" Because it was winter and there were roses. The ghost said, "Roses grow."

The real reason the ghost said "Roses Grow" is because I've long been a Concrete Blonde fan and this was one of my favorite songs. I thought it would be cool to slip in the title as a line of dialogue. Once there, it fit so well it became the novel's title, the first in a projected trilogy. I wrote the second book, and you won't see that, either.

I still have them, and some 60 or 70 thousand words for the third, but 20-something year old me didn't write as well as the me of now, didn't know what he was doing, and maybe put together a decent ghost story but knew nothing about structuring a trilogy. It didn't work.

But music has always inspired me, even if not always directly. The story was in no way based on that song, or any song Concrete Blonde had ever recorded, but the tiny inspiration still snuck into the story and became something greater.

When I put together my soundtracks, I usually set them up specifically for the story. If I'm writing something set in New Orleans, I'm likely to include more jazz and blues than if it's set in New York. What I put in a soundtrack today is different than what I would have done 5, 10, or 20 years ago, and it'll probably be different again 5, 10, and 20 years from now. It feeds into the moment and becomes part of the process. In a way, it's a thread underneath everything. I pick the music because it contributes thematically or atmospherically.

I know other people can't listen to anything at all. Like I said, they need silence – and there's nothing wrong with that. I've written with silence. Even silence can important to a particular project.

TOOLS

I want to talk about using what you've got. The tools of the trade. If you're a writer, you don't need fancy notebooks and thousand dollar pens. The fountain pens I use cost much less than a typical Mont Blanc, and there are pens that cost even less than that. You can buy a package of Bics for a few bucks and get a dozen perfectly usable pens.

A photographer will need a camera and lenses, so there's more costs involved. Lights cost a lot of money, but sometimes you work with what you've got. On this photoshoot this past weekend, I traveled a lot – hours to get to Jacksonville, hours to get to Daytona, and all those hours again to get back to home. I didn't bring lights. Since all the shooting was outdoors, I used natural light and natural shade to help craft the photos. (Photography is the juxtaposition of light and shadow.) When you're shooting a model, you are collaborating; the model is equally as important as you; the clothes (and their designers) are important; the makeup artists and hair stylists all contribute. All of these require someone to put time, effort, knowledge, and experience to work.

This shoot cost me only gas and time. But some of the artistic expressions we want to pursue are not cheap.

The other day, someone told me a story about a saxophone he wanted. He doesn't have one anymore but used to love it. I said go get one – which seems pretty obvious and simple and straightforward, and if you have the cash, it's an easy thing to do. I couldn't buy a brand new saxophone today if I wanted to, or even a used one, and neither could he. He was struggling. He didn't always have enough to pay the rent and all the bills. I suggested making one of his monthly bills, when possible, a contribution toward a saxophone fund. It's vital to pay rent and buy food. That's all necessary if you want to continue to live.

Living is important if you want to be an artist. To be blunt, you can't be artistic if you're dead. You have to put your physical needs first sometimes. Some people insist art must be first – you *must* do this, you *must* do that. Anyone who says you *must* do something is probably mistaken. There are times when the balance is more difficult to strike. It can be painful. It can be soul deadening. It can be numbing to have to give up time that could be spent on something exciting, engaging, interesting, and artistic. What you're really doing is trading that time for the money necessary to keep a roof overhead and food on the table, and buy that saxophone.

Finding balance is tough but necessary. Consider the tools you need to pursue your art further. Perhaps a saxophone – or a notepad, a computer, an animation desk. Maybe you need to travel somewhere. Photographers need certain lenses. Chefs may need a set of Sabatier knives. If you can't go out and buy them today, what do you need to do to make it happen?

That saxophone cost about one thousand dollars. Determine how long it will take to save that much, then make the effort. Develop a sketch of a plan to obtain whatever is required. Make a plan that is achievable, but don't hold yourself so strictly to it that you can't fluctuate from it. Things come up. Rent has to be paid; you might get sick and lose time; unexpected medical bills, car repairs, or the water heater blowing up can cause delays. But if you have a sketch of a plan, if you have an idea of your goal and how you're going to get there – it's much easier to achieve.

ADVENTURER

My business card says I am a writer, photographer, and adventurer. The first two are relatively easy: I write; therefore, I'm a writer. I take pictures; therefore, I'm a photographer. Not difficult to define. But then there's that third one: Adventurer. How do you define that now? It's not like this is the Age of Discovery and I might wander the world leading a crew into uncharted territories toward lost treasures, lost tribes, all sorts of wondrous things no one has ever seen – if not *ever*, for at least hundreds, possibly thousands of years. [Author's note: I acknowledge that "never seen" is generally from a European vantage point, inaccurate at best, and oftentimes xenophobic if not outright genocidal. That conversation is beyond the scope of this book.]

Today, there's a lot less uncharted territory out there. So what does it mean to be an adventurer in the 21st Century? I think it means being brave.

Brave is not running headlong into danger. Brave is not standing up to an undefeatable adversary or obstacle and throwing yourself at it until you die. That's foolish. That's reckless. That's not conducive to art. What would, in fact, be conducive to art is taking risks. Pushing beyond familiar boundaries. Explore horizons you've not personally seen. Find out what you're capable of, then go further. Otherwise, you'll end up rehashing the same things that have already been said and done – if not by you, then by someone before you. You don't want to do that. It gets boring. It gets dull. It's uninteresting and forgettable.

Being brave is taking on opportunities when they're offered. I was once offered a chance to move to Sydney, Australia. That's well over ten thousand miles away from both the place of my birth and where I was living at the time. It was a place where I knew no one and nothing. Of course I went. I went without hesitation. [Author's note: I later did the same thing when I moved to Madrid, Spain, and I didn't even speak the language.]

Missed opportunities turn into regrets. I would much rather regret what I've done than what I've failed to do. When I reach the "golden years" at the end of my life and am rocking in a chair outside some Florida nursing home, I don't want wonder about the things I didn't do. I'd rather tell true stories no one will believe.

I'd never been on a motorcycle, but I'd always wanted to ride. For a recent birthday, I took the course and got my motorcycle license. I don't have a lot of experience, but it's tough to consider yourself an adventurer when you can't hop on a random dirt bike to flee wicked villains trying to kill you in some Medieval castle. I should also be able to pilot a helicopter – for similar reasons. You never know.

That's what I mean when I talk about being an adventurer. It's not necessarily being Doc Savage or any other hero from the pulp novels of the twentieth century. It's about consistently expanding your personal horizons, looking beyond what you've already done, experimenting, and exploring while willing to make mistakes and sometimes fail.

Traveling

If you're listening to this episode when it goes live, I'm on the road to California – I'll be seeing new things, meeting new people and old friends, buying and exchanging books at a writing convention.

Part of the point of travel is the opportunity for new experiences. You see new places, new people, and new things. You get new vantage points – and new sparks of inspiration.

The World Horror Convention in 2013 was in New Orleans, a wonderful place if you like jazz, bourbon, ghosts, vampires, voodoo, or anything dark. It seemed to be the right city for that kind of an event. There, the nature of my InkStains changed. From the day I arrived, my stories featured ghosts, bourbon, jazz, and sex. That's what my experience of New Orleans was all about. There for a weekend, I got a limited view – I only one time got out of the French Quarter. You can't experience every aspect of a city.

Travel is not always easy. You have to select what you'll bring because of limited space – you've got a suitcase, you've got a car, only so much – and sometimes your art seems to be left behind. Dancers, for example, rarely get to do much dancing, even in business class.

We often see travel as being about the destination. We go from here to there. Airplanes excel at skipping entire swathes of the country to drop where you want to be. Interstates are also good for that: essentially straight lines from here to there, and you don't have to get off. You can pull on and off the Interstate without ever seeing the places you're passing through. You don't see where you are, only where you're aiming for.

Focus travel more on the journey, and it becomes an adventure – and fuel for an artist. Those new sparks of inspiration don't come from truck stops on the side of I-10. They come from the magic shop in the middle of a town like Galena, Illinois.

To be fair, inspiration *can* come from anywhere – even an interstate truck stop – but you're more likely to see the color of a place, the depth of it, and its breadth when you're away from what's familiar. Interstates are highways on steroids and everything is all the same. Jump off the Interstate for a gas station, it's the same gas station you would've seen 400 miles and four states back. It's the same place and the same fast food over and over again. You don't get a good idea of what's really out there.

I am planning to make an adventure later this year. The trip I'm on presently is not that kind of an adventure – I'm taking an Interstate to an airplane, I'm hopping from one side of the country to the other, and I'm only exploring that specific area.

This summer, I plan a more relaxed adventure. I'll meander a bit. Get out and do some book signings. I don't have an itinerary. What should I see? Where should I go? What should I do? Who's going to buy me dinner on the road – you?

One thing I'm sure of: I'll use the experiences of that trip to write something. Last summer, I was on a book signing tour – just a few cities in the southeast United States – and I wrote a story called *On the Road with Brian Keene*. It's mostly based on true information, though the things I don't tell are more important than the things I do. That was a real adventure: two writers in a red Jeep Cherokee, traveling from here to there, hitting every bookstore along the way.

AIMING HIGH

To celebrate Brian Keene's 50th birthday, I picked up author Wrath James Wright at the airport in Baltimore. Together, after sunset, we drove into the backwoods of Pennsylvania. If you don't know Wrath, he's a former kickboxer, he towers a good foot or two over me, he's a wall of solid muscle, and he writes very extreme horror. We could barely squeeze him into my car.

The woods were dark and mountainous. I said something like, "All we need now is a scarecrow in the middle of the road." Everything was going well until the phone, the GPS guiding us to Brian's house, the GPS that claimed we were ten minutes away, decided to – er – give up the ghost. "No Signal."

How could I not use this? In the metafictional story, however, I thought having Wrath with me would be an unfair advantage, so I wrote a solo adventure. This is how real life and fiction blur.

We did reach the party, and a number of other writers and artists were already there. I can't tell you about all the things that happened. I'm good at keeping secrets. I can say there was a lot of talk about writing, setting goals, and aiming high.

The way I see it, you should always aim high. Always try to do better than you've done in the past. Strive for what's just out of reach. If, for instance, there's a market, some anthology that sounds really cool, but they're going to pay in peanuts or exposure or some other worthless thing, is that really the first market you target for a story you just spent weeks working on, agonizing over, and perfecting? Aim high, shoot high, do more, do better.

I realize not everyone has the same goals when they write.

If you want to be a professional, if you want to make this your day job, ask why you're submit to someone who isn't paying you. There may be legitimate answers. I'm not saying there aren't. I'm not saying you can't be supportive of your editor friend. I'm not saying there's no market where exposure will help you. I'm not even saying I've never done it myself. What I am saying is: if they're not paying you money, what are you getting in exchange for your words?

When considering your long term goals, your dreams and aspirations and intentions, does this help you achieve those goals? The answer may be yes. The answer may seem like yes until you examine it. Exposure in a market that pays in exposure most likely won't deliver you into the many eyes, and it's unlikely to lead to a book deal or movie deal or a date with the singer in that band. I'm not saying it *can't* happen. I believe in impossibilities, I really do. I'm just saying it may be an impossibility you're looking at, and you might be better off sending that story to a different market that will pay you. The competition will be stronger, you'll prove more to yourself and others when you get there, and the exposure provided by a well-known paying market is substantially more beneficial than being exposed by a market nobody knows.

ADVENTURE AND THE STICKS

I forget to go out sometimes. I don't mean I forget to leave the house utterly and completely. I go for walks almost every day, even if it's just around the block – partly to explore this new place where I live, partly to make sure the blood doesn't coagulate in my veins. And I go to the store sometimes because a man needs bread and wine.

This past week, I drove to Norfolk, Virginia, less than two hours away. I didn't tour battleships and submarines, I didn't even hook up with a friend who can get me a badly needed behind-the-scenes tour of an old movie palace. I went, instead, because my partner had a speaking event at the Hermitage Museum. We spent a good chunk of time at the museum before the event; then I hid in a coffee shop as she did her museum talk thing.

This is remarkable for several reasons. I don't drink coffee. But before I get to what happened at the coffee shop, I have to tell you more about the Hermitage.

It's a house museum with gardens. An amazing lighting system was set up in the original foyer, something I'd love to somehow mimic in my own place – assuming I ever have money to buy a light again. There was much about this house I liked: Chinese art, wooden sculptures within the architectural elements, a lot of wood, and something called the Small Library.

Any house with so many libraries you have to differentiate between them has got to be a good house. The place meets my needs, and I'll be happy to live there.

I found much to be inspired by. Then, in the gardens, I found something more.

I should go back further. I've been reading some classic horror stories, like Shirley Jackson; H.P. Lovecraft, whose work always felt impenetrable to me; and Karl Edward Wagner. I mention him last because the story of his I read is called "The Sticks."

"The Sticks" features stick lattices, which I assume weren't anywhere near the size of the stick structure I found at The Hermitage.

Before I tell you what it did to me, and what happened there, I should attempt to describe and explain it properly: it's an outdoor sculptural element made entirely of *Stickwork*. The artist, Patrick

Doughtery, according to the Hermitage's website, has been combining carpentry and nature over the past 30 years to build some 250 stick structures. (Check him out at www.stickwork.net.)

At the Hermitage, the stickwork is basically a large hut. The sticks are woven around each other to create a circular structure you can walk through. This is what I entered after reading a bunch of cosmic horror stories, including, not insignificantly, "The Sticks."

The trip to the museum and gardens was great because it got me outside my usual four walls. (Admittedly, more than four walls: this house is a warren of interconnected rooms – well, four or five interconnected rooms – four walls is a common expression!) The truth is, I needed to get away, to go somewhere new, to see a thing I'd never seen before, and experience something very nearly unworldly. The stickwork was exactly what I needed.

While my partner gave her talk, I was in a coffee shop. I just happened to have a fresh, unused notepad. As luck would have it, I also had a freshly inked fountain pen. So I scribbled. I started with:

I CAME UPON A HUT MADE OF STICKS TWISTED AROUND EACH OTHER TO MAKE WALLS AND WINDOWS AND ENOUGH OF A DOORWAY I COULD SQUEEZE THROUGH WITHOUT STABBING MYSELF. INSIDE, I FOUND MORE OF THE SAME: STICKS, WRAPPED ROUND EACH OTHER TO FORM SCULPTURES, A DANCER AND A BULL AND A SICKLE MOON.

You'll notice I incorporated stuff I didn't actually see in the stickwork, in the gardens, or in the museum. The inciting incident, of course, was that stickwork, which I never would have seen if I'd never left the house.

It's important to take a day off, to explore, to go beyond the boundaries of your regular life, to find something new, exciting, invigorating, and inspiring. I forget sometimes, and I assume you forget too, so this is your reminder. Go outside and discover something.

Find something local, something within an hour's drive, someplace you've never been to or heard of.

I don't only mean the big, obvious places, like the Museum of Modern of Modern Art. Seek something small and intimate, someplace where you might find a moment for breath, for reflection, for simply seeing whatever it is that may inspire you.

It may just mean getting out of the house and using those legs to take you in a direction you don't often go. Discovery is, of course, the key. I had no idea there would be stickwork at the Hermitage when I went. I didn't really know anything – except that there was a talk I couldn't attend.

I sat in a coffee shop, though I don't drink coffee, and wrote a story inspired by, but not about, something I saw. I ordered hot chocolate and a cookie. I don't believe in stealing the space; I paid my rent.

Find something. Do as little research as you can and allow yourself to be surprised. Go to a park, go to a garden, go to a house museum, explore a neighborhood, get into that old antique shop you've never entered, wander into an art gallery. Inspiration can come in any form at any time, but it's almost always a function of apparent randomness and the collision of separate ideas.

INKSTAINS STORY:
OBJECTS NEEDED BY ADVENTURERS

FORGET ABOUT IMAGINATION AND OBSERVATION, FORGET WORDCRAFT AND SKILL AND TALENT. FORGET ALL THOSE INTANGIBLE THINGS. AS A WRITER, PHOTOGRAPHER, ADVENTURER, AND MAN, SOME TOOLS — REAL PHYSICAL OBJECTS — ARE REQUISITE.

YOU SHOULD HAVE A MESSENGER BAG TO CARRY THOSE OBJECTS. THINK INDIANA JONES, AND YOU'RE HEADED IN THE RIGHT DIRECTION.

NOW YOU'VE GOT THAT BAG, LET'S FILL IT UP.

YOU NEED A PEN. I DON'T CARE IF YOU WRITE EVERYTHING ON YOUR DESKTOP, LAPTOP, TABLET, SMART PHONE, OR WATCH, YOU MUST ALWAYS BE PREPARED. FIND A GOOD, SMOOTH FOUNTAIN PEN. REMEMBER, YOU'RE A WRITER. STYLE IS VITAL.

YOU NEED AN ASSORTMENT OF NOTEPADS. THE SMALLEST SHOULD FIT YOUR FRONT POCKET AND FUNCTION AS REMOVABLE DATA STORAGE. ANOTHER SHOULD BE AS BIG AS A TRADE PAPERBACK. YOU'RE FREE TO CARRY MORE, IN A VARIETY OF SIZES, DEPENDENT ON YOUR SPECIFIC NEEDS.

YOU NEED A PAIR OF DICE AND A LEGITIMATE DECK OF PLAYING CARDS. BE PREPARED FOR IMPROMPTU GAMBLING AND ILLUSION.

YOU NEED ROPE. OR A WHIP. A WHIP WILL ALMOST ALWAYS WORK IF YOU DON'T HAVE ROPE.

YOU NEED A KNIFE. I MEAN A FRIGHTENING, SHARP, DEADLY KNIFE, PREFERABLY A FLASHY ONE. IF YOU INSIST, A SWISS ARMY KNIFE WOULD PROBABLY BE USEFUL, TOO, BUT THESE ARE DESIGNED FOR UTILITY, NOT TO IMPRESS.

A HANDKERCHIEF IS REQUIRED IF YOU WANT TO BE CONSIDERED A GENTLEMAN ADVENTURER. YES, YOU CAN BE BOTH ROGUE AND GENTLEMAN. THESE ARE NOT MUTUALLY EXCLUSIVE.

WHILE YOU'RE AT IT, YOU SHOULD PACK A FRESH CHANGE OF SOCKS.

CARRY A SMALL ATLAS, EITHER OF STREETS OR OF COUNTRIES. DON'T WORRY IF IT'S OLD AND OUT OF DATE; EVEN NEW MAPS LIE.

Bring extra business cards.

A toothbrush.

A razor.

You should carry an old photograph of your mother. If you don't have a picture of your mom, anyone's mom will suffice.

Take your favorite book of poetry — someone else's poetry, not your own.

Your camera bag — yes, that's a separate bag — should have a remote, an extra battery for the camera, lenses for wide angle, telephoto, and portraits, and one regular everyday zoom lens. Bonus points for having an external flash and extra batteries.

Don't carry your photographic portfolio. You don't have to prove you're a photographer. However, you should always carry a copy of one book you've published, even if it is a book of photography.

It's the 21st Century. You'll need a GPS, a smart phone, spare flash drives, and a tablet of your choice. Rely on none of these.

Carry extra keys. You never know when you'll find a lock that needs one. And you can never go wrong with a good set of lock picks.

If you're reading a book — of course you're reading at least one — bring it. Wouldn't you hate to be two chapters from the end and trapped without that book in a cave with no hope of escape?

Did I mention a flashlight yet? You might take two.

Carry a stick. A walking stick, a fighting stick — it should be versatile.

You can't really carry flowers, but in a pinch, good, quality paper can be used to make origami flowers. Freshness is important, so don't fold the paper until absolutely necessary.

Don't forget your hat. Gloves. And a tuxedo. You never know when a spontaneous formal occasion will break out.

BEYOND YOUR USUAL SELF

Exploring beyond your neighborhood in search of new experiences is one great way to get new ideas. Another way, especially for writers, is to read outside your genre. You write horror? It's not a long stretch to fantasy or romance. You write nonfiction? Grab a pulp mystery novel.

Just like those same four walls, if you always read – or ingest – the same types of things, you'll be stuck repeating them. Inspiration often comes from the juxtaposition of ideas; they cannot collide if they're already intimately familiar. Read a historical novel or a true history book. Explore something that's entirely opposite to your beliefs and knowledge. You're religious? Read someone else's religious texts. You enjoy painting? Check out some sculpture. Even the animators at Disney made three dimensional macquettes of their characters so they would understand how a character looked from every angle.

That's a little off-topic. Okay, some animators now paint landscapes in oils or have set up tattoo parlors in Costa Rica.

It's always good to have depth in your own field, to know its history, to know what came before you. But it's also important to nurture a broad foundation, and break through your own limitations and pre-conceptions. Get outside of your comfort zone.

That story about the sticks: I didn't know where I was going when I started, but in the end I called it a Cosmic Horror Love Story. Which is, I think you'll admit, an odd juxtaposition – and for me, it's a mixture of ingredients I rarely play with. But it means I've read cosmic horror and I've been exposed to love stories – and, let's be fair, I've lived my fair share of both.

Not everything will work for you. Not everything will speak to you. You might find some of it distasteful or just bad. That's okay. Put it down and go elsewhere. I was once asked to name the single most important piece of literature everyone in the world should read. But that's an impossible question. There's no single piece of literature, or art, that can possibly affect everyone in that way. I can recommend individual pieces, but I often tailor those recommendations to what I know about the person asking. I'll start broadly: if you want to know fantasy, you might start with *The Lord of the Rings*. I say *might* instead of *have to* because I don't believe it's up to me. I don't have any real say in how something will impact you.

(If I had to choose right now, I'd probably go with James Thurber's *The Thirteen Clocks*, and I would read it aloud to children if I could, because it's filled with wonderful imagery and wonderful language, and is essentially an extraordinarily well-written fairy tale.)

If that's outside your norm, and you're not sure where to look when I say look elsewhere, start there.

More Travel

This past July, I took a day off in Westchester, New York. The night before, I'd gotten maybe three hours sleep before driving four hours from Necon – the Northeastern Writer's Conference – in Rhode Island. But I'm getting ahead of myself.

The week started simply. I left Tallahassee, Florida, in a car filled with books and clothes. I drove for days, making stops along the way. I met with Armand Rosamilia, who, with his wife Shelley, runs Project Entertainment Network. I stopped in a random hotel just north of South of the Border on 95 and was not carried off by the insects. I had dinner in Virginia, thank you Jeff Prettyman. And I stopped briefly in New York on my way to Rhode Island. After some fifteen hundred miles, I reached Necon and pulled into the parking lot. I was tired. Hot. Thirsty. I climbed out of my car, but didn't make it halfway to the front door before Weston Ochse emerged from another and said, "Turn around, you're taking us to lunch." By us, he meant he and his wife Yvonne Navarro. We went to the place with the best clam strips ever. (Just a few years before, Wes led us to the best razor clams in Portland, Oregon; Wes lives in the desert, so when he goes out for seafood, he only goes to the best places.)

Necon is not like other conventions. There's a lot of time to talk with old friends and make new friends, and there's only a single track of programming so you're never forced to decide between panels. I took home a stack of books and art.

While surfing couches and stealing guestrooms up and down the east coast, I made time to write InkStains stories. I made an explicit effort to keep disciplined. And I found odd inspirations on the trip.

Many years ago, I shot a photo of a freight elevator at the Museum of Modern Art. I gave my friend the only print I ever made. We had talked about modern art, our opinions on it and some of the specific pieces on display. We probably spent an hour with *Starry Night*. But I had captured this moment of an open freight elevator and said, "This, right here, is modern art. I can make a single print twenty feet wide and charge six or seven figures for it."

That print – slightly smaller – was on his desk in Westchester the morning after I returned, beaten and battered and bruised by my journey to Necon. That print stared at me, grinning and winking – I'm sure, now, this was a hallucination, despite the ten hours I'd slept after the convention. I wrote an InkStains story, based on that picture, from the point of view of a freight elevator in an art museum after it's closed down.

Later on that same trip, I spent a few nights with one of my closest friends in this industry, Brian Keene, along the Susquehanna River. I caught up with Geoff Cooper, whom I hadn't seen in years, tried Mike Lombardo's pizza and survived, and visited a friend from elementary school I hadn't seen in over twenty years. I also stumbled upon the Frank Frazetta museum.

You want to be inspired? Go to the Frank Frazetta museum. I brought home only one print. But this week alone, that picture has inspired two vastly different InkStains stories.

I was on the road over two weeks. I got a lot of work done. I also wrote my InkStains stories every day – except for my one day off every month – and I drew inspiration from the road, the destinations along the way, the people and places and art. There are always fifteen or thirty minutes when I can write a little something . And there's always – *always* – new inspirations that can spark a story.

QUESTION: WHERE DO YOU FIND TIME TO ART?

I'll be honest. I don't. I can't find time to do something as massive that. That's insane. Do you realize how big a project *InkStains* is? 353 stories over the course of a year? That's just nuts. There's no way I can find that kind of time.

So what I do, instead, is *take* time. Make time. I carve time out of my schedule. I use lunch hours at the day job. I stay up late or get up early. Individual stories might not take all that much time – some are as short as 15 or 20 minutes. Many clock in at 30 or 40, and a few might be an hour or two – or five.

But can't be a matter of finding time, because you're never going to. Something always needs to be done. There's always something demanding your attention. There's always something on the periphery saying hey, you need to pay attention to me. And it may be right. You have to pay attention to some of those other things. But you make time to do what you believe is important. If art of any sort is important to you, you will make the time. It might be tough. There are occasions when it's not just *seemingly* impossible but *actually* impossible. It's okay to take a break when you need it, and it's okay to deal with external obligations. The point is not to let any of that bog you down. You can make time in your schedule. Maybe not every day, maybe not every day for year, but you can do something on a regular basis. I know you can. I have faith.

QUESTION: HOW DO YOU MAINTAIN MOTIVATION?

There are times when you feel like you must make art or you'll burst from not doing it. Write or die. Blow that horn or stop breathing. One thing or the other must happen.

Other times, however, are tougher. You don't seem to have that motivation. You're no longer a locomotive barreling down a track; instead, you're pushing that locomotive up a hill. Should you continue pushing? Take a break and seek other inspirations?

That's one thing I do. I'll read a book, something I hadn't read before, maybe outside my own genres. I'll take on new experiences or a new adventure of some sort. I'll go zip lining, or walking alongside the beach. There are plenty of things to do. Museums. Films – where you can study the filmmaking techniques, not just watch it for the escapism. You're an artist. Pay attention to what other artists do, even outside your field. Pay attention to the choices they make.

When you're watching a film – say *Casablanca* – don't just fall for the storyline or the love affair. Watch Rick's transition. See if you can spot the precise moment when he transforms from who he was at the beginning of the film (and, in flashbacks, the moment he became that man). Question and understand the choices in lighting and shot composition.

A lot goes into filmmaking and story writing and music making and dance and everything. It's not just about the final piece – I mean, it is definitely about the final piece, and it's important to present a seamless finished piece whose parts aren't obvious and blatant. But, as an artist, it's part of our job to play the mechanic, take it all apart, and figure out how it works together.

When I examine the process of, say, filmmaking, which is not something I've done a lot of, it inspires me, re-motivates me, and gets me going back onto my own projects.

Nurturing Creativity

I believe we are all born creative. We this innocence at birth, and curiosity. These are important tools in developing creativity. Then we go to schools – institutions designed like assembly lines intent primarily on producing good workers – not creatives, not good people. This is not how most teachers think, but a systemic function of the institutions. Others have discussed this kind of thing much more than I will. I don't want to focus on these shortcomings. I want to focus on the fact that, even after going through such institutions, you can still foster your creativity.

If you think you lack creativity, or merely feel a need to expand yours, there are things you can do.

One of the most important things is to seek *experiences.* Experiences are the parents of creativity. You write, you paint, you sing, you dance, you act – about things you've experienced, positive or negative. Everything in your past is fuel. This is what you draw upon. This is what inspires and motivates, and this is what you use to make those creative ideas become a reality.

Start using those experiences as fuel, and you'll find the more experiences you have, the further you can go. Somebody once suggested you shouldn't write a novel until you're at least in your 30s. I don't know if that's true – age is irrelevant, and there's a lot of craft to be learned by writing no matter your age or life experiences – but that's what they were talking about. You can't write about life if you haven't actually lived one.

Another method for increasing your creativity is to ingest creativity as part of your experiences. Read more books, watch more films, visit museums, watch live shows. Do interesting and find what inspires you. If you're a musician, other performances will fuel your motivation. If you're a writer, read extensively, not just in your genre. Watch more films. If you're a filmmaker, be aware of what other people are doing and or what others have done. Look at the history of your favorite art forms. There's hundreds of years of experience already available for you to draw upon.

If, for example, you're interested in film or photography, its history stretches further back than its existence. Early photographic portraiture was often staged to mimic the styles of paintings. Study the influence of

Renaissance masters on early fashion photographer Edward Steichen. If you're writing in the horror genre, you might be inspired by writers from 20 or 30 years ago, but they were inspired by writers 30, 40, and 50 years before, and them by the generation before, until you reach beyond Shelley and Poe to find similar themes in Shakespeare, Sophocles, and the tales of Gilgamesh. You can find a lot by looking backwards – and looking around you now, at what's going on today – not just in the art, but in your life, in everybody's life, in the news – don't just limit yourself to the headlines. Dive deep. Examine articles in *The New Yorker* or *The Atlantic Monthly.* Understand what other people think and why. Writers should be able to show the other sides of issues. Try thinking like somebody who doesn't think the way you do. That's what you're doing as a writer: putting yourself in the shoes of somebody else.

I recall Billy Joel in an interview saying he can write a song about Vietnam veterans and their experiences, not because he shared them, but because he talked to people with these experiences, and he empathized. There are a lot of ways to communicate; if you can't interview someone, read about the things they've done, watch films or biographies. You can spend hours with documentaries on the history of New York City before writing about New York; it might be helpful to know not just the names of the neighborhoods of the city, but who they were name for and what these people stood for. Who was Stuyvesant? Carnegie? Astor?

Don't forget to pull from your own experiences. Your experiences, as unique as they are, are often universal. They touch upon the same ideas, emotions, fears, and joys everybody else knows, even if their specific experiences are different. Use all of it, and find ways to express it. I don't think this is an extraordinarily difficult thing to do, but it needs to be nurtured. Do it frequently, and frequently enough that it becomes second nature.

Living the Artist's Life

What is the artist's life, and how do you live? What are its secrets?

Loaded questions, don't you think? Are we asking for the secrets of living as an artist, or are we asking how do we live more creatively? It might be semantics, but I'll approach the latter – because how we live as an artist is bogged down by all the stereotypes of what an artist is – the black shirts, the clove cigarettes, the bottles of whiskey, coffee shops with Moleskines filled with poetry scribbled hastily and often in incomplete fragments – or paint splattered all over your fingers – living on the road, going from show to show with a guitar on your back. Those artist lifestyles have not just been imagined, they've been thoroughly romanticized.

Let's forget about all that for a moment. What is it to live a creative life? Creativity is a lot more than just being an artist. I had a conversation with a person at my day job the other day. She insisted computer programming was not an artistic endeavor. That depends on how we're defining *artistic endeavors.* Is it an act of creativity? Yes it is. Do you create *art* with it? Not necessarily. Some of those programs being coded by people in cubicles in office parks across the world are purely functional. They're not necessarily what you consider art. Yet, they are acts of creativity.

Anytime you engage in problem solving, you are performing an act of creativity. Applying creativity is how you solve issues. To get from Point A to Point B sometimes involves thinking outside the box. And I hate saying things like *thinking outside the box.*

What are the secrets to living creatively? What do you need to do to really be a creative person and think innovatively? One answer is persistence. Don't stop. A martial arts teacher once told me a black belt is just a white belt who never gave up.

There's a story – I don't know if it's true – about Picasso being asked in a bar to draw something on a napkin. He did something in just a minute or two and said, "That'll be one million dollars." Or something. I don't remember. She protested. "That's only a few minute's worth of work." He said, "Yes, but I used a lifetime's worth of experience." That's persistence – you a lifetime's experienced learning, finessing, perfecting, and acquiring your skills.

Determination goes hand in hand with persistence. If you have a goal, artistic or commercial, it could help to create a plan and follow it until you can get from Point A to Point B. It's also important to deviate from that plan as necessary because of unforeseen obstacles.

Another important aspect to living creatively is to always be *on*. Pay attention. Observation is a huge part of what creative people do. I have a collection of notepads. *Collection* is not quite the right word, because I don't display them. I have drawers full of notepads of all sizes, shapes, and colors for various and myriad purposes. Small ones that fit my jeans pocket so I'm always carrying a notebook. Bigger books for particular projects. Even larger for when I need note-taking. The point is to always have one, or almost always, so you're able to record anything that inspires you. When you have an idea, jot it down – you can't always be scribbling these things napkins – under certain circumstances, napkins are perfectly fine, and if you have nothing else, use that damn napkin.

Finally, be prepared to be motivated, be prepared to be inspired, be prepared to be challenged, and face those challenges head on. Be brave, too. And bold. Luck favors the bold, luck favors the brave, and luck also favors the fool – so you've got that going for you as well.

INKSTAINS ABOUT FOOD?

Can you do an InkStains challenge focused on food?

The answer, obviously, is of course you can.

You can do an InkStains challenge about almost anything, any kind of art you want, so culinary arts to count. For a three day challenge, you can make three new meals. You can eat at three restaurants you've never dined in before. You can stretch this to every other day for six days – on day one, you go out; day two, you stay home; day three, you go out; etc.; on day seven, decide if you want to do it all over again. InkStains don't have to be writing exercises. They can be anything. There are no requirements. No rules. The rules, if they do exist, are: what can you do to expand yourself, expand your own horizons, expand the depth and breadth of your knowledge and experience, to become somebody more than you are now while learning to do something you've never done. What's important is the pushing of personal boundaries.

ANOTHER ART CHALLENGE

I AM A WRITER, BUT ALSO A PHOTOGRAPHER. THESE TWO FORMS OF ART DO NOT NECESSARILY COINCIDE. THEY USE DIFFERENT PARTS OF MY BRAIN, THEY USE DIFFERENT PARTS OF MY EYES, THEY USE DIFFERENT PARTS OF MY FINGERS. SHOOTING A PHOTO IS NOT ANYTHING LIKE WRITING A STORY.

HOWEVER, THESE ARE TWO ART FORMS I'VE BEEN DABBLING IN FOR DECADES. THERE ARE OTHER FORMS OF ART WHERE I AM NOT SO EXPERIENCED. FOR INSTANCE, I HAVE NOT HAD A LOT OF PRACTICE WITH MUSIC. I LEARNED THE RECORDER IN THIRD GRADE LIKE EVERYBODY ELSE ON LONG ISLAND. I PLAYED THE TRUMPET BRIEFLY. AND EVEN THE XYLOPHONE ONE WEEK IN MIDDLE SCHOOL — AND I WAS AWESOME. I WOULD HAVE BEEN AN EXCELLENT XYLOPHONE PLAYER. UP THERE WITH ALL THE OTHER FAMOUS XYLOPHONE PLAYERS.

OBVIOUSLY, I DIDN'T MAKE A MISTAKE BY NOT CHOOSING THAT DIRECTION. OR MAYBE I DID. PERCUSSION IS STILL A THING THAT USES DIFFERENT PARTS OF MY HANDS AND DIFFERENT PARTS OF MY BRAIN. IT'S STILL AN ART FORM. AND IT CAN GET ME MOVING. RHYTHM IS ACTUALLY VERY IMPORTANT IN BOTH PHOTOGRAPHY AND FICTION.

ANOTHER FORM OF ART I DON'T DO A LOT WITH IS MAGIC. I AM NOT VERY GOOD WITH CARD TRICKS. I AM NOT A DEFT COIN PERSON. I CANNOT MAKE A WOMAN DISAPPEAR — I MEAN, I CAN, BUT THAT'S NO GREAT TRICK. I CANNOT DO THINGS WITH ROPE, EITHER. THE BEST I CAN DO WITH MAGIC IS ENJOY IT. ILLUSION IS GREAT. I WROTE ABOUT THE DIFFERENCE BETWEEN ILLUSION AND MAGIC IN ONE OF MY NOVELLAS. *POCKETFUL OF SMOKE, FISTFUL OF GLASS* WAS A PLAY ON THE WHOLE SMOKE AND MIRRORS THINGS WHERE AN ILLUSIONIST HAD TO DEAL WITH AN ACTUAL MAGICIAN CHASING HIM.

MUSIC AND MAGIC AND EVEN ILLUSTRATION ARE ARTS I AM NOT VERY SKILLED AT, BUT I STILL PLAY WITH THEM OCCASIONALLY. I THINK IT'S IMPORTANT TO PLAY ARTS OUTSIDE YOUR FORTE.

MAYBE YOU DON'T NORMALLY DRAW, YOU'RE NO ILLUSTRATOR. BUT MAYBE FOR THREE DAYS, YOU SHOULD TRY DRAWING SOMETHING, MAYBE FASHION SKETCHES, MAYBE ARCHITECTURAL SKETCHES, MAYBE FLOWERS. IT'S VALENTINE'S DAY, FLOWERS ARE GOOD.

QUESTION: DOES WRITING
ENERGIZE OR EXHAUST YOU?

This assumes art can't do both simultaneously. I'm energized, first, by numerous other arts. I find inspiration in so much already out there. I am energized by own persistence, my determination, and the images in my head – characters and places and scenes and conflicts, the wonder of it all – and I go until exhausted. I go until I've given everything I've got and physically cannot do more. Then I do it again. Both energized and exhausted during the process.

It's a beautiful kind of exhaustion. When you've given everything, when the reserves are empty and you're laid flat because you have nothing left to offer – that kind of exhaustion is bliss. I hope you can work till you experience it. I hope you experience that energy, too.

Even going to conventions, seeing other people and talking to them, re-energizes me and leaves me physically exhausted. These two states are irrevocably connected.

WRITER'S BLOCK

Do you or someone you know suffer from Writer's Block? That immense weight that is an inability to be creative, to think coherently, to produce anything worth producing?

Sure, everyone feels the pressure of Writer's Block. But let me tell you a secret. It's not even a little known secret. All the best professionals do this one thing. When Writer's Block comes: they don't suffer it.

They get on with their work. They get over it – this Writer's Block – *then* get on with their work.

Let's define this a little. I'm not talking about what happens after your spouse or father or daughter dies. That's grief. You deal with the grief, and I can't begin to tell you how. I'm talking about something not tied to grief, not tied to financially induced stress, not tied to overzealous bosses assigning tasks clearly outside your area of expertise. Those are different kinds of problems that require different kinds of solutions. I'm sorry, but none of what I'm saying here will help you *heal*.

I'm talking about the moment you sit in front of the blank page or blinking cursor, when you've got the guitar in hand and only a monotonous strumming, when the brush hangs limply in your fingers and the canvas stares back like an abyss and laughs.

I'm talking about that stupid thing that stops you from moving forward and probably doesn't even exist. Not a lack of ability – but a lack of ability in this *moment*. I'm not talking about the self-proclaimed *auteur* who has been wrestling with Writer's Block for the past three years and hasn't written more than 500 words on their damn novel.

I'm talking about Writer's Block. True writers, artists of any kind, do not *suffer* Writer's Block. They deal with it.

Your personal method of "dealing with it" may differ from mine and the person's next to you. What it comes down to is this: your creative battery is low. Wasted. Out of energy. Fortunately, creative batteries have been forged with the best available technologies and can be recharged. This may mean getting out of your own headspace by reading something else, watching a film, browsing a gallery, enjoying the fruits of someone else's creative labors. It might mean a change of environment, a trip to the country (or the city), even if only for an hour for a walk. Introduce yourself to a different perspective. See things you don't always see. Spend five bucks on a fidget spinner and spin to your heart's content.

But recharge those creative batteries.

Sometimes, it requires a short break. This is not suffering Writer's Block. This is dealing with it. If you tend your batteries, if you make an effort to keep them always charged, if you seek out other music and other tastes, if you selectively expose yourself to all the various stimuli bombarding us daily – I don't mean by reading about it on Facebook, but by involving your own blood and sweat – you will not merely stop suffering Writer's Block, you can probably avoid ever having to deal with it at all.

When you're working on a project like InkStains, daily stories or self-portraits or sketching architectural designs – I've designed my version of this project with a mandatory day off every month that is a built-in opportunity to recharge. Take advantage of your own kindness here. You won't always need that day for a sick day or to ride the rails up the Atlantic coast. You can use it to give your creative batteries the kind of kick that prevents them from stalling. Then, when the blank page stares at you, when the canvas mocks you and the song remains unsung, you can take a breath to clear your head, lean in, and get down to business.

QUALITY VS. QUANTITY

I don't get asked about this often. I feel like I should. Someone should walk up to me and state, categorically, that this idea of writing a story every day for a year is absurd. Because it absolutely is. They should tell me there's no way all of these stories will be good. Because they're absolutely not. They should tell me the idea of quantity should never be put over quality.

That might give me pause. Not because it's not true.

When I write these stories, these short stories, these little flash fictions I call InkStains, I average under a thousand words a day. That may sound like a lot to you. If you're not a writer, it's an immense number. Count them all up at the end of the year, that's over three hundred thousand words. By hand. In a handwriting practically indecipherable to the average eye – and to many above-average eyes.

InkStains are exercises. I admit, I have packaged and sold some in monthly volumes. Because they're also an art project – and the covers admit include everything is included, failures and successes alike. Above all else, InkStains is an exercise in discipline. Can I steal the twenty or thirty minutes required every day to write a little *something* for an extended duration? Some of these stories are bad. I admit it. I wouldn't read those on this show. Yet, while some stories are successful, some fail as stories but are successful experiments.

Because InkStains is not merely an exercise in discipline. I have played with language, with metaphor, with sound, with point of view. A project like this, an exercise where the end goal was never to sell any particular story to a particular market, allows room to play, to experiment, to write that second-person point of view action adventure that relies heavily on the personification of rocks and excessive consonance. When most of these exercises can technically be considered throw-aways, there's no harm in devoting one to synesthesia, attempting a story without visual cues but only smells, trying your hand at poetic prose, or crafting a memoir from your own life about something that never happened.

Throw away all the usual rules. Play with ideas and concepts, not just for the stories themselves but in the way you approach writing them, the way you attack them, the way you massage them into something potentially greater than the sum of its parts – or something that fails to coalesce. *Even from the failures, you learn.*

That's part of the point as well. Writing these daily stories is an exercise not just in discipline, but also in building and honing the tools at your disposal. Until you've purposefully overdone a metaphor, you run the risk of not recognizing when you've done it inadvertently. You run the risk of your top choice market sending it back with a big ugly red *Rejected* stamp.

The InkStains stories are *practice.* The only way to learn a thing, to become good at it, to become a master, is to practice. Daily when you can. With discipline and rigor and intention. This applies to more than just the arts. You can easily adapt what I've just said to illustration, to animation or to sculpture or to cooking, but you can also apply it to spreadsheeting and office filing and accountancy and law. The more you do, the better you'll do it. Quality versus quantity is a poor dichotomy because it's through quantity that you attain quality.

ART IS HARD

The idea of leaving for an adventure is thrilling when you're stuck dealing with obligations and responsibilities. Some people's lives can be considered an adventure. Think Indiana Jones, the archeologist – but you forget the scene when a crowd of students demanding his time forced him to flee out his office window.

Responsibilities are like that. They'll crowd you and haunt you and stalk you. They're like hungry little beasts in the real world. They'll erode your energy and your strength and your vitality.

The trick is to figure out how to maintain that vitality, how to reclaim your own energies and focus them on your art. This is not an easy thing. Those obligations can be mighty and overwhelming.

I'm talking, essentially, about making time for your art. Even when you have no spare time, find a way to build it into your schedule. That's what the InkStains project has always been about: making my writing an obligation. Forcing me to answer for my time and ability.

What I've found is simple. The more I create, the more I want to create. The act of making art feeds itself. When I'm writing a novel, I have ideas for other novels. When I'm writing the daily InkStains stories, I never run out of story prompts. Objects in motion and all that.

Conversely, inertia begets inertia. It's easy to not write, to not paint, to not sing. It's easy to turn on the television or collapse under the weight of your day job or run the kids to soccer practice and karate and high school dances. It's easy to do all of that and not do your art. The less art you make, the less you want to make. Objects in motion and all that. If the motion is away from the art, you move away from it.

Writing is hard. Art is hard. I don't mean hard like digging ditches. I don't mean hard like engineering corporate mergers or defending accused criminals in court. To do anything, and do it well, is hard. It involves effort. It involves sweat. It involves sacrifice. Sacrifice is never easy.

At the end of the day, if you've taken time to make some art, you've created something tangible. Something real. It doesn't even matter if it's good. You've attempted something, worked on something, and completed something. In society today, it's easy to focus on making money. I'm not going to say there's anything wrong with that. Money's necessary. It's required. You need cash for the essentials: food, shelter, medicine, and the like. To maneuver through this world requires money. You will have to make decisions around that need.

But there's a point where the making of money overrides the making of art – not just for individuals, but for society – making it even harder to choose to make art. It's hard to choose to write or sing or sculpt when it goes against the apparent norms of society. It's hard to be an artist.

It's hard, but it's worthwhile. It's satisfying. It's enriching. It adds depth and breadth to your everyday experiences. It allows you to pursue a truer version of yourself, and to see a truer version of the world.

It can be very hard, sometimes, when the news is filled with death, violence, destruction, and chaos. When politicians seem to act directly to your detriment. When friends fail to understand. When family doesn't want to be supportive. It can be hard when everyday realities draw you back to a harsh, cold, vicious world. But those may be the times when you most need to make art. Those may be the times when you most need to look internally. Those may be the times when you most need to remember that life, even when it's harsh and cold and vicious, is also beautiful.

Art reflects the beauty and the cruelty of the world, and therefore becomes the best means of preserving our culture and history, of showing the future who we were and what we did and what was important to us, as well as how we reacted when things didn't go our way. There's probably nothing more important than that.

ARTISTS ARE MAGICIANS

I've heard writers compared to gods – not gods in real life, not disguises for Zeus or Odin or anyone familiar, not even characters from *American Gods* – but when their characters pray to a god, they're praying to the writer. Which seems entirely wrong. I don't consider myself a god. If so, I'm especially cruel, and I don't think of myself as a cruel person.

However, I do think of myself as a magician.

Not a David Copperfield kind of a magician – although we share a birthday. More like a sorcerer. A wizard. Not in the sense of Merlin or Dumbledore or Gandalf. Nor Dr. Strange or Dr. Fate or any other character you can think of.

But writing stories is a kind of magic. Writers create whole worlds with a twist of their fingertips. A few special words in the right order, abracadabra, presto change-o, you've transformed mere ink and symbols into beauty, terror, hope, and awe. The magic wand has been replaced by a fountain pen. Incantations have become paragraphs and scenes. Words, simple everyday words available to everyone to use, paint places, rooms and homes and cities and worlds; and also people, human people, fantasy creatures, and science fiction aliens, complete with failings and faults, hopes and dreams, biases and beliefs.

Created out of nothing.

Nothing.

What else can this be, but some sort of magic?

Musicians are the same. With a set of strings, a rod full of holes, or a pair of sticks and a stretched bit of skin, a musician can conjure melodies and harmonies and rhythms and songs that can reflect or incite the deepest, scariest, and most wondrous emotions within us.

Illustrators and painters are the same. With lead, graphite, dye, ink, chalk, and oils, they connect a series of lines, straight lines and curved lines, until they take on form, capture a moment of stillness or a frame of activity, and evoke a scene, a person, and a story. They do this with nothing but canvas and a few practiced slashes of color.

Artists are magicians.

A magician who practices, who hones their skills, who works

diligently on achieving perfection in the illusion, can build anything.

If you wonder why you do this, why you practice whatever form of sorcery you dabble in, maybe I can't tell you. For me, a big part of it is the magic. We, as artists, create something from nothing, using tools that at first glance seem ill equipped. A mere pen to build a world.

A great many sorcerers came before me, some of them masters in their arts. Edgar Allan Poe. Robert E Howard. Ray Bradbury. Salman Rushdie. Neil Gaiman. Haruki Murakami. Some, as you see, are still alive. There's magic being tapped from all corners of this earth. Not merely sorcerers. Alchemists. Miracle workers. Oracles. Storytellers.

It's no wonder I write so often about types of magic and the things that surround it, the mythologies, histories, and mysteries of it all. From a young age, we're taught to write what we know – which is both excellent and terrible advice, a topic for another day – and I'm gullet-deep in magic.

As sorcerers, whether adepts or masters, we need to practice our arts. We need to study our craft and hone our skills. This can be done through classes, practice, how-to books and videos, and thorough examination of the spellcraft of masters who came before us.

You also learn through critique. Not just the critique of your work, which can be enormously helpful, but through your critique of others.

The most important thing to remember when it comes to critique is that everyone has an opinion, everyone's opinion is valid, and no one's opinion overrides that of the artist. If a person suggests something may be wrong with a particular section and offers a solution, they may be right about something being wrong but not about the solution. If a dozen people look at something and have issues with the same part, then probably something isn't working. You have several options when a person gives you a critique: accept what they say and make the changes they recommend; accept what they say and make your own damn changes; or acknowledge what they say and make no changes whatsoever. In the end, it's your work and no one else's.

When critiquing someone else's work, you get an opportunity to see what works and what doesn't work, and you'll likely see how that's reflected in your own spellcraft. If you notice someone relying heavily on the word *very*, which oftentimes add nothing, you'll likely pause when you start to write the word in your own work. You'll ask yourself, "If this didn't work in that other story, why do I think it will work here?"

Maybe the answer is yes, it does work here, so you use it and go on. But you paused and asked the question. You chose deliberately.

You sharpen your skills not just by having someone react to your art, but by examining your own reactions to the work of others. It can be difficult – very difficult, even – to find a good critique partner or group. But long ago, in the dark ages before universal internet access, I found one. (A library sent me to a bookstore where the owner was a writer gathering like-genre writers.) Today, you can find a group on Facebook.

FOCUS

Focus seems easy. As a photographer, either you focus on the subject or the shot is bad. But that's not necessarily true, and nowhere near a complete picture. [Author's note: Groan with me at my terrible word play!]

What you focus on is a decision. Consider two people in a movie scene, one near the camera and one in the distance. Their relationship is established by the framing of the shot. In a visual medium, elements like this can and should contribute to the story. What you show the viewer is an image, even if it's not static, and you have to choose. It's not a red pill, blue pill kind of decision, but where you want to focus the audience's attention.

You might focus on the character in the foreground or the one in the background. You might, during the course of the shot, shift your focus, perhaps to reflect the rising importance of one of those characters in this scene or the diminishing of the other's.

You're deciding what the audience should see. This is true in filmmaking, this is true in photography, and this is even true in poetry and prose when you choose what to show and what not to show.

Sometimes, what you don't show can be just as important as what you do.

There's a thing in photography called selective focus. When a person in a photo is framed and in focus but the background is out of focus – that's selective. That's usually a decision on the part of the photographer. By changing the aperture, you change the focal length of the shot and determine how much to show and not show. You blur the less important elements.

You've seen that picture of the sailor kissing the woman in Times Square? Galf a dozen other people are clearly visible in that picture, and dozens more behind them, all out of focus, all providing ambience, scene, story, and background to the photo. But only that couple is in focus because that's what photographer Alfred Eisenstaedt wanted you to see. (If you're interested in the story behind that photo, Google it.)

The men breaking for lunch on a steel girder high above New York City? The city is not in focus because it's not the focus of the photo; but without it in the background, it's just a bunch of guys on a beam.

Focus is only one tool by which you compose your shot, but it's possibly the most easily visible. And focus is important beyond just the photographic arts. In fiction, for instance, I'll give you an example of poor focus: spending five pages in a book describing a door and its history despite that it will be opened just this once and never seen again. By giving it that level of focus and attention, you're implying it's somehow important. The door matters. There's story weight attached to this door; and we, as readers, damn well better be paying attention. When there's no pay off, when it turns out that door isn't important at all and those five pages were just flowery description for the sake of flowery description, you've drawn our focus erroneously away from what is important – the story, plot, and characters. You've basically just taken a portrait in which the background is in focus and the subject, even if perfectly framed, is out of focus – but not for any purpose.

When you choose, no matter your medium, to focus (or not focus) on a particular element, do so with deliberation and intention. You should not do so because you have your camera set to autofocus. You should not do so because you don't know any better. Happy accidents can happen, but if you're relying on happy accidents, I'm not sure you're actually trying to make art.

INTEGRATION

In my mind, it's nearly impossible to separate the various arts. They're all interconnected. I could spend hours trying to sort it out, trying to explain the similarities between sculpture and martial arts, between piano and pastels. But it's probably best if I go with a single illustration of it.

I'm going to use *Baby Driver*. The movie, directed by Edgar Wright, incorporates music more tightly into its script than any other I've seen. More so than a lot of music videos. I blame Dave Thomas, of The Horror Show with Brian Keene, for pushing me to see this. I went alone, in a lonely theater in the middle of the Florida swamps. It was intense. It spoke to me. I identified with Baby.

I'm not going to spoil anything. I will say Baby suffers from tinnitus and they illustrate it so beautifully, and so explicitly, that I recognize it in myself – the high-pitched buzz he hears all the time, that he needs the music to drown out – I have it, too, albeit not so constantly.

Maybe I play the music too loud. Maybe my tastes are too diverse. Depending on my mood, I can listen to torch singers like Stacey Kent, classic rock like The Who, much of the best stuff from the 80s that I grew up with, pop stars like Kylie Minogue, blues, jazz, modern rock, even a bit of rap.

I listen while I'm working. While I'm writing. Which is why I don't listen to a lot of rap music – t's too close to spoken word. I don't listen to the radio when I work because commercials and deejays disrupt me. Music, however, does not. Music becomes background. Soundtrack. I know some people cannot listen to music while working. Everyone has their own way of approaching the work, and no one way is better than any other. Hell, I don't even approach every project I work on in the same way.

Often, I'll put together project soundtracks. I'll throw songs into a mix to play while I work. I pick songs that can somehow inspire the project, or at least work off the same energy.

When I'm working, music is a secondary activity. It falls into the background. Every once in a while, though, I prefer music as a primary activity. When I go to a concert. When I'm sitting on the couch in my office with the lights down and a glass of bourbon. During *Baby Driver*, the music wasn't merely a soundtrack; it didn't play a subservient role to the visuals. It was integral. The music was the film, absolutely and thoroughly. I'm not sure I was ready for that. I watched, but I need to go back and specifically listen.

There's a lot to learn through the study of arts other than your own. I watch video essays on film production, in part for the parallels between the construction of a movie and the construction of a book. Not physically – film and paper are not the same – but the structures underlining the plots and the development of characters. Lighting in film directly correlates to what you, as an author, choose to accentuate in your prose. The way Edgar Wright integrated music into this film makes it unique, and offers a lot of opportunity for exploration on paper.

But I won't explore the specifics of the film and the music. I will, instead, explore some integrations of my own.

INTERCONNECTIVITY

I'm a story person: a writer, wordsmith, and poet. I play with words, with ideas, with characters, and themes. I'm constantly striving to be better than I am, or better than I was. I always want to do more than I've done.

With that in mind, I often read books about writing, like Tom Piccirilli's *Welcome to Hell: A Working Guide of the Beginning Writer*, Richard Layman's *A Writer's Tale*, or Stephen King's *On Writing*.

But I'd be foolish if I only paid attention to people who write in the fields I write. In fact, I'd be foolish if I only listened to writers. So I've read books on the creative process of dancers, models, and tight rope walkers – Philippe Petit's book *Creativity* wasn't about his walk between the Twin Towers in 1974, but the creative process which led to that and other adventures.

When I'm wasting time on YouTube, eating lunch or taking a brief break, I watch film analyses – the things wrong with Peter Jackson's *The Hobbit*, the things right with *The Matrix* – because story beats in film work the same as they do in fiction. But also, so does lighting.

Lighting, in film, sets a mood, directs the audience's attention, and reveals or keeps things hidden. Writers do the same thing in fiction. Painters do the same thing on a canvas.

It's another creative process. I'm all about encouraging creativity, and also learning how it works for other people. Though we all function differently, we function within the same parameters, the same overall ideas, the same tools.

I also play. By play, I mean I make maps. I'm terrible at mapmaking, but I do it anyway. I've tried figure drawing. I'm terrible at figure drawing. I have attempted pastels and charcoal, edited video, and mixed music with varying degrees of success. If I have one place where I feel like I'm working on mastery, where I can really shine, it's my writing.

So why do I waste my time with other artistic pursuits?

Good question.

Let me think.

Maybe I'm just a Renaissance Man, like da Vinci, and I need to excel at a variety of things. That might even explain my rudimentary interests in science and technology. But I'll never be a master painter or inventor, and it's an unlikely title for anyone born in 1970.

I'll try again.

Maybe creativity is a muscle, and we can exercise those muscles in all sorts of ways. We don't have to just put pen to paper to work creatively. The more we work, and the more broadly we reach, the stronger all those muscles become. We improve as writers when we understand photography. We improve as musicians when we understand filmmaking. There's a level of interconnectivity between all these things, not always so obvious as the connections between dance and music. These connections can be personal. But you can make those connections and improve your writing, even if it means spending a few hours studying Faberge eggs or watching videos about Spielberg's use of long takes.

OBLIGATIONS

You might not realize this, but I am under obligation to write my daily InkStains stories.

I am not obligated to a publisher. No editor watches a calendar and points out the days demanding new words for each and every. No one is publishing these but me. I consider InkStains an art project rather than purely writing: a challenge to my discipline, and an exercise for my skills and talents. There's no discussion around big New York conference tables about my timetables and ability to stick to them.

Which is a shame, really. External obligations can be quite motivating. "Get us that group of words by this date, and you'll get a check for this amount." Even artists have to eat, and everyone has to find their comfort zone between art and commerce.

I have an obligation to Project Entertainment Network to get my show produced, uploaded, and available by a certain time. If you haven't met Armand Rosamilia, he's a big guy, quite imposing, and he's from New Jersey. I've never seen his bad side. Maybe he doesn't have one. *Maybe* I can take him in a fight – but we'd probably both get hurt, so why risk it? I also have an obligation to you, the listeners. [Author's note: this is no longer true; the podcast concluded with its hundredth episode. Armand still hails from New Jersey.]

I'm talking about the actual InkStains stories. No one waits at home for me to turn in pages every night, threatening me with a paddle if I don't. I'm not e-mailing stories to an online vault to keep attack drones at bay.

There's absolutely no external obligation to write my InkStains stories. Theoretically, I can skip writing today and no one will complain.

No one, that is, but me. Because I do have an obligation. To myself.

When I first took on this challenge, it wasn't a test of whether or not I could accomplish it. Before the first year of InkStains, I'd dealt with major health issues, I worked a full time day job that required at least forty hours every week, and I wasn't getting a lot of writing done. Yet, the year before the InkStains, I managed to write five novellas and almost a sixth, but it was too short to be called a novella. It sounds like more now than it felt like then. Going into 2013, I felt like I'd not been focused, that I'd forgotten who I was and who I was meant to be, that I hadn't been true to myself.

I often refer to InkStains as a challenge, but in truth, it's a promise. A promise to myself to not lose focus. A promise to remember who I am and nurture that side of me. A promise to never again lose track of me or my vision.

Fulfilling that promise involves more than merely writing my InkStains stories. But as artists and creators, it's important to have something to focus on. It's not enough to want to write a novel. You have to set parameters. But there's no need to be unrealistic. If you know you can only write for an hour a day one day every week, then set aside that hour and aim for a target.

I use targets rather than quotas because I disagree with the idea that it's a failure if you don't make two thousand words – or whatever the intended goal. If you write half that, because it's been a tough week, you've still made progress and that's a very real kind of success. Maybe you'll find an extra half hour to squeeze in more time next week. The important thing is setting that goal and striving for it.

Someone once said if you shoot for the moon and miss, you still reach the stars. (Weird, considering how much further all the stars – even our sun – are from us.) Here's a variation: Aim high, and you may not reach your goal but you will still reach higher; aim low, and you will succeed – so congratulations on that?

The thing that makes goals effective, however, is having some means to measure them. If you aim for one to two thousand words weekly, with a longer goal of completing a novel in a year – from fifty-two to over a hundred thousand words – then, provided you fulfill this obligation to yourself, you'll write that novel.

It's hard to look at and accomplish the long goal. Write a novel? That's insane! It takes too long. It's much more possible to look at short goals and accomplish them. Every two thousand word week brings you closer to that novel.

"It Feels Like Failure"

I was on a spectacular road trip. In Nashville, my nephew, aka *The Baritone*, performed his final undergraduate concert before leaving to work on his Masters in music at the Boston Conservatory. Then Indianapolis for Mo*Con. (I didn't realize I'd be driving through Louisville the day before the Kentucky Derby. That – wasn't as bad a mistake as it seems.) Though an exhausting weekend, it was basically a family reunion – where maybe you bring parts of the same family together who haven't yet met. We all have the same interests, and it was fantastic. Then I drove through Ohio – which I guess is allowed – then onto the Pennsylvania Turnpike, which had me singing Billy Joel's "New York State of Mind," and finally to a secret, undisclosed location along the Susquehanna River, where my friend Brian Keene was waiting with a bottle of bourbon. I was really there to do the Horror Show with Brian Keene telethon, which raised over $20,000 for the charity. It was fantastic and exhausting, and a gathering of that same family I'd seen in Indiana. Around midnight, Mary SanGiovanni, Mike Lombardo, and Joe Ripple, CEO of Scares that Care, interviewed me.

They asked a lot of good questions. People at Mo*Con and the telethon asked me great questions. Brian and Mary, when it was just the three of us, asked me great questions – and since we've known each other for half our lives, they know exactly the questions that matter.

It's been about a year since I left the day job and started writing fulltime. Creatively, it's been fantastic, and I've never been so productive or content. Financially, it's been – let's say *rocky*. Car repairs, moving costs, and tax bills combined to devastate the little money I'd acquired as a kind of buffer between working full time and writing full time. It was never expected to be an easy transition, but it got more difficult and more complicated much more quickly than anticipated.

So I took a part time job. Nothing fancy, nothing like the industries I've worked at in the past. Something meant to get me through the summer: a movie theater. It was low pay, but I didn't need a lot. I had a lot of advantages and a lot of support. But what I didn't have was my audience. I'm still finding you out there, slowly, one or two at a time, in an attempt to make this whole *writing full time* thing possible

In the quiet before the telethon, Brian asked me about retreating to a day job, even a part time job, and how it made me feel.

I'll tell you what I told him in private.

It feels like failure.

The artistic life isn't always easy. It's hardly ever easy. There are the obstacles you face *in* the work, and there are the obstacles you face *to* the work. On the podcast, I talk about facing and overcoming those obstacles, learning from mistakes, fighting to make your voice heard. I talk about these things because I'm still in the middle of it. I'm still on that battlefield. I'm getting old and I ache all the time and sometimes I'm afraid it's all pointless, that I'm going to lose, I'm going to destroy myself doing it, I'm going to wake up one day and, well, just not wake up, never having achieved my dreams.

If at any point I gave you reason to think any of this is easy or without sacrifice, if I've led you to believe there isn't opposition and resistance to what we're trying to do built into the very fabric of our society, I apologize. That was never my intention.

I can slip easily into melancholy, but I try to avoid it. It's not a good place, not a happy place, not a productive place. Instead, I'm going to do what's necessary. I'm going to take this part time movie theater gig and use it to pay my bills, I'm going to watch a lot of movies this summer, I'm going to break through whatever obstacles are still ahead of me, and I'm going to find my audience.

Failure, even this type of failure, this step backwards and away from what I want, is temporary. Until I'm dead, I'm still able to fight, and this one little step backward is not the end of the world. I know I have it better than many. I know I'm capable of finding my way through. I know I'll find my audience, or my audience will find me.

And I know I've got more stories to tell.

FAILURE

How do you define failure?

This past week, I failed to meet my daily writing goals. I've been fighting a cold, I've been worried about Florida friends and family and the impending hurricane, I've been distracted by the fact that I'm still in boxes. Excuses, all of them, and none particularly good. I'm still getting work done, but I have not succeeded every day.

I have written my InkStains every day. That's something. And I've been making good progress on a novel that's been gestating for a few years. So it's not a total, complete, absolute failure.

Most importantly, I haven't given up. I missed a few daily goals. Who cares?

If I cared, I would have given up a long time ago. If you miss your goal one day, just go on to the next. It's okay. Real failure doesn't occur until and unless you give up and stop.

If you stop writing, stop painting, stop dancing – then, maybe, you can call yourself a failed writer, painter, or dancer. But isn't that a bit of a stretch? You try a thing, you do it for a while, you realize it's not for you or you've explored as much of it as you want – that doesn't equal failure. You do something, never reach the level of success you wanted, and stop to pursue something else instead? I'm not sure I'd call that failure, either.

I think we overuse the word failure.

But we also underuse it.

I write InkStains stories every day, even on days when I'm sick, even on days when I'm preoccupied with external forces that have aligned to eradicate my joy, and some of those stories don't work. They're not great, not good, maybe not even decent. There's nothing to resonate with a reader. Maybe I've attempted a second person point of view tale in future tense, and although it's not completely senseless, it's actually rather pointless. A failed experiment. Sometimes, the only success is the fact that I wrote a story at all.

Those failed experiments, however, are extraordinarily important. Vital. They're how we grow and learn and improve. I think Thomas Edison once said of his first, wildly unsuccessful attempts at the light bulb, "I have not failed, I have just found one thousand ways that won't work."

Another good quote, from Winston Churchill: "Success is not final, failure is not fatal; it is the courage to continue that counts."

We learn from mistakes and failures. Failure is a sure sign we've made an attempt. That effort is important, regardless of the immediacy of success. We learn to write first by scratching out crooked lines and curlicues that don't make any sense to anyone. It takes effort and time to develop those into letters. We learn which letters go together in what order to create words, and later how words fit together to form sentences. We write hundreds of sentences before our first story, and we write dozens or even hundreds of stories on our way to writing the first thing someone else may want to read. Those first stories, which we never sold because we didn't yet know characters could have secrets, or that we could write our own stories rather than re-tell tales we've already heard – all those failed stories and false starts and abandoned premises and silly mistakes – everything before every epiphany that didn't merely improve our writing but defined our voice – those are the failures upon which we've built tomorrow's successes.

These failures are instructive. By applying a certain attitude toward failure, they can be used as fuel and inspiration. I will do better today than yesterday. I will learn from my mistakes. I will improve as a writer, as an artist, as a human being.

If you won't give yourself permission, then I will: *you are permitted to fail.* It's okay. You can fail today and you can take something from it. You can fail tomorrow. All the failures that have led you to where you are today, they are the fundamental building blocks of who you are – not just as an artist – and I want you to be comfortable with the fact that failure is inevitable. Embrace failure. It means you're not standing still, not just letting the world happen around you.

All those so-called failures from which you've learned and experienced and grown make the successes we ultimately achieve all the more wonderful.

I failed to meet my daily goals this past week. I'm okay with that. The words I didn't write last week will still get written. I'm not that easy to defeat. I still have a book to write, and I will still meet my deadline. That's partly because I know how life can get in the way sometimes.

When I draw out my plans, I expect things to go awry. I build days off into my schedule.

It's a great sentiment, to write every day, but in practical terms it's nearly impossible. Especially when you fall ill. It's okay not to count those days, to move on and say you're still doing it. Because you are, in fact, still doing it, and you didn't give up because of some stupid self-imposed deadline.

Just as I haven't given up.

Over ten years ago, as I wrote the first draft of *Once Upon a Time in Midnight*, halfway into the book I discovered I didn't know what was needed next. I didn't know how to push forward. I failed that manuscript, that novel, that story – and I put it aside. I didn't give up on it forever. I was very particular about how I phrased what I was doing: "I'm putting this book aside for a while. It may be a short while. It may be a long while. I may never pick it up again, and that will be okay. I'm not giving up on it, I'm just putting it aside. I'm releasing my mind to think about it underneath everything else."

I don't really remember exactly what I said, but that was the gist of it.

No one was expecting the manuscript. I was under no deadline. Those factors might have changed my approach. I was free to fail, or not to fail, that story, and I felt comfortable doing so.

Six months later, maybe less, I picked up the book again, read through everything I had written, including all my notes and background information, and went back to work. A year later, I sold the book to a small press publisher.

When that publisher cancelled its upcoming books, including *Once Upon a Time in Midnight*, it had once again achieved failure. A few years later, Maelstrom, an imprint of Thunderstorm books, requested and accepted the manuscript. The book came out as a limited edition in 2012. It's now available as an e-book. Despite all the failures along the way, internal and external both.

DARK NIGHT OF THE SOUL

The way I talk about the joys of being a writer, artist, and creator, you would think it's all roses and butterflies, that I have a champagne toast every night to celebrate my day's accomplishments, that I and the other self-proclaimed artists put our feet up and smoke cigars and laugh about the lesser artists trying so very hard to join our ranks.

I can't say such a place doesn't exist. I can tell you I'm not there. I work hard, every day, sometimes for all the hours, often in the dark, sometimes hearing the whispers in that dark tell me I'm never going to make it, I'm never going to succeed, I should do something else and make other plans. I'm not talking about imaginary voices or signs of psychotic breakdowns, I mean the friends and family around me who aren't artistically inclined and say, "That's just a hobby." Maybe they're right. Sometimes, they are right.

But I'm not making a hobby of this. I'm making a lifestyle choice. I'm attempting to build a career. I've seen friends celebrate their successes, and other friends wallow in their failures. I've seen people struggling to scrape together enough money to pay the rent not have any energy left to make their art.

It can be a terrible world we live in. It can be brutal. Harsh. Unforgiving.

It doesn't help when you can look back at a lot of the work you did twenty years ago and objectively state it's crap. I can pore through old files looking for something I didn't sell, or even something I sold that still represents me, but they're difficult to find. Not only do we have to compete with a world that doesn't want us competing, we compete with the ghosts of our past selves and our past expectations.

When I started the first InkStains, when I sat and said I'm going to write a story every day for a year, I did it because I knew I wasn't working on my writing nearly as much as I should. I handwrote those stories. I used fountain pens and notepads that weren't absolutely necessary. They were just tools. Playthings. The only important part was the writing. I wrote till my fingers ached, I wrote till my hands were claws I couldn't unfold, I wrote until my head had nothing left to say. I stared down empty pages and wrestled demons inside me and told everyone – everyone who would listen – I was doing this because I am a writer, more than any other thing, and I had been letting that part of me die.

Die. Yes. It sounds dramatic because it's true. This *writer's life* can be filled with highs, but also lows. There are days, what I call *Dark Nights of the Soul*, when I question what I'm doing and why, when I wonder if I'll ever be good enough, when I wonder when or if I'm going to find the break or advantage I need to reach the next level.

The truth is, I don't know how these levels are defined.

Another truth: I have had breaks. I have had advantages. I have had help and support along the way. But in my darkest moments, I can only look back and see failures, mistakes, and missed opportunities. I see the opportunities that were never mine to miss, and it can be heartbreaking.

What I'm trying to say is, this isn't always easy. When you're alone in the dark, you are truly alone. It doesn't matter that other people have been alone in the same darkness or that others have gotten through. All you see ahead of you is nothing, because that's all that's promised. The myth of hard work leading to results is proven true for the people who have succeeded, but shown to be a lie by the many more who cannot manage to make it to that next step.

There's a belief that only the strong survive. I think I used to believe it, at least a little bit. I'm not so sure anymore. I'm not really sure I ever *believed* so much as *understood* the concept. There are plenty of concepts I understand. My belief is not required.

I believe in myself. My potential, if not always my skills. I tell you this because I also believe in you, whatever stage of your career you're at, whether you think you've already peeked and are slipping downward or you're just starting out. I believe in your potential as well as mine.

I believe the InkStains projects have changed me, fundamentally, as a writer. I can look at what I wrote before and say that was someone else, a different person who wore my skin and used my fingers, but he didn't always understand what he was doing. Sometimes he thought he did. Sometimes, he did okay. But the sheer volume of words, work, and effort that went into InkStains made me realize there was so much more to learn. I assume there's as much more for me still to learn.

All I can do is push forward. Work hard. Seek opportunities. Sharpen my skills. Share what I've learned. Do the best I'm able. That's all I can do, and I encourage you to do the same.

QUESTION: HOW DO YOU DEAL WITH DARK NIGHTS OF THE SOUL?

Dark Nights of the Soul: this is when you feel the numbness of the life outside your creative activity. When you feel the frustration of not achieving whatever you're attempting to achieve. This is *not* clinical depression; for that, you probably should see a professional. I am no professional. You might need medication, you might need guidance, you might need therapy. This is not that. This is for those occasions that are not everyday occurrences, when the weight of everything just seems to hit at once. How do you deal with Dark Nights of the Soul?

I can tell you I don't always deal with them well. And rarely easily. They're not easy to deal with. Like I said, it's not clinical depression, but it's still a melancholy that envelops you. Primarily, I try to weather it out by shifting my attention away from the probable causes and focus instead on solutions. Probable causes might include the day job getting monotonous, overwhelming, or stressful. I try to not pay too much attention – which is hard when you're actually at the day job. But when I get home, when I'm out and away from it, I should be able to stay away. I don't take that home. Maybe you do; it depends on the job. If so, you'll have to find another way to shift that focus.

Solutions for me, for example, would be to write. Writing, for me, is always a good solution, but it's not always that easy. Sometimes, it's easier to sit, maybe read for a while, watch a film, or just go for a walk. Anything that can shift focus out from what's dragging you down; even if you don't know exactly what it is, a change of environment, gets the blood moving. Go to the gym and walk the treadmill for thirty minutes. Even at a slow pace, it gets the blood circulating, it clears the mind, and it might get you out of that rut.

The InkStains project itself is an example of that.

InkStains was initially because I wasn't devoting enough of my time and energy to the things that nourished me and made me whole, which sounds like a weird thing to say but is absolutely true. I needed to find myself again. I was lost. I was lost and adrift and I didn't know what I was doing. I was probably trapped within a Dark Night of the Soul, but it stretched for weeks if not months and I didn't even know it. But I did know something was wrong, and I found a way through it. InkStains was one of those tools I used to get through it. A project like that might work for you as well. You might not need a daily, year-long project; it might just be that you devote a certain amount of time to it. It's remembering that you are, in fact, a creative person; in some way, in some aspect, in some capacity, you have a creative spark smoldering inside.

If you don't, I'm not sure why you're reading this.

If you've got that spark, the InkStains project is a regular reminder that it's inside you. You can access it and tap it and use it. It's only potential until you start using it. But if you allow yourself to get muted, if you allow yourself to lose sight of that, it can be hard to re-ignite. That doesn't mean it necessarily goes away.

It's not always impossible to find. But why allow it to go away if you don't have to? It doesn't have to take a lot of time and energy. You can do it, I know you can. I've done it. I've gone through spells of darkness that have lasted longer than others. I've gone through spells of what some people call writer's block. I'm not entirely sure I believe in that, not in the way most people use it. It's not a crutch, not an excuse; it's a matter of distraction – a distraction from the creative aspects of you, a distraction from who you really are. Are you going to let yourself be distracted from who you are by things happening around you? I don't think I want to. I don't think you want to, either.

This is one of reasons I do InkStains. I write that story every day – it may only be 15 or 20 minutes at a time – but it's a reminder that, despite the Dark Nights of the Soul, despite the muted sensations that may be overwhelming and blanketing my existence at the moment – despite all that, I still have a creative spark, I still have that energy and drive, and I am going to use it. I am going to use it again today, and I'm going to use it again tomorrow, and I'm not going to let it go. You don't have to, either.

The Pasture

The Pasture is a section of disk space on my computer's hard drive where story fragments, false starts, and failings go to die. It's a graveyard for words, for the computerized and electronicized words I've purged from my throat onto a blank page. I go through them once in a while to see how haphazardly I strung sentences together twenty years ago. I re-acquaint myself with characters from novels no one has ever seen and never will, some of whom had entirely disappeared from my memory.

I've got thirty thousand words of one novel I don't remember writing at all. I have no idea who those people are, and I don't even know for certain I wrote it. Those words, those sentences, those paragraphs – are clumsy, ill-shaped, without any sense of poetry.

If nothing else, walking through the Pasture reminds me of how far I've come, how much I've grown as a writer, how right those publishers in the early 90s were when they didn't throw contracts my way.

The oldest, non-novel related file is called *Time in a Bottle*. I just re-read it, and I've already told you more than you want to know. It's from twenty years ago. I didn't have this computer twenty years ago, nor the computer before it, not even the one before that. The return address in the header is a place I lived in so long ago, I barely remember it. I don't remember the story. It's not memorable.

But other things in The Pasture, bits of ideas, might want to be re-worked. It's wrong to think of the Pasture as merely a place for old stories to rot. Some might still catch a bit of light. It's a garden, that Pasture, and I've left ideas to grow wild and flourish like weeds in an abandoned field. There's a four hundred word review Chris Kosarich and I wrote after DragonCon 1997. The oldest file seems to be from one of my first novels in 1994. I think I wrote it by hand, originally, and typed it on my first IBM compatible computer and a very early Microsoft Word.

Sometimes, I wander the Pasture, not in search of anything in particular, to remember things I've done and thought, to see where I've come from, even to find those fledgling ideas that deserve to be re-visited. I have rescued the errant sentence, or even whole characters, from the gardens of my Pasture. They're my past, and my weeds, and my seeds I've let grow.

I know much of it, most of it, deserves to be let go and forgotten.

They may have personal meaning, but mostly they're just words I thought might go well together when I didn't know what I was doing. Those words do not go well together. Best to leave them alone, undisturbed and unseen, like ghosts.

I recently moved. Among all the things I've left in storage are several boxes filled with old journals. Long before I started writing InkStains stories, I had gotten three notebooks for a dollar and started something that wasn't quite a diary. These weren't collections of stories so much as fragments, ideas, song lyrics, snippets of conversations, musings on my disastrous and/or non-existent love life, and possible future scenes from novels I was working on. (A few of which made it, virtually unchanged, into actual manuscripts; others were discarded entirely.) These journals started as cheap spiral notebooks and later graduated to the hard cover notebooks you might find in special sections at the front of Waldenbooks or Borders. Once or twice, I might've even tried a Moleskine, or something else fancy. I got what I could and wrote inside them; I scribbled, and planted seeds of ink in a garden of dead trees. I explored ideas and concepts and thoughts, sometime poorly and sometimes crudely, and sometimes I drew irrational conclusions.

The Pasture and The Garden have, for me, been the same thing, a place where ideas are nurtured, tended to, discarded, forgotten, and when appropriate, re-discovered. I'm willing to bet writers aren't the only artists that do such things. As a photographer, I have hundreds of thousands of files, almost every digital photo I've ever shot. In that storage unit, I've got another box filled with developed film going back at least as far as my first trip to Europe circa 1984. If I look through them, I can see my growth, not just as a photographer but as a person – my journey from then till now illustrated clearly in the quality of my skill and the quality of my ideas and subject matter.

I don't believe my Pasture is a safe place for others, whether lovers or strangers. There's a lot that should probably be ignored, forgotten, lost, and dissolved into nothingness. The Pasture is not meant to be shared. But I do think this pasture, this garden, serves a purpose. It helps us learn. It helps us hone our skills. It gives us the freedom to explore, and to make mistakes, and to hide our embarrassments. And it gives us the perfect field in which to play with our InkStains.

QUESTION: WHAT ARE THE
FUNDAMENTAL BUILDING BLOCKS OF ART?

Is this supposed to be an easy question?

The most basic would be vision, right? In order to create something, you have to see it – or hear or feel it – or taste it – the specific senses involved will vary depending on your art. But I suppose, no matter the art, you have to feel it. Somewhere deep inside, you need to have an understanding of what you're trying to create. It may be only a skeletal structure to begin with, or a starting point with no clear end in sight, depending on how you work. So instead of saying vision, let's say *sense* – sense is one of the fundamental tools of art. A blind man can create art. And you certainly don't need to see music – unless maybe you do. Experience and interaction with the arts are a unique experience for everyone.

You might also need *direction*. Direction is one of those things that's not easily definable, yet we all know what I mean. You're moving from A to B in your life, in your general acceptance of the world around you, in your understanding of our variation of reality, and that direction – even if it's different from anyone else's – will guide your artistic endeavors. It's maybe the underlying essence of what you're seeing, or sensing, in the first place. So perhaps direction is, ultimately, the more important ingredient.

Education? Is that important? A great many artists of all types have had more or less education than their peers, and you can rarely judge their level of success by their degree of formal education. Of course, there are other types of education – all experiences teach us something. Maybe *experience* is the better choice. Sometimes, even a limitation on experience can lead to an interesting angle from which you see the world. The amount of formal and informal education, the degree and severity of that experience, will directly impact the art you create, but no measure of education can effectively predict your ability to succeed.

So it must be something else.

Definitions, I suppose, are important. How do you define success? Success for one person may look very different than success for somebody else. All the commercial success in the world may leave you feeling like you've failed the *artiste* inside you. All the artistic success in the world may leaving you cold in winter and hungry always. Is it a success when you complete the artistic project, or when you refine the artist project? Can you over-refine it, and perhaps ruin something by removing its roughest edges? Can you critique yourself beyond what might be a reasonable level of success? Are there, in fact, reasonable levels – and therefore, by inference, unreasonable levels – of success? Too little and also too much? Is the definition of your success buried in the degree of your ambition?

Is *ambition* a vital ingredient to the creation of art? There are so many different types. What if one person's ambition is to become a bestselling novelist, while another person's ambition is to write the most perfect novel in history? These are not necessarily diametrically opposed. You can have both. But does the striving for one, and the success in one, make it more important than the other?

There have always been arguments over the *balance* of art and commerce. You must eat to create art. You must sell out to eat. If you cater to your fans, are you eroding the integrity of your art, your artist vision, and achievements? Perhaps balance is the most vital ingredient in the creation of art. Does understanding your own personal balance, how far you can edge either to the artistic or commercial aspect of your chosen art, even play a role when you create? It might be successfully argued that *imbalance* is necessary to create art. When you're off-kilter, sliding over the edge, unsure of what's going to happen next – maybe those are the times you are most creative.

I think there are answers to these questions. I'm sure of it. And I'm sure any successful artist, however they've defined success, will tell you without ambiguity exactly what they think is vital to becoming an artist. Hell, people do this all the time. They may say something different at fifty than they said at fifteen. That doesn't make either answer more or less correct. What's right for one person at one time is, well, right for that person at that time. Another person, another time, another set of circumstances, you'll find your own balance and needs will change. Paths to success followed by your idols from previous generations will not be the same paths you follow today. Paths to success followed by your friends yesterday will not be the same paths that lead to your success today. The variables are too great, too innumerable.

The fact that there's not one single answer to all these questions capable of binding you and me and Stephen King and Van Gogh and

Mozart into a single, unifying theory of art doesn't mean there's no point in pursuing these questions. You should understand your own needs, your desires, your intentions. *Self-reflection*, I guess, is another important tool in the creation of art.

Maybe the most important tool is a pen, or a pencil, or a paintbrush. Maybe a guitar, a spatula, or a pair of ballet shoes.

The Most Important Tool For InkStains

What's the number one most important thing to have when working on an InkStains project? If you're writing, perhaps it's a pen, paper, or a computer. For musicians, it might be a guitar. For sculptors, maybe it's clay.

But none of that is more important than creativity.

I've defined creativity as the ability to resolve a problem. To put it in corporate speak, it's the ability to think outside the box. It's getting past obstacles, whether those obstacles be in the classroom, the office, the warehouse, or on the page. We all have some degree of creativity, though I think a lot of us learn at an early age to bury it and color inside the lines. We ignore the voices that belong to the more adventurous parts of ourselves saying go on, take the risk, do the thing that's not been done.

Without creativity, all the ink, guitars, and clay in the world won't do you a lot of good.

However, there's something more important than creativity. It's not talent; talent is something we're born with and can nurture. It's not skill; skills are abilities we learn and hone. It's not hope and it's not love, even if love is the answer to most the other questions.

It's persistence.

The ability to keep going when you're tired, when you're struggling, when you're facing impossible obstacles.

I'll use a stupid example. It's really stupid, and trite, and you'll recognize it immediately. But the river, facing a mountain wall, just kept hitting that wall despite being told it would never get through the mountain. It eroded a little bit at a time until eons later, the day finally – and inevitably – came when the river broke through the mountain. Yay stupid examples!

The InkStains project is an example of that. Some days, the writing doesn't flow easily and I push through. Some days, the writing flows like another damn river, and I run with it and mix my metaphors and everything. You're not in control of the external factors that affect this. Any day can be a good day. Any day can be a bad day. You push forward anyway.

I'll admit, the world can be a vicious, cruel, uncaring, and downright nasty place, and there will be days when you put everything aside and wonder how you're possibly able to work on something that seems so frivolous compared to the enormity of life. Death. Destruction. Tragedy. Catastrophe. I'm in no way trying to tell you to keep writing through that. I mean, yes, you *can*, and I encourage you to make the attempt if you think it will help, if you think it'll heal you. But if you need time for some *life event*, if you need to step away, that's understandable; I am not suggesting you're a lesser artist or a lesser person for doing so. In fact, you'll probably be a stronger, more capable person and artist, after overcoming those kinds of challenges, and you can't fight everything with a pen.

The normal daily emergencies, the regular curveballs of life, the everyday drama – that's the kind of stuff you have to be able to work past. Your coffee machine broke this morning? Fine. Fix it and move on. The water heater broke? Fix it and move on. You don't know how to handle the transition from the first chapter to the second? Fix it and move on. Sometimes, fixing it means giving it to someone else – a plumber, for instance. Sometimes, it means putting it aside but continuing anyway. That chapter transition will still be there tomorrow, so maybe today you skip it and move on anyway.

It's the persistence of struggling forward, or sailing forward, every day – on whatever schedule you've set for yourself. Some writers start young and never give up, and reach my age or older before becoming a success. Don't let success define you as an artist. Keep at it. Be productive. Be better than you were.

Influences Challenge

Inspiration comes from everywhere, sometimes where you least expect it, but those earliest influences stay with you for life. These days, anything can inspire me — which sounds a lot like I'm saying everything inspires me, but that's not true.

Politics, for instance, do not inspire anything positive in me. They do not inspire wonder or awe or creativity or anything powerful. I can list a number of things that have an anti-inspiration effect. They're diversions. Sometimes, they're very worthy, important, necessary, and profound diversions, but they don't add to my creative arsenal, so I try, when I can, not to focus on them.

Sometimes, you have to. Sometimes, the car has to be fixed, and it'll cost $1,400 you don't have. Can't be avoided. Money has to come from somewhere. Yes, you're going to worry about where the money's coming from, or how you'll pay for this month's medications or rent. That type of thinking is detrimental to making works of creativity — but that doesn't excuse you from thinking about them.

The separation of those types of things is important. You can worry for days, but you don't accomplish anything by worrying. Worry is a useless activity that steals your time and accomplishes nothing. It's an emotional outlet, perhaps, and more necessary for some people than others, but some people don't do anything but worry. I'm fairly sure some people don't worry enough. Balance, as with all things, is important. But there are better ways to approach the challenges of everyday life than worry. You can plan and plot, you can find or create solutions. Not easily. Not simply and quickly. But hell, you've got a creative mind, you can put it to good use in overcoming every obstacle thrown your way.

JUST BE CAREFUL NOT TO GET BOGGED DOWN IN THE THINGS THAT SAP YOUR CREATIVE ENERGY — THE THINGS YOU CAN AVOID, DEFER, OR IGNORE.

SOMETIMES, IT'S IMPORTANT TO FOCUS ON THE THINGS THAT REFUEL YOU, THE THINGS THAT SPARK YOUR SENSES OF WONDER AND AWE. MAYBE IT'S MUSIC OR FILM OR BOOKS, FRIENDS OR FAMILY, RACE CARS, YOUR CAT. ANYTHING CAN INSPIRE YOU.

I FIND A LOT OF INSPIRATION IN MUSIC. AND IN MOVIES. IN LITERATURE. AND IN JUST WALKING OUTSIDE. MOVE THE LEGS, MOVE THE BLOOD, CLEAR THE BRAIN, THAT SORT OF THING. I'LL PLAY STUPID LITTLE VIDEOGAMES, ON THE OUTSIDE, WHILE INSIDE I'M WORKING ON STORY PROBLEMS, EVEN IF ONLY SUBCONSCIOUSLY. I CAN'T EXPLAIN HOW EVERYTHING WORKS. I'M NOT A NEUROSCIENTIST, A PSYCHIATRIST, OR A THEOLOGIAN. I'M A WRITER, A POET, AND A WORDSMITH. I'M A PHOTOGRAPHER. I'M AN ARTIST CONFIDENT IN MY TALENT AND MY SKILLS.

I CAN MAKE A LIST OF THE THINGS THAT HAVE INFLUENCED ME. IT'LL BE A LONG LIST. IT'LL GO BACK AT LEAST TO THE AGE OF 6, DECADES AGO, AND WILL INCLUDE THINGS THAT ARE VERY MUCH OLDER THAN THAT. AND THAT'S YOUR INKSTAINS CHALLENGE TODAY: CREATE A LIST OF THE THINGS THAT INSPIRE YOU. BE TRITE AND SENTIMENTAL. BE OBSCURE. INCLUDE THINGS THAT INSPIRE YOU BECAUSE YOU KNOW YOU CAN DO BETTER. MAKE A LIST, A FULL PAGE OF INSPIRATIONAL THINGS. DO NOT MAKE A LIST OF WHAT LIMITS YOU. DO NOT MAKE A LIST OF WHAT OBSTRUCTS YOUR CREATIVITY. MAKE A LIST OF THE SPARKS AND FLAMES AND BLAZES THAT SET YOU OFF IN ALL THE RIGHT WAYS. MAKE AS LONG A LIST AS YOU CAN, A FULL PAGE OR TWO OR TEN, AND KEEP THAT LIST. RETURN TO THAT LIST WHEN YOU'RE STRUGGLING, WHEN YOU'RE FALTERING OR FAILING. NEVER FORGET THAT LIST OF THE AWESOME THINGS IN YOUR LIFE — ESPECIALLY DURING YOUR DARKEST AND SCARIEST MOMENTS. YOU MAY BE A POWERFUL CREATIVE ARTIST IN YOUR OWN RIGHT, BUT YOU'VE BUILT YOURSELF ON THE BACKS OF INNUMERABLE POWERFULLY INSPIRING THINGS. AND IT'S ALWAYS GOOD TO REMEMBER WHAT MAKES YOU GO.

Golden Apples

A few years ago, I went to the wilds of Maine, to a house on the outskirts of a town with a population of fewer than 1,000 people – I've worked in buildings with larger populations, and this was the outskirts – for the Golden Apple Art Residency. It was only two weeks of my life.

Those two weeks gave me a chance to immerse myself fully into my art, to ignore the details of real, regular life, to walk through the woods and risk my neck on the rocks, to listen to seals and lobstermen, and to spend time with a few other artists – there were four of us – and not have to contort myself to fit into everyday society.

I don't live in an art enclave. This was the closest I've ever been to one.

And I loved it. Shelley and Greg Stevens run the residency. They fed us, they brought us on excursions to places like Wild Blueberry Land, and they gave all of us the space and time we needed to work: a studio and a cottage on the edge of the water.

I had my camera and I shot a lot of photography. I had never seen the Milky Way so powerful, bright, and wonderful in the sky, and I'd never seen as many stars. Most importantly, I went with a project in mind, a project I'd already begun. I was about 20,000 words into the manuscript, and it had taken me six months to get there. During those two weeks, I wrote another 40,000 words, fully half of the novel. I spent the next six months writing the rest.

That book became *The Corpse and the Girl from Miami.*

Golden Apple game me something I'd been looking for: a chance to focus exclusively on my writing. The photography, the hikes, even the meals – all of that was extra and complementary. None of it took away from my writing time.

In the real world, there's always something eroding our art time. There are day jobs and mortgages and electric bills, there are cars that break down, family that needs the laundry done, and social obligations. A thousand things demand your art time. Many are necessary, some are in fact wonderful – not everything that wants to steal from the art you haven't made is evil or wicked.

There are other kinds of art and writer residencies. Some are only a weekend, others go for months or semesters. Every once in a while, an escape like this is a good idea. Maybe you can't right now; that's okay. There are plenty of times and reasons we can't get away. But the change of environment, the elimination of distractions, and the immersion are extraordinary.

You don't have to go to Golden Apple. But if you want to apply, they're at www.goldenapplestudio.com, and you can tell them you heard about it here. I don't get anything for that, but it's still a nice thing. The Clarion Writers Workshop accepts applications until March 1, Odyssey Writing Workshop through roughly April 7, and other kinds of workshops and retreats accept applications year round. [Author's note: these dates probably change from year to year and were accurate when I read them on the podcast.] Workshops are different from retreats. At Golden Apple and other such places, you're left alone and encouraged to explore your creativity when and how you wish. The workshops require, well, work, similar to classes. But both serve a similar purpose: immersion.

You don't need to go to an established workshop or retreat. I've always loved the idea of taking a weekend and running to a hotel, any hotel, not even far from where I live, where I can be alone to work and where I can wander outside safely. (That feeling of safety is important unless you need the sense of urgency that comes with knowing your life might end the next time you step outside.) Maybe even that's beyond reach at the moment. There's family all around and cash can be low. In that case, send *them* away – to a park or museum or movie – and give yourself at least a two hour retreat.

You deserve it.

Brainstorming and Notepads

Brainstorming, as traditionally structured, has never worked for me. I do variation all the time, in my notepads, where I write and scribble, take notes, and play. I have notepads devoted to particular projects, but I also have others that are blank, random, and meant for anything.

In one, I have a page listing several of my projects – the glass book, the Boston book, InkStains books and DarkWalker books – and columns checked to indicate whether they needed to be written, edited, laid out, submitted, or whatever else. On the next page, I have written: "Write another book. Write another book. Shoot another picture. Art another art. Write another book. Medusa. Echo. DarkWalker 1 2 3."

It's a small notepad, 3 by 5 inches, and that's the sum total of one page. That barely qualifies as brainstorming. I'm not sure it qualifies as much of anything. Was I psyching myself up for something? Getting ready? At the time, *Echo* was only a title, and *Medusa* was – well, we'll get to her another day. [Author's note: *Echo* is scheduled for early 2020 from Eraserhead Press.]

Another page in the same notepad says, "No good can come of something like this."

Another says, "Someone should put some effort into making lawn equipment quieter."

And on another, there's this little story-like thing playing with an idea older than I am:

In the big ballroom, Harry sat alone drinking spiked punch when he heard footsteps.

"Hello, Harry."

He turned.

"I'm here for the time traveler's party."

"But I haven't sent out any invitations yet."

"I know. But you will in the morning."

On another page, I play with possible episode topics for the very beginnings of the podcast – which means this particular book, still on my desk though all the way filled up, was begun over a year ago.

It's still here because there are titles for projects so secret even I know only their titles and whatever's contained on this page of ink devoted to them. Looking through it now, I'm reminded of things I'd forgotten. That's part of the point of these notepads: an extra bit of creative storage.

But they also work for brainstorming.

If I were a musician, my notepads would be filled with musical notes and phraseology, questions I want to explore, possibilities, terrible sketches of instruments new and old. If I were a cook, I'd have lists of spices and maps of where to find them, recipes I'd only begun to imagine, and notes on these notes to point out where I went wrong and where I went right.

Brainstorming is one of those things you can return to at any time. The notepad remains on my desk because I can pick it up and scribble more on some of those already used pages any time I feel the urge. I can stare at my brainstorming sessions, dip my fingers into any runoff, and catch a thunderbolt. I can do it today. You can do it today.

Brainstorming exercises don't have to be about specific story ideas. You can explore methods and techniques. You can scribble notes, like *try telling a story in future tense.* A list of meals that can be roasted. Colors you might restrict yourself to. Your brainstorming might ask why a particular chord resonates the way it does and how shifting just one note to make it a minor key changes everything. You can write a title, over and over again, varying it slightly, varying the way you write it, changing words and shifting letters, employing different color inks, just to understand the sound and shape of it, and the next day's painting or poem or photo can be made with that title in mind.

Wasting Time

I've worked boring dead end jobs. I once ansswered phones for a bank. People called every day to ask if this check cleared or that check cleared, or why we bounced their check. When holidays gave us a day off, I often stayed home and wrote.

Finding time to do your art can be monumentally challenging. We have to do things for other people, we have to go to the day job to earn salaries so we can pay rent and buy the food that sustains us so we can go back to work and keep it all going. In the minutes you steal for yourself, in the time you're able to devote to actually working at your art – that's when I was always happiest. I dive into my worlds, into my words, into whatever art I'm creating.

Here we all are, travelling through time the long way, taking a full sixty seconds to get one minute into the future, and we have devised countless methods of wasting every one of them. We have mastered the art of burning up time. When we're young, we think we're invincible, we've got all the time we need, and we'll never run out.

But we will. One day, we will create our last piece of art, our final poem or story, our last painting, our swansong. One day, we'll go – and maybe we won't go quietly. Our art will be part of our legacy.

We don't get credit for the stories we didn't write while we were watching *Game of Thrones*.

But sometimes, when we're wasting time, we're not wasting time.

In the back of my mind, of course, I'm always thinking, gestating, tossing around all the ideas and characters for the *DarkWalker* novel I'm writing. There comes a point in the day where I've written all I can, emotionally, intellectually, and physically.

When I was younger, there were days I wrote 10,000 words. I won't say the words were good. Actually, the words were good; I probably didn't have them in the best order. But I wrote them, and if I didn't I would not have learned whatever lessons I needed then that contributed to my abilities now. If I'm at all good today, it's because there was a day in my 20's where I put over 10,000 words all in the wrong places.

I believe Jack Ketchum said – I cannot verify this – that sometimes, staring at walls *is* writing. The mind has to be given free rein to wander. You work consciously, staring at those walls, twirling your pen or paintbrush in your hand like some mad conductor – or twirling your conducting baton like a mad painter – attacking obstacles, considering possibilities, exploring whatever it is you're trying to create. Sometimes we work subconsciously while watching *Game of Thrones* or aimlessly walking city streets or playing games. The subconscious work happens all the time. It's subconscious, so we don't always know it.

The trick is finding balance. How much time are we supposed to waste? The time we spend at the day job – maybe that's not a complete waste, because it keeps us in food and shelter, it gives us the toys and tools we need, or maybe it just barely manages to keep us afloat. The quality of those day jobs varies. If the time we waste re-energizes us, re-ignites us, re-inspires us – how can you call that wasted time?

Physically, I can no longer write 10,000 words in a day. I did once, not too many years ago, and hurt my fingers so badly they still hurt and will always hurt. If I try it again, those might be the last 10,000 words I write.

Emotionally, when I create art I'm draining myself, my wells and internal resources. Wasting time – vacations, days off, silly romantic movies, whatever you do – allows those resources to replenish.

Intellectually, there's a point – even if you outline your novel all the way through, or know every stroke of the brush or every chord – where you've reached the limit of what you know and what you can create today. Like any muscle in any sort of workout, you work to the ends of your limits, then push beyond those limits – and then you stop, and do it again tomorrow or the day after, and you find you're fully capable of pushing just as far and farther.

There comes a time when we feel guilty about wasted time. I think that's partly us being too hard on ourselves, or someone else being excessively hard on us, or – and realistically, this is probably the biggest and truest reason – we're out of balance and wasting too much time. The subconscious stops working on problems and possibilities if you never apply those results to actual work. If you stop creating for too long, you risk having your subconscious abandon the effort.

Fortunately, I believe you can re-start that whole process anytime you're ready. Get back into the poetry, the sculptures, the movie making, whatever your art happens to be. It may not happen immediately. You'll have to go through the motions and kick-start that subconscious back to life, but it will return. We were all born with it, almost everyone has neglected it at some point, almost all of us have had to rein it in. But it's there, inside me and inside you, and if you think it's beyond reach anymore, if you think you can't tap into it anymore, if you think you've lost it – you're wrong. You're wrong, and it's time to stop wasting time and get to work.

FUEL

I've talked about inspiration and I've talked about the mechanics of writing and other forms of art. Somewhere in the middle of that, between the spark and the art, are the artists and creators and maniacs. Yes, I think there's a level of insanity involved in the creative process, but that's probably better covered by some psychologically based podcast, a YouTube video, or a textbook written in the 18th Century. Have I talked much about how we consume our inspirations, how we learn from our lessons, how we make something out of nothing?

As artists, we find inspiration in all the usual spots – not exclusively in bars at 3am. There's other art, our friends and family, our enemies and nemesai and obstacles. We find inspiration in music and theater and literature by masters, novices, students, and children. Where we find inspiration isn't the question here. It's what do we do with that inspiration.

We transform it.

An idea can strike me and demand immediate attention, or it can burrow into my brain to gestate and blossom. Other ideas, unrelated things, may get attached, and that initial seed explodes in a variety of ways. I explore avenues I maybe didn't think of before. Sometimes the results are exponential. When I'm working on a particular project, some of those ideas and thoughts, the results of other inspirations, integrate themselves into that project; the mind is already at work in a particular world and it sees everything, everything it can, by the filter of that world.

Inspiration, ideas, thoughts, hints, suggestions – these are all the raw materials that keep artists going. They're what drives us – what drives me – and I can't shut off the valve. Sure, there are days when it gets stopped up and the ideas don't flow so freely. But other days, words pour out of me like a monsoon, like a cat 5 hurricane, like a rain of meteorites from space hell-bent on annihilating the eastern seaboard.

The other day, someone told me they weren't a writer. He had tried several times and didn't have the skills. More importantly, he didn't have the drive. He didn't want to write. But he had an idea, and he was sure it was good. I warned him, right at the start, because he wasn't going to let me go without telling me his grand idea, that I already have plenty to do – but that's okay, he said, because maybe after those. He didn't understand there is no *after*. I warned him only he could write his story. He said he couldn't. I didn't argue that. What I was trying to say, politely, was that I *couldn't* and *wouldn't* write his story.

He shared it with me anyway. There were some decent thoughts in there, a foundation of facts and a good amount of extrapolation. He had the fuel, he had the ideas, but his engines – the engines at the source of him – didn't run on that kind of fuel. And that's fine. He's not a lesser man because of it. And I'm not a lesser man because I won't take his idea and run with it.

The best I could do in that situation was allow him to talk, to encourage him to write it himself and not worry if it was any good – but since he refused that, there was nothing else I could do. I won't write his story. His fuel won't work in my engines.

But fuel isn't just about the ideas. It's also about the abilities, the talents, the things we know about our art that allow us to pursue these ideas. For me, as a writer, I know a lot of words, I know how to twist them to my needs, and in many cases, I know enough about the minute differences between similar words to choose the best ones for the job. I know story and story structure and plot, I know how those things are not the same, and I know how they're related. I understand character and point of view, and I know how to unleash my imagination.

In other words, I have an amazing, albeit incomplete, toolbox. I'm always on the lookout for new weapons in my war against the mundane. I recently moved to Spain and I'm struggling to learn Spanish. One thing that's helped is the depth of my knowledge of English and the roots of words. I recognize similarities between the languages – not just when the words are the same or almost the same, but in cases where the Spanish word – like *el libro* – is related not to the English word – *the book* – but because of its relationship to words like *library*, a house of books, and its Latin root *liber*.

This kind of knowledge is a lot like the kindling of a bonfire. This is what I use to start the fires, the stories, the epic sagas – this is part of what allows me to do what I do.

What do I do?

I'm a wordsmith. A storyteller. If you'll forgive the humility: a master of dreams.

I'm the kind of artist who builds his tools by hand and is invigorated by the prospect. No, I can't make a pen or a computer, and I don't know how to pulp paper, but those aren't the tools I mean.

There are things we're taught in school that don't matter. The difference between a metaphor and a simile? Is that important if you use them effectively? Symbolism? Do you need to think about symbols, or can you allow your subconscious to do the work – or better, the Ph.D.'s who can spend entire dissertations discussing and interpreting your use of the color blue?

PART TWO
WRITING

ATMOSPHERE

Let's discuss atmosphere. As you probably know, the earth's atmosphere is almost 80% nitrogen with enough oxygen to support humanity and other kinds of animals that live on this planet, but that's not what I'm here to talk about.

In fiction, atmosphere is more than just the setting; it is the mood, and it is struck in part by the setting, struck in part by the choice of words, and how you put those things together.

Look, for example, at Van Gogh's *The Starry Night*. There's a definite tone set by the color choices in that painting. One of the earlier sketches shows more yellow than blue; it feels very different, and that change in atmosphere has a tremendous impact. [Author's note: I cannot confirm this yellow version I saw that one time was legitimate.] Atmosphere may be what most survives the art you're working on. Look at film noir, or photography, for examples of setting atmosphere. There's a huge difference between a photograph of a 1950s pinup model in a yellow polka dot bikini on a beach at sunset and the same model wearing a long black dress in a low key black and white picture sharply lit from one site. That difference in approach makes an impact on what the piece says and does. It's more than just being fantastical, it's being fantastical and dark – or not dark, as the case may be. The atmosphere in a movie like *Lilo & Stitch* from Disney, sets a mood – it's got its own atmosphere – vastly different from what you would find in *Casablanca* or *Salem's Lot*.

It's important to establish an atmosphere and work within it. It can dictate the types of words you use, as well as the way you're going to use them, but it can be a little difficult to pin down – like voice and style, it defies easy definition. It's not like you can say, this character has *this* in their background. That doesn't make atmosphere. Atmosphere isn't made by the fact that the building has existed for a hundred years, but when you see those years in the bricks that have started to crumble in the corners, where spiders have abandoned their webs, and where the floor perhaps doesn't quite want to support you as you walk. That presents an atmosphere very different than solid marble floors and pristine statues and tapestries hanging from the walls.

Atmosphere is all of the setting and the characters and the plot and the history and the background combined to create something that isn't specifically spelled out. You don't have to tell us, "It was a dark and stormy night." That might set an atmosphere, and probably did the first time it was used long, long ago. That's one way to set a scene, but it doesn't really set much for atmosphere. They're just words, they don't exude dark and stormy; they just say, hey, I am dark and I am stormy. This is where you'll see the difference between showing and telling.

It's also the things you leave out and the way you say things. When it works, you know that it works, and you remember it. When you're trying to work on something, when you're trying to create an atmosphere, you'll know when it feels right. Because it is about *feel* here.

Word choice is vital when establishing an atmosphere. Is the basement dank, muddy, sterile, or claustrophobic? Are the trees bright and leafy, hunched over from their own weight, scorched by the sunlight they're struggling to prevent from reaching the earth, or dripping with sugary syrup and sap?

We're trying to elicit an emotional response to the setting and the scene and everything going on, to the atmosphere surrounding and permeating the characters and their story you're telling.

The atmosphere is what transports your readers into that world.

REVISIONS

When writing the InkStains stories, I never went back for revisions until it was time to include them in a book or read them on the podcast. The stories I read, however, are not first drafts; that would be rude and disrespectful.

The first time around, I write the stories every day throughout the year. After I've written those stories, or at some point during the following year, I start typing them. This is Revision Number One. I have to type them because the rest of you cannot read my handwriting – I can barely read my handwriting – people I have known and loved for decades cannot read my handwriting. I make little corrections as I go – choosing better words, aligning the grammar, correcting the punctuation. I'll change little things here and there. With the InkStains, I am explicitly avoiding massive changes. There's zero structural or content editing, just making sure I get the words right.

I print out the typed stories and, with a blue pen, go through and lay down another layer of ink. I make additional changes – not always a lot, but there are pages with more blue ink (editing) than black (printed draft). Sometimes the story just needs more tightening and tinkering. I'm not doing any content editing, merely shuffling words, choosing better words and better phraseology, making it more interesting and more successful as a story. Additionally, I'll correcting tense, subject-verb agreements, and the like.

Then, reading it on the podcast, I make other corrections on the fly to make it sound better. The words may have seemed okay in print, but not after reading them aloud. Doing your own out loud reading before submitting or showing a story to someone is often a good idea

At the moment, I'm deep into revisions on several projects – novel projects, not just InkStains. Usually, when I talk about revisions, I don't mean just making sure I've got a few words better than what I'd had, and I'm not just correcting grammar. I'm doing content editing. I'm switching scenes around and making sure I have continuity.

There's always going to be a later time when you look at it and realize this word needs to be changed, this letter needs to be removed, something bizarre happened to the formatting on this page, I don't understand why this doesn't look like I remember it. That's just how it happens. There's always going to be another change. There's got to be an arbitrary point where you just put it down and say I'm done.

You can't just put it down and say I'm done after the first draft. I get a great sense of accomplishment when I finish the first draft of a major project. When I put END at the bottom of that manuscript, I am thrilled, I am excited, I break out the bourbon, I go out for a fancy dinner, I celebrate in some way. Maybe I'll buy myself a new fountain pen because I'm stupid that way. But that's not the end of the process, that's just the beginning. That's the end of the biggest, first step. The next step is to do that revision.

The first step is getting the words down. The second step is getting them right.

Obviously, some people do this entirely differently than I do. They agonize over a page for days before moving on to the next and never look back. While I may do that during the revision process, I am a *dump it all on the ground and clean it up later* type of first drafter. There's nothing wrong with doing it differently; but the successful writer who tells you they don't go back and edit is most likely editing as they write. I'm not prescribing how you should do it, just telling you how I do it.

In my process, I'm checking for grammar, spelling, formatting, and continuity, and I'm confirming all the subplots that need resolving are resolved. I'm making sure I've been true to the story and haven't included anything extraneous. This is a big effort, and it's usually easier if I allow some space between drafts. I'll write the first, then do something else. I may shoot a photography project, write an entire other novel, or edit something different. I may take a short break and read three or four novels by some of my favorite authors. (I have an overabundance of books in my To Read Mountain.)

Then, after I've cleansed myself – it's like when you're at a wine tasting, a beer tasting, a chili cook-off – that *something else* has basically cleansed my palette. I'm too close to the story when I finish the first draft. I know everything in more detail than the story, and I need to attack it from a more removed perspective. If something I know is missing from the story, and it's necessary, in order to even realize this, I have to forget a little bit. Part of the revision process is filling in the blanks, making sure there aren't holes that shouldn't be there. It's a long process, a difficult process, and it can sometimes take as long to do the second draft as it did to do the first. But you might miss these holes if your subconscious fills in the gaps for you.

I always use a blue pen because it stands out in contrast to the black ink on the paper, and I usually edit hard copy. That's my process —other people edit on a computer or tablet.

Perfection is something we aim for, but it's not something we'll ever actually achieve. There's no such thing as perfection except as a goal to strive for. Striving for excellence is important. You can achieve excellence. Striving for perfection may be the path to insanity. Let it go.

Make it better. Make the words matter more. Make them stronger, give them more punch and immediacy. Make the story work the way it was intended to work, not just the way it ended up when you scribbled that first draft. That's how I think of my InkStains stories: I'm scribbling. And even those scribblings deserve to be clear and evocative.

Themes

I've been revising old InkStains, I've been reading through even older InkStains, and I'm writing new ones presently – so I'm working a lot of different stories – and I've noticed certain themes I return to regularly and images that come up over and over again. For example, I have written lots of stories set during storms, and I have numerous times personified storms or storm gods.

The mechanical nightingale from Hans Christen Anderson's fable makes appearances in several of my stories, seemingly any time I have an opportunity to throw it in there. You'll often pass a copy of *The Book of Lost Fates*, which I quote from at the beginning of multiple stories. (The novella *Necropolis* is the first I remember.) *The Book of Lost Fates* is fantastic because I can make it say anything I want because it's mine. I invented it, I created it, and I have it appear, not just in the InkStains stories, but throughout the worlds I've created in my books and novels and short stories.

I'm not the only person who does this.

The first year of InkStains, I didn't have any topics; it was just go at it, do whatever you want. The second year, I had a theme every month (i.e., *The Months and The Days*). The third year, I didn't want to feel obliged to tie every story to a singular theme, so I chose touchpoints I could visit repeatedly. The first month, I returned to a character who has appeared in a couple of my stories, Cool-Eyes. That did not mean every story was a Cool-Eyes story. March's touchstone was *The Book of Lost Fates*. This allows me connect stories that would otherwise be, or seem to be, disconnected. I'm not the only person who has ever done this. Stephen King has several cities you see over and over again, Castle Rock for instance. Brian Keene's Labyrinth has featured in a number of his stories in a lot of interesting and unique ways.

Sometimes an image just sticks with you – that mechanical nightingale from Anderson – but sometimes they represent issues you're still working through. Consider the femme fatale I wrote about consistently when I was young and single and not doing well in the realm of romance. Where could I *possibly* have been emotionally then?

The difficulty with recurring themes is returning to the same well runs the risk of going stale, of pulling out the same stories over and over again, the same imagery, the same situations, the same characters. It's important, when you purposefully return to the same types of themes, images, and worlds, to attack them in different ways. Show them differently. Highlight them, accentuate them, or hide them in fresh ways.

Musical themes, for instance, can continue throughout the entire length of a series of songs to tie them together in a bigger way (think opera or rock opera), and do not have to just be the same series of notes repeated. Repetition can be useful, but repetition should be used as a tool, as a means of showing progression. It shouldn't happen because you're not paying attention.

Be conscious about what you're doing when you approaching your recurrent themes. I hope you're making progress on a personal level with whatever issues you're facing, that you're not stuck writing the same story because you're stuck in the same place in life. It's great if you can make some sort of movement, not just in art but also in life. Like I said, don't let it get stale. Don't let it get old. Don't let it get boring.

That's really important.

The worst thing you can do as an artist is bore, not just me as your audience, but yourself. If you're boring yourself, I guarantee you're boring everybody else. If you're writing the same story again, that is no longer a recurring theme – that's paint by numbers, and is rarely considered great art.

Themes Continued

A lot of artists return frequently to their themes. Tom Piccirilli, for instance, had a number of characters who were drivers of some sort, for the Mafia or a crime syndicate or a team of thieves.

I wonder sometimes if we're trying to work something out internally when we return to our themes.

These aren't retellings of the same stories, but explorations of similar ideas from different angles. Over time, I like to think we're growing, all of us, that we're learning from our past explorations. So when I write another story about a thief, I don't intend to focus on the same aspects of thievery every time. My thief characters have different backgrounds, different methods, and different skillsets. I highlight magic a lot, illusionists in particular, the ideas of sleight of hand – and of course these can be easily linked to thieves.

The second set of InkStains stories had monthly themes. This restriction forced me to move beyond the obvious and dive deeper into my own inner workings. What is it I find so fascinating about folded paper and origami that I've featured it in a half dozen stories and at least one of my novellas? I can use my own stories to explore those kinds of questions, and ultimately I might come to realize that folded paper and magic are intricately linked, but maybe I'm no closer to discovering all my own hidden secrets.

These themes I'm talking about are almost superficial. They're the themes on the surface. When Tom Piccirilli was writing about getaway drivers, he was actually writing about his complicated relationship with his father. That's the thing with themes: some of them are obvious and apparent, and some are folded deeply into the fabric of our stories. When you read a Brian Keene story, you can get a real, palpable sense of his nihilism. When you read one of mine, you hopefully get an idea of what I think of the power of imagination.

In art, you see themes represented in color as well as subject matter. It's the same with music and writing. The recurrent themes resonate. They become so much a part of the story, they're impossible to remove.

Some themes are disguised as morals. No, I've got that backwards. Morals are disguised as themes. Unlike the tropes we return to as writers – the vampires and thieves and ghosts and drivers – morals are the kind of themes that are carefully considered and consciously inserted into the tale. The truest recurrent themes are subconscious. They only become apparent after a number of different works, tales, stories, or paintings. Looking at the work of Van Gogh, you don't see a man struggling with insanity, but an artist in extraordinary control of his creations. Look at the work of Steven Spielberg, and you'll see the flawed relationships of parents with their children. Through the vampires of Anne Rice, you'll witness an author working through loss and grief.

Anthologies often have a theme tying the stories together. Sometimes, that theme is another author – like *Clickers Forever*, in which authors paid homage to the late JF Gonzales. (For transparency, I am one of those authors.) Another kind, where I did not contribute, would be Ellen Datlow and Lisa Morton's *Haunted Nights*, which explores Halloween and related subjects. But when you work to a theme that's assigned or suggested, you'll still incorporate your own themes – the conscious or the subconscious – into them.

Language, imagery, and conflict all contribute to the themes of the work. If you find yourself referencing the same things time and time again, you're possibly exploring something deeply psychological or philosophical inside you. One advantage of being a writer: you may be exploring either your fears or your hopes. Or maybe your truths.

DAILY GOALS

I had a discussion with another writer this week. He was having trouble attacking his novel. Basically, he was working on an epic fantasy and had a question I'm going to answer here: how do you start writing something like a one hundred thousand word epic fantasy? It seems like too massive a thing to do.

There's only one way to write such an epic: one word at a time.

But divide it up. I don't start a project needing to write that many words so I can have a complete book. I can't write a hundred thousand words. That's ridiculous. But it is possible to say I'd like to finish the first draft by the end of three months. That many words over 90 days is just over a thousand words per day. But I don't even divide by *all* days, so how many weeks is that? I do a little bit of math. Yes. Math.

How many words do I need every week to reach one hundred thousand during twelve weeks? Less than ten thousand. I break that down further to how many words is a day for five day week. I build in the idea that I'm going to be interrupted. Two days every week makes it like a regular work week, Monday through Friday, with Saturday and Sunday off. But I'm not specific. It doesn't have to be Saturday or Sunday. Floating days can be used anytime. Maybe I get sick, maybe there's a family event I have to go to, maybe there's a day I have technical issues that prevent me from working. Something comes up all the time, so my schedule includes flexibility. It's possible I won't take two days off every week and I'll write more words than targeted – that's fine. The goal I'm aiming for on a daily basis, based on this calculation, is not the cut-off point where I have to stop; it's the minimum I want to achieve for that day.

Of course, there will be days where you don't reach that goal. You can't be deterred by the fact that you don't achieve it every day. Some days just don't work no matter how hard you try. If your goal is 1,000 words, approximately four pages double spaced, and you write 900 or even 600 or 300, you still have those two floating days. You can still make them up later. And if you don't – you're still going to achieve what you're looking to achieve because you have a long-term goal, you have a road map, you have a plan of action, and you have a means of fulfilling that. Don't let a single day's disruption put you off.

That's part of the reason I include those two free days. Maybe one day you only get 500 words out of the 1,000 you're looking for –these as arbitrary numbers, nice, easy, and round. Maybe on one of those free days you write another 500 and only take one day off. Maybe some weeks, you don't take any days off. Maybe some days everything is working so smoothly, you find you've doubled your intended minimal goal.

All of those work. All of that is beautiful and wonderful and helps you achieve your goal. You want to write a hundred thousand word epic fantasy? Break it up into smaller pieces. Further: give yourself rewards for achieving certain goals. After the first month, if you're on target, celebrate somehow – make a point of saying yes, I am working on and achieving my goals. Celebrate those little victories. The celebration might be something small. I'm not saying take a vacation to Acapulco. Maybe have a piece of chocolate and say, I've done a good thing today, I've made it to this point, I've made it to this – I hate to steal words from Corporate America – *milestone*, and I can make it to the next one and the one after that.

As long as you look at the steps immediately ahead of you on a smaller scale within the bigger process, you will eventually have your hundred thousand words. You'll have that novel. In fact, if you write a thousand words a day, five days a week, you'll have a quarter million words by the end of the year. That is a lot. Just so you know.

KEEPING UP THE WRITING PACE

The writing pace for InkStains is interesting. In a very real way, it's more a marathon than a sprint. I'm not running a race where I'm trying to get there as quickly as possible; this is an endurance exercise. The idea is to write just one story a day. One story could be 15 or 20 minutes. They don't always take a lot of time. I sometimes squeeze that into a lunch hour at my day job. I can do it first thing in the morning as a form of exercise, of getting my mind situated with reality – or non-reality, as the case may be.

I once heard poets tend to fill a page when they wrote a poem. If their page was only five inches long, their poem would end up being five inches of whatever their handwriting happened to be. If your page happens to be 11 inches long, then it's going to be 11 inches worth of poetry. I don't know how true that is, but when I'm doing the InkStains, they tend to end near the bottom of a page. They very rarely leave more than an inch of empty space, though they do sometimes curl around at the end to finish in the margins.

I think the same is true of the time. If I've only got 20 minutes to write a story, I write a 20 minute story. Like in a marathon, I'm paced so that I'm not running flat out – or writing flat out – from the start. I'm just doing a little bit, a little bit, a little bit every day until I reach the finish line. The trick is to not get repetitive. Sometimes you examine a theme from multiple points of view, or return to a particular image or icon or character. There's no rule that says I can't. Referencing the same character or location or theme isn't inherently a bad repetition if it's not the same story over and over again. I'm writing it from different points of view and examining it from different angles, different attitudes, different vantage points. Plots change. Characters change. The reactions and interactions vary greatly.

(I'm not saying none of my stories are repetitive. I definitely have bad days on the InkStains, and sometimes that's just what you've got to do: burn through bad days.)

It's just like running that marathon: you're in the last mile before your second wind kicks in – I'm not a runner, so I don't know the actual terms. There's a point where you just keep pushing until you reach that second wind. Sometimes there's a day or two where the stories turn out to not be as exciting or engaging as others, and it's a disappointment.

Don't let that stop you. Don't stumble, don't trip and fall and sit on the ground and say, oh, I can no longer run my marathon. That's not the case at all. Get back up. Get running again. Get writing again. Get performing again. Whatever art you're doing. It's just a little bit of time on a daily basis. It is every day, but that small bit of time on a daily basis goes a long way.

CELEBRATE THE FIRST DRAFT

DO I CELEBRATE COMPLETING THE FIRST DRAFT OF A NOVEL, OR IS THAT PRE-MATURE? AFTER ALL, THERE'S STILL A LOT OF WORK AHEAD.

THE FIRST DRAFT IS ONLY ONE OF MANY, MANY STEPS BETWEEN CONCEPT AND A FINAL NOVEL. YOU SHOULD PROBABLY DO AT LEAST TWO ROUNDS OF REVISIONS — ONE TO CORRECT ERRORS, ONE TO MAKE SURE YOU DIDN'T OVERCORRECT — BEFORE YOU START SUBMITTING THEM. AGENTS AND EDITORS WILL WANT EDITS. THERE WILL BE GALLEYS TO REVIEW, AND MAYBE ADVANCED READING COPIES. EACH STEP CAN BE ARDUOUS, AND SOME CAN TAKE AS MUCH TIME AS WRITING THAT INITIAL DRAFT.

ALL THAT SAID: HELL YEAH, I CELEBRATE THAT FIRST DRAFT. THAT'S A MAJOR ACCOMPLISH. ESPECIALLY THE FIRST TIME YOU COMPLETE A FIRST DRAFT; IT'S SOMETHING YOU'VE NEVER DONE, AND SOMETHING MOST PEOPLE WILL NEVER DO. THAT FEELING NEVER CHANGES. NO MATTER HOW MANY NOVELS OR OTHER PROJECTS I'VE COMPLETED, NO MATTER HOW MUCH TIME AND SWEAT AND BLOOD WAS DEVOTED TO IT, IT'S ALWAYS A RUSH.

AS TO METHODS OF CELEBRATION — I DON'T THINK I SHOULD DICTATE HOW YOU CELEBRATE. ENJOY THE DAMN MOMENT. YOU'VE EARNED IT.

WHEN THE WORDS WON'T FLOW

A listener asked if I ever have days where the words don't flow smoothly and, if they're not flowing, how do I power through that?

Like the spice, the words must flow, and I make every effort to keep the roads clear. The InkStains project, for instance, is a method of letting words flow. If I'm writing every day, I get accustomed to writing every day, and I find myself itching to write even on that day off every month.

Sure, there are times when it's more challenging. I have taken – I'm not sure what to call them – *sabbaticals* from writing. Breaks. I put down the first draft of *Once Upon a Time in Midnight* because I'd run up against a stopping point I couldn't push past. I didn't know if I'd ever pick it up again, but I did, and six months later finished the first draft. But I put it down knowing if that particular path was stalled, there were other roads I could travel, other stories I could write, and I didn't need to get caught up in a web of my own design.

Don't you love how my metaphors swing in such violently random directions?

I power through it by powering through it. By maybe taking a moment as a break, by seeking other inspirations and a change of environment – maybe a vacation or just a day away. And sometimes, I just accept that this particular piece is done, if not complete, and I should focus elsewhere.

WHO IS IN CONTROL,
THE AUTHOR OR THE CHARACTER?

I've been asked, "Do you control your characters, or do they determine who they are and let that inform you how they'd react to a situation?" And variations. "Do you ever have to reign your characters in?"

Characters, in general, are amalgamations of people I've known and haven't known, the ways in which they are or were and aren't or weren't. A single character can be a patchwork of a dozen different people.

In a past life, as a forms designer, I designed Character Sheets which I use to track information – height, weight, place of birth, relationships, important life experiences, that sort of thing. (I stole the idea from Dungeons & Dragons.) When I create a character, when I pull from all my various experiences and build a person, hopefully I imbue them with enough dimension that you, as a reader, can relate to them or at least understand them. But at all times, I am in control. Never once has a character leapt out of the pages and started making demands.

However, if I've created a fully realized person, they'll react to situations in ways consistent with their character, their thoughts and beliefs and experiences. So, while I am in control, I am also very much restricted by how a real person (or non-person, depending on the type of story) would react.

The characters are afforded opportunities to learn and grow – or not to do so. Ultimately, that's what most stories are about. Like everything else in this world I created, whether it be an alien or fantasy world, or the City of Night from my Midnight stories, everything within the story must remain consistent with itself.

If I establish that the city Midnight has no bats but does have crows and magpies, I cannot forget that partway through the third book. By the same manner, if a character has blue eyes, I cannot forget that. And if a character has consistently reacted in a non-violent way to threats on their life, there better be a damn good and convincing reason for them to suddenly start throwing punches.

DO OUTLINES KILL CREATIVITY?

No.

Wow, that was easier than I expected.

No, outlines do not kill creativity. For some writers, it's an integral part of the writing process. Many won't even start until they know every plot point, every beat, every side story, every subplot.

I know at least one writer who starts with an outline and expands it, then expands it some more, then keeps expanding it until they've got a fully fleshed-out novel. It sounds like a fascinating process, but it's not mine.

Outlining, like any other part of the process, is subjective. It's personal. What works for me might not work for you. What works for you might not work for me.

I have done outlines. I have done them in the classic style with Roman numerals, and I have done them as sketchy thought clouds. I find those structures to be a good start. But I never feel obligated to stick to them. Once upon a time, when I was still very young, I re-outlined a single novel so many times, as I was writing it, the story changed from one about psychics to a story about aliens, then witches, and finally developed into a particular kind of never-before-seen supernatural race. In this way, the outlines served more as sketchpads. I played with ideas, explored possibilities and themes, determined what wouldn't work for the story, and got rid of it before it became too intricately entwined.

I have written completely without an outline, just diving straight into something. A lot of the InkStains stories are like that. But the InkStains stories only take a few handwritten pages. They rarely have the time, space, or need to develop as fully and richly as a novel. I have several failed novel beginnings that will never go any further because I never had any place to take them.

I always sketch out possibilities and explore options. It's part of who I am and part of what I do. This is how I fill notebooks. I've been known to write possible future scenes, things that might happen later in the book, things that seem like they have to happen. Sometimes, these scenes end up inserted exactly as written in precisely the right place. Sometimes, events in the story make these scenes unlikely or even impossible.

On big projects, novels and novellas, and sometimes short stories, I at least know where I'm going. I have something of a map, if not a richly detailed and fully annotated atlas. But I have a goal, and all efforts in the story are aimed toward that goal.

To avoid pitfalls, I take notes as I write, I keep character sheets, I have index cards with questions that need to be answered so I won't accidentally leave something hanging. If I plant a seed, I make a note so I don't miss a payoff. If it turns out the seed withered and died, I determine whether the seed itself still serves a purpose or should be removed in revision.

An outline might prevent some of those bad seeds. But when I'm writing, I consider it an exploration. An adventure. I may have an idea of where the book is going, and I may know some of the paths I'll take to get there, but I'll probably have additional ideas as I go. I may discover something needs more attention – or something doesn't belong at all. When I write, it's not purely an act of creativity, it's an act of discovery. I don't always know how I'm going to get to the end I have in mind.

Those pre-supposed endings can change. During the first draft of *Breath of the Moon* (my second novel, circa 2006), I reached the ending I expected to discover it was only the halfway mark. It's not merely okay, as the creator, to be surprised by what you uncover as you write; it's exciting.

The short answer is no, outlines don't kill creativity. They provide a guide rope through what can sometimes be treacherous terrain. But the depth and breadth of everyone's outlines varies. In fact, the nature of the outlines and/or maps and/or plans I set for my own works changes from project to project. Every project is new, and every project must be approached in its own way. There's no single right answer as to best method of outlining. I cannot prescribe the perfect approach. The best way is always the way that best serves the project.

DOES MY PHOTOGRAPHY AFFECT MY WRITING?

Does the visual nature of my photography affect how I creating my fiction? Do the stories impact my photography?

I believe all arts can be interconnected. Not that they are or have to be, just that they can be. I've always had a very cinematic approach to my writing. In my first novel, *Sins of Blood and Stone*, the climax begins when a demon crashes into a cathedral through the stained glass rose window.

Take a moment to visualize that.

I'd written the first draft of this book in the 90s. That's a long time ago. When I wrote the scene, I saw it, in my mind, very cinematically. I had studied video and audio production in college (but never worked in the field), and I had taken one photography course. By the time the novel was published in 2002, I'd only had a fistful of other stories published. I couldn't be called a photographer; despite that photography class in college, I hadn't actively shot for years.

I renewed my love for photography when I borrowed my partner's digital camera during a trip to Savannah. Digital was relatively new then, at least to me. I think I caught some amazing things, even if I had no idea what I was doing or how the equipment worked.

As with the writing, I learned through experience. Years of it. Experience and self-guided study. I read the books, I took online courses, I even convinced a day job once to send me to a course in Photoshop.

The writing and photography did not necessarily go hand-in-hand, but I learned both over the same stretch of a lifetime, each in spurts as I expanded my knowledge and did more.

So, to the question of how the photography affects the writing and vice versa, it's not that the relationship is *between* them. Instead, the writer in me and the photographer in me share a similar ancestor – me – and therefore are fed by similar attitudes and proclivities.

I think that's true of many artists who work in different fields. The musician who also paints. The dancer who keeps a journal of poetry. The chef who posts pictures of interesting doorways on Instagram. The different means of expression don't compete, and they probably don't express the same things. However, they have the same source, which is to say me, or you, whoever the artist might be. Our experiences and knowledge and skillsets, our biases and prejudices and beliefs, our point of view on this world and our outlook on life – all these things feed all our arts.

It's been said that I write about unexpected cities and inconvenient women. I believe the same can be said about my photography. I believe the adjectives *unexpected* and *inconvenient* are reductive, restrictive, and incomplete. But I believe a lot of things. You're more than welcome to disagree with me.

To break this down: I write visually for the same reason that I shoot photos, not because I shoot them. Other outlets allow you to explore in different ways. They let you see the world from a vantage point other than your primary art. Sure, the two arts, or more than two, will grow together, will intertwine with each other in sometimes unusual and unique ways. They will intersect, and sometimes feed off each other, and they absolutely can affect each other; but they are siblings, born to the same place.

LANGUAGE, POINT OF VIEW, AND THE RIGHT WORD

Words matter. Word choice matters. When you're writing, there's a world of difference between *He staggered down the stairs* and *He hopped down the stairs*. Both can be simplified to *He went down the stairs*. The choice of *stagger* or *hop* provides a level of description, and a layer of story, to the sentence while provoking a stronger image. Language is often about creating images.

You want to use the right word for the job. Like any tool. You wouldn't use a hammer to screw in a lightbulb, right? You would completely and utterly fail.

Word choice and phraseology depend not just on the writer, but on the point of view being presented. You may be an Oxford educated linguist fluent in eleven languages, but if the point of view character in your story is a working class teenage boy from Detroit, he's not likely to say, *I presume from your stature a great deal of malevolency directed toward me and my fine cronies*. You don't just want to avoid that in dialogue, but in the language of the story.

When the story is from his point of view, even in third person limited, the language used should reflect his. Otherwise, you risk kicking your reader out of the story. We can have a whole conversation on points of view, and how this might not matter if you're writing in third person omniscient, and it might even change if you're writing about that teenager from Detroit sixty years after he's completed his post-doctoral treatise on the musicality of language and the excessive reliance upon pretension. On the other hand, if your teenager looks down at everyone around him, if that teenager puts himself on a pedestal, maybe he chooses his language to be dismissive of everyone around him. Maybe he *would* say *I presume from your stature*, and then lift his jaw to provide a better target because it somehow proves he's not a savage like everyone around him.

You tell a lot of story in the language you use, not just the way you use that language to forward the plot or paint a character or describe a setting.

Here's the thing, though. I am of the camp who firmly believes the first draft is all about getting the words down. Power through it. If you're stuck on a particular choice of word, do not let that derail you. I often take a minute or two to figure something out, especially when it's a stupid brain freeze and I know the exact word but for some reason think it starts with a C when it actually starts with a P. It's okay to live with that frustration for ten or twenty seconds. Then I'll leave myself a note in the manuscript, something in all caps that says *SMOKE DRIFTING*, so when I come back to it in my revision, the part of the process where it's all about getting the words right, I'll see that note, say, *waft, I can't believe I blanked on the word waft*, and fix it.

You'll find, when you've been doing this for a while, you often know exactly the right words, though that doesn't mean you won't mistype them, misremember them, misspell them, or something equally stupid. The word *waft* stands out for me because when I was younger, a lot younger, in the middle of a story I used it and it made me stop. It broke my rhythm. Not because I was searching for the right word, but because I had just written a word and wasn't sure if that was what I'd meant. I wasn't sure I knew the word, or how I knew it. I needed to open a dictionary – this was the dim ages of the early internet, but the truth is I still have seven or eight of them – just to make sure I'd used the correct word. I had. I'd used the right word in exactly the right way and the right place. It was excellent. Possibly the single best word of that long ago story.

Another time, I described a woman as *sillowy*. Go on, look it up. Use an online dictionary. I'll wait. You didn't find it, did you? Because it doesn't exist? I remember nothing else about the woman or the story except I'd typed the word *sillowy* and, when I went in for my revision, it made me pause. Not because it threw me out of the story. It made me pause because I wanted to get the words right, and I wasn't sure this was the right word. It wasn't even a real word. It took a while to realize I'd probably hit S instead of W, and that I'd probably meant to describe her as *willowy*, which is an honest and real word. But I couldn't change it. In this case, this unreal word, this thing I'd created by virtue of a mis-struck key, seemed somehow more appropriate.

The word *sillowy* still doesn't exist in any dictionary I'm aware of. However, you will find it, every once in a while, in other stories of mine. Not every story, not every novel, not every woman. Only when it's appropriate. Because even though the word doesn't exist, it's provocative, and in context you know exactly what it means, and because it is exactly the right word in the right place at the right time.

POINT OF VIEW

The stories we read and write could be utterly and totally without limits unless we, the writers, apply limits. We choose which scenes forward the story and need to be shown, and we choose which scenes serve no purpose and can be skipped. So we don't need to follow every step from the innkeeper to the room, only the exchange of money for a key, and only the moment we open the room door to find a baby dragon mewling inside.

Deciding on point of view is one of the most important decisions of any story. It sets the ultimate limitations. It restricts what we see, what we do, and what we are telling our readers. If the first line of *Moby Dick* had been *Call him Ishmael,* it's already lost all its impact. It no longer tells us who is telling the story, and it no longer signals to us, right from the start, that the narrator doesn't want us to know who he really is. It's not like he said, *My name is Ishmael.* Call me this, because I would use an alias, because I know you won't believe me and maybe you shouldn't. And if J.R.R. Tolkien had decided to make *The Hobbit* a first person adventure, with Bilbo Baggins telling the story, he couldn't begin *In a hole in the ground there lived a hobbit.* And he certainly wouldn't bother telling us *Not a nasty, dirty, wet hole,* because the hobbit already knows what a hobbit hole is and would feel no need to explain it.

A lot of today's fiction is written in third person limited, wherein most scenes are told with words like He and She but are still limited to the senses and knowledge of a single character. Third person omniscient doesn't have that limitation, and used to be in vogue, but is more difficult to pull off successfully without confusing readers accustomed to the more limited point of view.

First person is told with words like I. I did this, I felt that, I saw this. Like third person limited, it's restricted to a single point of view, but even more blatantly, and sometimes makes it difficult for readers to differentiate between the author and the narrator.

Second person is told with words like You. You go into the room, you pick up the book, you hoist the flute like a weapon. This is less frequently used, but for a brief time in the 80's and 90's it was predominant in *Choose Your Own Adventure* novels. Chapters ended with the reader deciding what to do next and turning to the appropriate page. Pick the pocket of the ogre magistrate? Lie to the princess? Boldly attack the prison guards with only a frayed shoelace and a thimble?

In the InkStains stories, I got to play with all of these points of view, even second person stories where I tried to make them as inclusive as possible – nothing to specify gender, height, or weight, and I even tried to not exclude disabilities I've never had or imagined. I wanted everyone to be able to get into the story. But I missed something, in doing so, as second person also gives the reader an opportunity to be someone else, even if only for a short time.

As a writer, being someone else is important, especially if you want to include characters not directly familiar to you. Examples could be women writing from a man's perspective, or Catholics writing from a Hindu point of view. The intent isn't to demonize the person who is *other* than yourself, but to understand their struggles, their beliefs, and their experiences, even if in a small way, and make their characters feel real, honest, and authentic. Consider it an exercise in empathy.

The future for all of us is a great open road into the unknown. Catastrophe may await, but also opportunity and experience. A large part of what we do, as artists, is distill our various experiences into something readers can recognize and, hopefully, relate to. Even in the most fantastic literature, even when the characters aren't human, we generally know them through our human experiences. We empathize, or at least sympathize, with their emotions and their situations, because those emotions and situations reflect our everyday lives.

Even when the primary purpose of a story is to serve as an escape, it works because we can put ourselves into the shoes, and into the minds, of the characters. We can understand how they would react to a situation, any situation, because we know how we might react. Granted, we might not make the same choices as the characters in the story or on the screen. We may even scream at them, "Don't be an idiot, don't investigate that noise alone, don't go down into that cellar in your underwear!" Because we know we would never do such a thing. But in a well-crafted story, we should at least comprehend those choices. We should understand why they're doing what they're doing. We should realize that, in the same situation, we might do the same thing.

We might not, for instance, bury our recently dead toddler in a pet cemetery hoping he'll return. And we might not choose to avenge the murder of our parents by chasing after clowns for the rest of our lives. But the emotions that lead to these decisions, the grief and despair, are very human emotions we can all tap into.

That empathy we feel as an audience is an essential tool for the artist. Some artists might successfully portray only their own point of view, but I'd be afraid that would lead to unsympathetic and unrealistic characterizations when think at all differently than you do. If there's one thing this modern world has taught us, one thing it drills into our head every single day because so many people can't seem to understand, it's that we don't all think alike, and some people are willing and even eager to kill in order to defend their point of view.

In fiction, we have to be able to step into somebody else's point of view in order to understand the character. They may be despicable people, they may have not a single shred of decency within them, but we have to be able to understand what fuels them, why they make the choices they do, how they lived their life to this point, and how they'll continue it in the future, beyond the confines of our specific tale.

It's a dangerous, dark thing, sometimes, diving into minds like that, essentially examining hatred, recognizing complacency, understanding fear. I certainly wouldn't claim to have a thorough understanding of these things through experience. At least I hope I can't. But I've lived my entire life as a human being, with human thoughts and human feelings. I've seen how some humans treat other humans. I've witnessed the best and the worst of humanity. And I have human reactions to what I see. I feel, and I care, and I hope. I remain hopeful. Optimistic. Even when I don't trust, I'm still hopeful. I've seen so much stupidity, but also so much compassion, so much generosity and love, that I believe we, the whole of humanity, continue to have a future.

POINT OF VIEW RISKS AND LIMITATIONS

There are several types of points of view you can use, but the most common are first person and third person limited. Quickly, second person is anything where the main character of the story is *you*, the reader. [Author's note: I've written one of these, and hopefully you'll get to see it soon.] Third person omniscient is not limited to a single person's point of view. When done well, it can be amazing – one example off the top of my head is Brian Lumley's *Necroscope* series. But you have to be careful with omniscient point of view, because if you hop from head to head – the heads of your characters, I'm not trying to describe some Cirque du Soleil act – you run the risk of confusing the audience. Often, it is done very, very poorly.

The risk with first person point of view, especially for younger writers – which doesn't mean that you're young; you might be eighty, that doesn't matter, I mean people who haven't had a whole lot of experience writing stories – younger writers will often confuse their protagonist with themselves. I used to do this when I was in high school and junior high – don't be surprised, I've been writing forever – but first person also has the distinct advantage of bringing the reader closest to the main character. It is of course limited to what the main character knows, says, does, and thinks.

Third person limited has the same limitation. The entirety of the scene is from a single point of view character, even though, as authors, we're still maintaining some distance. He says this or she does that. Again, we're limited – it's right there in the name – to what our POV character knows, thinks, and feels. For example, a young character with her father isn't going to think of him by his first name, she's likely to think of him as Dad, and would refer to him accordingly. Anything else could be confusing or require explanation.

This limitation also means you can't tell us what's happening concurrently in Prague without the point of view character being informed of this somehow, or by switching to another point of view character after a scene break – this is perfectly fine, but if you do it too frequently you run the risk of confusing readers again.

Clarity, as always, whether in entire scenes or stories or merely in sentences and individual word choice, is always important. When I talked once about the geography of an action scene, it was all about making the action clear. When I talk about the limitations of point of view, I'm talking about keeping the narrative structure, the presentation, and the story itself clear.

In fact, the word *limitation* is somewhat negative. If you think of it as a limitation, if you think it means you can't describe what's going on in Prague, if you think you can't get into the heads of the other characters and fully illustrate them as unique individuals – then I say you're taking this whole limitation thing the wrong way. Those other characters and those other plot points are still going to be witnessed and/or experienced by the point of view character in some way. Your narrator, in a first person piece, or your main character in third person limited, will know whether they like another character. Since those scenes are written from their perspectives, word choice is going to play a factor in what the reader thinks of these other people. Also what our POV characters choose to observe. For instance, if we say Bob's eyes are blue like twilight sky, that's a very different feel than saying Bob's eyes are narrow little needle points stuck under his brows. We can talk about the same person from two different points of view and get a rather clear idea that one of these POV characters really doesn't like Bob.

Poor Bob.

When writing in first person or third person limited, it's important to remember that the use of language and the sentence structure and the observations, as well as the story being told, will all be reflective of that person's point of view. It's much more obvious in first person, but it's still true in third. An eighty year old white American male will have a different voice, and notice different things, than a twelve year old from Sudan. Their life experiences, the ones that contribute to nothing else in this story and therefore don't need to be shared with the readers, will color their perceptions of the world, their opinions and beliefs, just as our own collective life experiences color ours.

Remember, a story is generally about a character, or characters, about how the plot impacts that character and whether or not they grow, learn, or even survive it. Even their use of language may indicate growth. If you ever read my "The Rag and Bone Man," you'll notice our point of view character through most of the story is Timmy. There are a few scenes from other points of view, including an opening section that is really omniscient and therefore probably never belonged. But you'll also notice that part way through the story, Timmy makes a decision that will have big implications for his life and change him forever; from the moment he makes that decision, it's no longer Timmy doing this or doing that, it's Tim. That was a conscious decision on my part, as an author, to help illustrate that yes, this is a life-changing decision he's made, and he's grown as a result of it.

POETICS

I've played with language in a lot of ways. Way back in fifth grade, I remember a language game our teacher, Mr. Schwab, had us do. He wrote *walk* on the chalkboard and asked us to identify other words that also mean *walk* but say something more. For instance: *stumble, strut, saunter, lope, march*. It was more than just a game of synonyms, because these words were also evocative. They said more than merely *walk*, and accomplished this with a single word. *Run* is not the same as walk, and *race* is not the same as run, and *speed* might shift the meaning even more.

I've found a great place to play with words and language is in poetry. I do not consider myself a great poet, but I've got a notepad especially for scribbling poetics, a Japanese-style *Moleskine* that unfolds as a single long page. Poetry often requires the most concise language, the strongest and best-considered words, and also gives you the chance to play with those words in ways you might not otherwise. Consider Edgar Allan Poe's poem *Eldorado*.

There are four stanzas, each containing six lines, the last word of every third line being *Shadow* and the last of every stanza *Eldorado*. Around those, every pair of lines but one rhymes. There's some serious wordplay involved here.

It's supposed to be playful, and you can have a lot of fun with it. You don't need to follow rhyming patterns or poetic structure to have fun with language and play with the words, though such structures force you to make choices you might not otherwise make.

GAILY BEDIGHT,
A GALLANT KNIGHT,
IN SUNSHINE AND IN SHADOW,
HAD JOURNEYED LONG,
SINGING A SONG,
IN SEARCH OF ELDORADO.

BUT HE GREW OLD—
THIS KNIGHT SO BOLD—
AND O'ER HIS HEART A SHADOW
FELL AS HE FOUND
NO SPOT OF GROUND
THAT LOOKED LIKE ELDORADO.

AND, AS HIS STRENGTH
FAILED HIM AT LENGTH,
HE MET A PILGRIM SHADOW—
'SHADOW,' SAID HE,
'WHERE CAN IT BE—
THIS LAND OF ELDORADO?'

'OVER THE MOUNTAINS
OF THE MOON,
DOWN THE VALLEY OF THE SHADOW,
RIDE, BOLDLY RIDE,'
THE SHADE REPLIED,—
'IF YOU SEEK FOR ELDORADO!'

Language

I've been uprooted. I took my cat across the Atlantic Ocean and ended up in Madrid, Spain, on the Iberian peninsula. While you've been listening to other shows, I've been acclimating myself to a new country and a new lifestyle.

There's so much to tell, but now is not the place. I could be here for hours, and we have a lot to do. But I had to welcome you back to InkStains, officially and formally, and I think this is the best way to do it. If you can't see me, I am dressed in full white tie regalia, drastically formal and well beyond a mere tux and black tie. I cannot say I have the official backing of the King of Spain, so I will make no such claim. I have bowed – you don't have to – and now I can get to what I'm really here to talk about.

Language.

I am new to this country, new to its history and culture and traditions and language. I've picked up a few dozen Spanish words over the course of my life. I've also got some French and German, but can't claim to be conversant in any of these. I have learned it takes thousands of hours to learn a language, so after just a couple of weeks in Spain I have no right to beat myself up over the fact that I cannot communicate effectively and elegantly with the locals.

Sure, I can use Google translate. And yes, since I'm here, I've started Spanish language lessons. I usually manage to get my message across. But it's easy at a store when I can point and say I'd like one of those please. Often, the people here speak as much English as I speak Spanish. Sometimes, there's someone who's at least conversant if not fluent. Fortunately, language isn't the only means of communication available to humans. We've got all that nonverbal communication stuff going on, too. Like I said, I can point. I can smile. I can shake my head or nod or at least say *No entiendo*.

But I exist as an island here, an English speaker in a sea of Spanish.

I'm perfectly fine with that. I knew what I was getting into.

Menus are the hardest thing, because there's so many words I don't understand, and all those words describe things in ways I don't understand. I'm a picky eater and cannot eat beans, for instance, and I'm not a fan of whipped cream. How do I convey this? How do I even order, when I look at a menu of a dozen items and I know one of these is chicken of some sort, because I recognize the word *pollo,* and one of these is octopus, because I recognize the word *pulpo,* and one of these is scallops because I recognize the word *escalopines* – but actually they're not scallops at all, that's actually how the meat has been sliced. That scallop dish was actually steak – and somewhere else, that scallop dish might have been chicken.

It can be so confusing.

When we write, we don't typically have nonverbal forms of communication available to us. Maybe if you're writing a screenplay, or a comic book script, or something similar, the end product will have artwork or imagery that will play into what you're communicating. But before that, all we've got to work with are our words.

It's good to know the right words to use, and when to use them, and when another word might be better. All that word choice is a function of our personal styles and can often be subconscious, at least in the first drafts. But as we revise, as we refine the work, we have the opportunity to review the words we've chosen and decide if they really are the best for the job. Are we employing language in its most efficient, most effective, or most elegant ways? Does it need to be all three of these at one time? Probably not. Are we doing what's best for the work?

I recently re-read *Something Wicked this way Comes,* by Ray Bradbury. It's much more stylized that I remembered. It's full of interesting language choices, even in the first line: *First of all, it was October, a rare month for boys.* It's not simply the choices of an author writing a book in the 50's, it's also the choices of the characters within that book. The language in dialogue should reflect the language of the speaker. The language in the narrative should reflect the language of the character whose point of view this is.

A person who works in fashion, for instance, is likely to know the difference between a shift dress and a sheath dress. A photographer will talk in apertures and f-stops. A chef will know when to use a boning knife and when to use a paring knife. People without these skills will see only a dress, a camera, and a blade, so when you tell me she's wearing a vintage Chanel cocktail dress, or that he's breaking out to a 1200mm lens, or she's about to julienne a plate of carrots, I'm making assumptions about these characters based in part on their use of that specialized language.

I'm also making assumptions when one character says the sky was blue and another says it's blue like ground lapis lazuli and another says it's blue like her lover's eyes.

As writers, language is our first and most powerful tool. Almost nothing exists without it. We can point and jump up and down like apes, like madmen, but that's probably not the most effective way to tell a story.

There are other, visual ways of telling a story, but even those art forms have their own specialized language and means of expression. As writers, as creators, it's our job to strive for a fuller command of the language we use and the way we use it, to take advantage of it when we can, to bend to its rigidness when we must, and to purposefully and intentionally convey the stories we're trying to tell.

QUESTIONS TO ASK AND ANSWER

What's one of the most important ingredients in the telling of a story? Questions. I don't mean just the mystery as characters try to answer questions to move the plot. Those are important, too. You, as the writer, should know the answers to the questions they used to train journalists to answer: what, who, where, when, why. The 5 W's, as they're known.

What happened? That's the plot. That's the linear, or non-linear, description of events that move your story from the beginning through the treacherous terrains of the middle all the way to the end.

Who? Who did the plot happen to, or around, or who is it about? As storytellers, we drive into the heart of who by striving to make characters believable and relatable with true motivation behind their actions. When the who is driven by the what, when you get characters who make choices to further the plot rather than their own agenda – even when their agenda is not mischievous or wicked or underhanded – you get a bad story. Watch any number of summer blockbusters and you'll see people making decisions because they have to bring the plot back home, rather than because it's what a real person would do in that situation.

Where? This is the setting, the environment surrounding the characters, and it's vitally important. A story about loneliness set in the heart of Times Square is going to be substantially different from a story about loneliness set in the heart of the Sahara. The answer to the question of where will help lead your story into specific directions related to your theme.

When? Like where, this can change the meaning of your story. A black man struggling against institutional prejudice in the present day would be different than if the story was set in the 60's, and would be different again if the story was set in the 1920's or the 1860's.

Finally: why? Why does the story happen? Often as a result of the decisions of characters within the story, but not always. Even a versus nature story should answer why the characters, pitting themselves against the might of a hurricane they know is coming, didn't flee inland. Or why they can't flee.

If you haven't realized, these are not simply answered. You don't sit down before writing your story and break out five index cards with giant

W's on one side and scratch out answers on the other before embarking on this particular adventure. Some of these questions will be answered inherently by the structure and nature of the tale you're attempting to spin. Some will imply the answers to other questions.

These are important questions, but storytellers generally don't answer them in the same way as journalists. We may want to impart this information slowly, perhaps over time. We might start with the name of the character and the color of her eyes while she's on a train – look, we've already started to answer *where* while establishing *who* – and we've also posed the question of *why* is she on that train in the first place. She's looking out the window, but we don't yet know if it's wistful or hopeful, we don't know if she's leaving something or going to something.

At this point, as a reader, I might want to know why we even bothered with the color of her eyes. This is the first bit of physical description you, as the author, have given me, so I'm assuming, based on its prominence right here at the start, it's somehow important. Prove that to me as the story progresses. Answer the why's while asking the other why's. Define the when, since she could be sitting on a train in 2019 or 1819. You have two where's to answer, in addition to the train itself: where is she going and where is she leaving. All of these questions are interrelated, and the substance of these answers is what makes the story. All of these are important questions to ask, and to answer, or to at least hint at.

But perhaps you want to hold something back. Maybe you'd like to set it in a generic city. Fine, don't say it's Baltimore or Columbus, but still establish that it is a city. The depth in which you answer these questions is defined by you and your story, not some guidebook that dictates just how much information you should impart to the reader and when.

These are fundamental to the creation of your story. But there may be a more important question than these.

The 5 W's, what, who, where, when, and why, all important questions and vital in the construction of a story, are only the component parts. You need more than that to tell a story. You need a reason for the story. Not a why so much as the answer to another question, possibly the most important of all the questions.

No, not what is the Matrix. The question is *What If?* What if a woman traveling by train met a magician and fell in love, but the magician was actually an alien from Mars? Now there's purpose behind the story and a hint at conflict. You don't know why she's on the train, what she's leaving or where she's going – not necessarily – but you're back on that train between places with a green-eyed woman and a magician from Mars who has never seen green eyes in his life, and suddenly you have – not a plot, not yet – but a premise, a theme, an idea.

The idea is important. Most good stories – I'm sure some don't – pose the question What if. What if a man's parents are murdered in front of him and he happens to be a billionaire? You get *Batman*. What if we exist in a simulated society that exists only in our minds while our bodies are harnessed for energy? You get *The Matrix*. What if scientists invented and lost control of a superflu? You get Stephen King's *The Stand*. You don't get the plots, you don't get answers to the 5 W's, not all of them at once, but you get the impetus to explore those questions.

What if aliens made contact? You get *Close Encounters of the Third Kind*. Or you get *Contact*, with Jodie Foster. Or *Men in Black*. Or *Mars Attacks!* Or you get a woman on a train meeting a magician from Mars and falling in love as she travels to or from some place for some reason.

STRUCTURE

On a story level, structure is about how the story is organized. You'll see and hear things about three act plays and five act plays, you'll read advice that states categorically you must have this kind of event happen on page ten of a script, or you must open the story in the middle of the action, or any variety of well-meaning and wrong-minded things you must do.

The only thing you *must* do is what's best for the story. And while sometimes that might mean following those kinds of strict guidelines, the story may demand something else. And while you should be free to build that story the way it needs to be built, you should also be aware of the rules and guidelines so that you can use them. You don't have to tie yourself down with them, but you have to know what you're doing.

You have to be able to build suspense, to give the story a foundation, to deal with inciting incidents and resolutions. You have to be aware that a story is about something, it's not merely a series of things that happens. I say *something*, but what I mean is character – the story is about a character, generally, and about that character's growth or failure to grow.

That doesn't always seem to be true, either. Look at series like Sherlock Holmes, where the main characters, the recurring characters, Holmes and Watson, unravel mysteries but don't necessarily grow as characters. There's no overall character arc. There is, however, a revelation; the revelation here is that different types of stories require different types of structure.

You've got narratives that flow linearly, and you've got three-act narrative, and you've got films like *Pulp Fiction* and *Memento* shifting everything around.

The story is structured around the desire of its primary character, the one whose story is being told, to either accomplish or avoid something. The story is all the things the character, and the other characters around them, do to achieve their goal.

Narrative structure is something, as a storyteller, you need to be aware of, so you can break those rules when you need to. Think of an architect designing a house. They don't need to re-create the idea of what a house is every time they put pencil to paper.

There's another, more granular kind of structure underlying the story. That's the grammar, the sentence structure, how the paragraphs are put together, how chapters break, how books in a series end. These are the nuts and bolts you use to put the story together. This is where you can employ some artistry and style.

And again, there's all sorts of great advice out there, like varying the lengths of your sentences to avoid a repetitive monotone; mixing up sentence structures; minimizing adverbs and using strong verbs. A lot of it, like how to determine when you've reached the end of a chapter, feels intuitive, and can tie back into the narrative structure.

Music is structured. Paintings are structured. Meals are structured. When you're working on exercises to strengthen your skills, be aware of the structural choices you're making. Practice using the tools so that, when you're not practicing, when you're working on the next novel for publication, you don't have to be consciously aware of how to form sentences. If you don't have to think about the mechanics, if they've become part of your muscle memory, you can focus on what you're saying with confidence that *how* you're saying it isn't getting in the way.

I think about structure a lot. This week, a friend, another writer, sought advice on doing a collection of stories. My response was to start strong and end strong, and to include variety – not just in the types of stories but the lengths and even the approaches. Like putting together a sentence, a story, a novel – or composition, poem, illustration, or sculpture – there are structural choices to be made. Aesthetic and architectural decisions. How do the stories flow, one to another, and how do they resonate together? If there's a theme of some sort, does it wind through the selections in a way that makes sense?

I can't tell you how you should approach the structure of your art, but you should be aware of it, you should be familiar with it, you should make conscious decisions rather than unknowingly defaulting to *whatever*, and you should, like our architect friend, be thoroughly familiar with the idea of what makes a house – or a story.

Structure Challenge

Think about the structure of a collection of stories.

Stories or songs or dishes or paintings. Whatever your art, put together something bigger, something that combines disparate things — yet somehow thematically linked so they form a cohesive whole.

Use pieces you've already created or pieces you only have concepts for, that's fine. The idea is to practice pulling things together, to see what works and what doesn't work for you. Take ten stories or songs or paintings and put together an exhibit, an album, or a collection.

If you've never done this before, do it with the understanding that this is only practice, and that this is merely a foundation that might change over the course of the next weeks, months, or years.

In college, a teacher (for a repeating class we were meant to take every semester) had us create resumes at age nineteen. There was nothing to include except the idea that I was going to school, I had flipped burgers, and I liked to write. The purpose wasn't to have a resume we could send to potential employers right away — and the purpose of this exercise isn't to have something complete that's ready to go right now, either. It's about familiarizing yourself with the structure of it, on a scale you've maybe never played with before.

Look at other collections and other albums to see what is or isn't successful, in your opinion, in the work of those artists, and apply what you learn. Think cohesion, but also variety, and think of this as a kind of showcase.

If you're early in your artistic career, maybe you'll be doing this just for fun and experience; but like that resume I made in college, it can become something you build from. That original resume looks vastly different than the one I used most recently because I've had decades to use, revise, update, and refresh the information. You'll do that here, too. Your first version may include story titles that aren't written yet. You'll later realize the third piece isn't as strong as you thought and you'll replace it. You'll decide the final piece isn't strong at all, and though it was your favorite last year when you put these together, it simply doesn't belong.

My first collection, *Shadows, Legends & Secrets*, long out of print, was published by Flesh & Blood Books in the early 2000s. I've learned a lot since then — about me, about my art, about how I would put together a collection. In a way, that was my practice collection, my learning collection, and that experience helped me when putting together my 2014 collection, *Tales of the Fantastic and the Phantasmagoric*. The lessons from that latter experience will carry forward into my next collection.

The point of this exercise is to play with structure on a different scale, so that when the time comes, you're at least familiar with the tools and have given the structure some thought.

STORY V. PLOT

There's a gargoyle in my office. He sits on a stone – he is stone – reading a book, and I know it's a book about a gargoyle in New York City because I wrote the first draft back in '96, the same year the gargoyle came into my life. He was a going away present, and a congratulations on finishing the novel, which was later published in 2002 as *Sins of Blood and Stone*.

He's not really reading. He's pretending. What he's actually doing is watching. Gargoyles, theoretically, are meant to keep water away from architectural structures to save the mortar from eroding, but there's no masonry involved here. He's probably actually a grotesque, but that's beside the point. He's performing the other function of a gargoyle: protecting the home from demons. He watches for infiltration, he and my cat Max, and together they keep me safe as I sleep.

And during the day, he makes sure I'm working. He's saying, "You've got words to write, so get to it. You have stories to tell and worlds to create and worlds to destroy." He's unflinching and relentless. He wouldn't allow a bathroom break if I asked, so I never ask and instead suffer the intensity of his glare.

He knows a great many things. He knows about climax and resolution. He knows about cardboard cutout characters who should usually be eliminated. He's forgotten more about tense than I've ever known – and I know there's more than just past, present, and future tense.

He knows the difference between story and plot. Do you?

I didn't, not for a long time. And when I look it up now, I'm still confused, because some places say, "the plot is a sequence of events and the story is how and why those events," while someplace else says, "story is a sequence of events, and plot establishes the relationship between those events."

I like this definition: story is what it's about, and plot is what happens.

I've seen *Lord of the Rings* used to describe this. The plot ends before the story, because the plot can be (spoiler warning) the defeat of Sauron and destruction of the ring, while the story is not about the ring at all but about Frodo and his journey; concluding the plot didn't bring his story to a conclusion.

However you define them – and one of these definitions is clearly wrong, since they're nearly opposites – story and plot are two different things, and during the course of fiction or film, the two are often very closely linked. In fact, typically, the closer the climax of the story and the climax of the plot are close to each other, the stronger the conclusion.

Back to my gargoyle novel: the plot concerns a demon alive in modern New York City and a gargoyle who can stop it. The story, however, is one of redemption. *Citizen Kane* is a story of Kane's life, but the plot begins when he dies and everyone wants to know what the hell he meant by *Rosebud.* The first *Star Wars* has a plot that involves blowing up the Death Star, but its story is the hero's tale of a farm boy who grows up to become a knight.

Sometimes, when you're writing, you may find a particular piece doesn't have a satisfying ending because, while you've wrapped up the plot, you haven't done anything to conclude the story. Once you realize what's wrong, this is something you can fix.

GENRE

When a listener asked for my favorite genre, I didn't know if she meant for reading or writing, so I answered with the story of me.

In ancient times, elementary school and maybe earlier, I started with comic book superheroes, though I'm not sure that's a genre onto itself. (At about the same time, I remember children's editions of *The Three Musketeers* and *20,000 Leagues Under the Sea,* as well as Golden Readers and *Curious George.*)

I moved quickly to science fiction and fantasy, reading *The Lord of the Rings* for the first time at about 12 years old (thanks Uncle John!). At the time, I wrote in those realms, though my knowledge of sciences was limited so my "hard" science fiction stories were just re-hashes of other people's hard science fiction. The first novel I wrote was a crappy version of *Star Wars,* because everything I did at the beginning was mimicry. *Dungeons & Dragons* led me to write more sword and sorcery.

By college, I'd been introduced to Stephen King and Dean Koontz, and I shifted from fantasy with dark elements to horror with supernatural elements. I also read mysteries and, once or twice, romances. I've since expanded to include literary fiction, which is often genre fiction from a different point of view in which language is often seen as more important than story.

When I write, I try to straddle the worlds of literary and genre fictions, fully aware that all such demarcations are arbitrary. What's most important is the story. Everything exists to serve the story – everything including the characters and the language and the theme, the message or moral or statement being presented. All of it serves the story, and all of it is equally important in sculpting that story. In the end, genre is only one of many choices that serve the story.

All that said, I tend to shift between genres, and would probably best be considered a writer of speculative fiction. When someone asks what I write, I tell them Fantasy, Dark Fantasy, and Horror – Fairy tales and ghost stories. Somehow, that gets my meaning across.

EDUCATION OR LACK THEREOF

I have a Bachelor of Science degree from the State University of New York College at Plattsburgh. If you're looking for it on map, find Montreal, in Quebec, and go south about one hour. It's in the valley next to Lake Champlain, where the Loch Ness monster has a cousin called Champy. I went to school there for three and a half years and spent my final semester in Albany, New York, working half an internship for the New York State Community Affairs Network until it was closed by the passing of a new state budget.

My degree was in Communications. Video and audio production, to be precise. Some of my classmates are now news or sports anchors at various television stations across the country, at least one works for the Major League Baseball Network, and one is a Vice President at the Children's Television Workshop. But outside that internship, which didn't last an entire semester because of politics, I have never worked a single day in the field.

Was my education important, then, or worthwhile? Probably. I wouldn't be where I am if I had gone a different path. I wouldn't be who I am, or the writer I am, if I had done anything differently. Instead of working in the field I studied, I worked at gas stations, I answered phones for Ticketmaster, I built cubicles in a publisher's office building, and I scheduled nurses and aides at nursing homes. None of these jobs required any of the skills I tried to hone in college, and none led me to a career of any sort.

Would it have been different if I'd studied creative writing or journalism? Maybe. But I cannot guess what might have been. I can only say what has happened.

What has happened is this: I didn't study my art, not directly, not wholeheartedly, at least not while in school. Sure, I had an English minor, and I took every writing class the school offered – creative writing, fiction writing, poetry writing, writing for radio and television, writing for regional magazines, expository writing, and others I've forgotten. Did any of that make me the writer I am today? Perhaps it contributed. But I remember one teacher telling me pointblank that genre was a waste of time and effort and that I would never amount to anything – and maybe he was right. Another teacher read one of my manuscripts, some novel I would never show you today for any amount of money, something that's long since gone, and said (quoting as best I can), "If you keep writing like this, you'll make a shitload of money."

At the time, fantasy and horror were still things you could make a decent living at. This was the late 80s, before the crash that eventually ended that horror and dark fantasy boom. All of which is to say, those teachers didn't really know everything they thought they knew. Salman Rushdie, for instance, the great literary writer who should be looking down his nose at genre, wrote books like *Hauron and the Sea of Stories,* which is most certainly a fantasy, and *Two Years Eight Months and Twenty-Eight Nights.* Do the math: that's one thousand and one nights, and they were fantastic and fabulous nights full of mystery, romance, and magic. Of course, publishers would never call these fantasy. Yet, when *The Golden House* was released in late 2017, it was touted as a "triumphant and exciting return to realism." So I guess you can be both genre and literary, you just can't admit it.

I admit it. I'm a little of both. I'm not the literary superstar Salman Rushdie is, but I do love a little magic.

This is all a long way of talking about my education, which wasn't geared toward making me a writer. F. Paul Wilson – I'm sorry, maybe I should say Dr. F. Paul Wilson – studied biology in college (according to his Facebook page). There are lawyers, nuclear facility managers, baristas, and foundry workers among my friends, none of whom studied writing officially in any school – just as there are people who did, who have multiple Masters degrees, who wear tweed suits and smoke pipes and teach at ivy league universities. People in both groups have had various levels of success in this writing career thing. Some never graduated college at all, or never set foot in one. Some barely graduated high school, got their G.E.D.s instead, or never finished at all.

In other words, we all studied writing by doing the same three things: reading a lot, writing a lot, and living a life that exposed us to situations, scenarios, characters, and storylines worth writing. There's no requirement that you officially and formally study your art. It might be helpful, it might point you in the right direction, it might introduce you to likeminded people, and it might open up opportunities. But there's no single path to victory here, no matter what some people might say.

There are examples of people who have failed English in high school and went on to be win great literary honors. There are people who studied and learned and followed all the right ways to do this thing and never found their voice. You are not defined by your education or lack thereof. You can make your own education. You can study, read, practice, examine, and immerse yourself in your art, and make yourself the best possible writer or painter or actor you can be, whether or not you earn a piece of paper doing so.

The best education is experience. You want to make good art? Make art. Make a lot of art. Make a lot of bad art. A formal or even informal education will teach you the skills. You can get lessons, tutors, YouTube how to videos, degrees, certificates, whatever. You can learn the skills out of books without anything formal about it. You can learn by poring through interviews of your favorite artists who do the type of thing you want to do.

There are a lot of good and even excellent reasons to get a formal education. Making good and better and intelligent art can be one of those reasons. But it's not a requirement. You don't need that formal education to nurture your talents, to explore the boundaries of your imagination, to express what you feel and what you know. You don't need me or anyone else dictating that you should read this particular book on sentence structure or color theory or film editing.

Two Week Challenge

I've always been a proponent of doing more, stretching outside your own limits, studying — formally and informally — your art and others. By getting outside of what's familiar, you can make discoveries and insights that are unique to you.

I started the original InkStains project because I felt I was losing touch with the realest version of me: the writer. Just after a heart attack, face to face with Death, I realized I hadn't accomplished most of what I'd intended. So I recovered, made changes, and re-focused my energies and intention. Six years later, I'm writing full time, struggling to pay my way every month, and feeling more artistically alive than ever.

There had been small pockets of that artistic aliveness — like when I spent two weeks at the Golden Apple artist residency in Maine — but for the most part, I felt like I'd been holding back and keeping a big, important part of me muted. InkStains was my first step toward unmuting myself, toward reaching into my soul and putting everything on the table. It was a long process, to get from that hospital room to where I am now.

It started with InkStains. I made them fun. I played with notepads and fountain pens. Ultimately, I even did the layout and design for a series of books based on that first set of InkStains — one for every month — the good, bad, and ugly of them, because this was an art project and even the failures were important to the overall statement.

The first InkStains challenge in this book was for three days. Now, let's go a little further. Two weeks. That doesn't seem like too much to ask, does it? One day off anywhere you want it. Whatever your art, whatever your passion, this is the time to do it. A complete something for every day.

There were rules when I did this: I had to start and finish on the day. I counted *the day* all the way until midnight or I went to bed, whichever came later. If I started in the minutes after midnight and went for an hour, that was fine. If I fell asleep at 9 and woke two hours later, I could still write that day's story. If I fell asleep at 9 and woke at 1 am, it was too late, the day was done and gone.

I DIDN'T ALLOW MYSELF TO WRITE THE NEXT DAY'S UNTIL I REACHED THE NEXT DAY. THERE WAS NO GETTING AHEAD. THE CHALLENGE ISN'T TO WRITE THIRTEEN STORIES OR MAKE THIRTEEN PIECES OF ART, THE CHALLENGE IS TO MAKE SOMETHING NEW EVERY DAY FOR FOURTEEN DAYS.

I'VE BEEN ASKED WHAT I WOULD DO IF I NEEDED A SECOND DAY OFF ONE YEAR. I DON'T KNOW THE ANSWER. IT NEVER HAPPENED.

I DID ALLOW MYSELF TO THINK ABOUT STORIES I MIGHT WORK ON. IT WAS OKAY TO GESTATE A PARTICULAR IDEA FOR DAYS BEFORE WORKING ON IT. SOMETIMES, I KNEW SOMETHING WOULD REQUIRE MORE TIME AND I WOULDN'T HAVE THAT TIME UNTIL SATURDAY, SO TUESDAY I WROTE SOMETHING ELSE AND WEDNESDAY I WROTE SOMETHING ELSE AND EVENTUALLY, REACHING SATURDAY, I SPENT HOURS SCRIBBLING UNTIL MY HANDS WERE RIGID CLAWS.

I'M NOT ASKING YOU TO WORK UNTIL YOUR FINGERS BLEED.

I AM ASKING YOU, CHALLENGING YOU, TO TAKE THE NEXT TWO WEEKS —START TODAY, IF YOU CAN — AND MAKE THIRTEEN NEW, COMPLETE, FIRST DRAFTS. IT'S NOT ABOUT GETTING ALL THE WORDS IN THE RIGHT ORDER, IT'S NOT ABOUT CREATING MASTERPIECES; IT'S ABOUT TRAINING YOUR HEAD AND YOUR HANDS AND YOUR HEART TO MAKE A HABIT OF YOUR CREATIVITY, TO MAKE A PRIORITY OF YOUR ART, TO CARVE OUT EVEN JUST A SMALL AMOUNT OF TIME EVERY DAY TO DEVOTE TO YOUR WORK.

RHYTHM

If you're a musician, you don't need me to tell you how important rhythm is to your art. But I mentioned this concept to a writer friend of mine, and they were surprised. Not just surprised. I don't know if they believed me. Not at first. Rhythm is all about sound, after all.

When writing, one thing I do frequently, especially when it comes to dialogue, is read it aloud.

Part of the idea is I want to make sure it sounds right. Rhythm isn't the only factor here – or meter, if you want to call it that – but meter applies primarily to the sound of individual sentences; it doesn't necessarily apply to the overall structure of the story or novel.

On a larger scale, we can talk about the overall rhythm of a book or a series of books. The narrative structure has its own rhythm, how you move from the inciting incident through building tension to the climax and resolution. When everything falls into place, it should be mostly invisible. But when anything is out of place, when anything's not right, it's disharmonious, discordant, distracting, and potentially disastrous.

Because of this, a lot of narrative structures sound very similar. They hit the same beats at the same points in the story, they follow the same natural progressions, and you might call it an act of laziness to allow your story to fall into the same rhythm as all the stories that came before it. It can also be comforting, when it sounds and tastes the same as what came before, which explains a lot of pop music. Similarities in time signature, and our complete immersion into what currently exists, doesn't just *allow* us, but *encourages* us to follow the same structural paths.

As an example, look at the *Star Wars* movies, *The Force Awakens* and *The Last Jedi*. The first, some people didn't like because it mimicked the original *Star Wars* almost beat for beat. The story wasn't identical, the characters were different, but there were so many similarities that quite a few people found it disappointing. (Personally, I thought it was an effective way of washing the taste of the prequels out of our collective mouths; and that echoing of the first movie, which I saw as a child, was a way for the filmmakers to signal they were returning to what made the original trilogy so impactful.)

The Last Jedi, on the other hand, didn't follow the same rhythms;

and because of that, a lot of the audience complained that it didn't feel like a *Star Wars* film. It stretched outside of the comforts that had been established over decades to do something different. Again, I think it worked. The filmmakers had already told us to expect more of what we love from *Star Wars*, and this was a very clear way of telling us it wouldn't be just more of the same.

In a story, in a book, we've also got the rhythm of the chapter construction, how all the pieces are put together architecturally. Not merely the story beats, but the physicality of the novel becomes important. I believe I was reading Douglas Clegg when I first noticed a chapter containing only one sentence. Technically a full paragraph, merely a sentence, it said everything that needed to be said. It moved the story forward, it helped establish a tone, it helped set the pace. Structurally, it presented some real variation. When the physical rhythm of the story become monotonous, whether it be repetitive sentence structures, paragraphs that mimic each other in style and form, or even the lengths of chapters, it can be boring. Dull. Distracting.

We've all heard, even in high school, about sentence structure. We don't want a story to say something like:

He woke up. He got dressed. He found an envelope on the kitchen table. He touched the envelope. He thought about the person who had left it there. He cried.

We want some variety to add emphasis, to illustrate emotion, to reveal character, and to move the plot.

He woke up and got dressed. An envelope waited on the kitchen table. He touched it. He touched it, and thought about the person who had written it, who had left it there, who had left him there alone, and he cried.

I'm not saying that's a good story, but it illustrates how the sound impacts what you're reading and what we're writing.

All of which, really, is to say: pay attention to the rhythms. The rhythms of the chapters and other structural elements, the rhythms created by your story selections in a collection or anthology or magazine, the rhythms of the paragraphs, the rhythms of the individual sentences, and even the rhythms of the night. To paraphrase Gloria Estefan: the rhythm will get you. As creators, it's our job to employ the rhythms to get our audience.

Titles

I love notepads and use a lot of them. I have notepads dedicated to certain projects and notepads that are freeform, and I always have a small one in my pocket for whatever random thing comes my way.

I started using notebooks and journals as writerly tools sometime around 1990, in college, with one of the three-for-a-dollar notebooks you could get at any supermarket or card shop. I used it partly as a journal, partly to write stories, partly for story ideas; I transcribed snippets of lyrics and poetry, overheard conversations, observations, questions, worries, and hopes. I spent pages at a time working out images that might apply to certain projects, and I spent pages working through variations of titles until I found the one that worked.

Titles have multiple purposes. They can tell you what's in the story, they can tell you about something within the story, they can reveal an artist's intention in a painting, they can be a defining pointer to the subject of the work. It doesn't have to be just stories. Look at *The Starry Night*, that painting of Van Gogh's hanging in the Museum of Modern Art in New York City, that painting I keep going back to because it speaks to me – it's called *The Starry Night* rather than *The Village Under the Stars* or *Cypress Tree* or *Study in Blue*, and the title alone directs your eye.

I have a list of project titles, some of which may never be anything more. I have possible titles for DarkWalker and Midnight books I haven't written yet, as well as standalone projects. I had titles like *Stale Reality* and *Once Upon a Time in Midnight* and *Echo* before I had anything else about those stories.

It also works the other way around. I didn't have a title for *Sins of Blood and Stone* or *The Corpse and the Girl from Miami* until well after I wrote the entire novels.

Those pages, where I work through titles to things I've never written, and maybe never will, serve multiple functions, not least of which is a form of brainstorming.

With art, with a lot of things, it's hard to know where to start. Where you start your song, your illustration, your story – all these things are important. And as creators, though we may not necessarily start with the title, that's usually where our audience starts.

LOSING INTEREST IN YOUR WORK

What happens when the story you're writing no longer interests you?

I'm not talking about writer's block, when you can't think of anything to write or say, but when a particular story loses all momentum.

That's happened to me once or twice. Usually, it's just a matter of getting away from it for a day or two. (I'm talking about longer projects, because most short stories usually take only one or two sittings to write.)

For an example, my book *Once Upon a Time in Midnight* came out in 2012 as part of Thunderstorm's Maelstrom series. Set in my city of Midnight, I started with the title. Sometimes I start with a title, but other times I struggle to find a title after finishing the first draft. Either method works.

I started writing the novel while living in Sydney, Australia. After a few months, approximately half way through, I realized I didn't know what came next. I didn't know what was going to happen, perhaps because I wasn't as familiar with the story as I should have been.

So I put it aside. I abandoned it. I put it aside saying I would save it for later, if and when it became appropriate to go back to it. I honestly didn't know if I would go back. It was possible the idea had just slipped through my mind and used itself up, ending up being nothing and nowhere.

That isn't actually what happened, though. Maybe six months later, I picked up the manuscript again. I started by re-reading it, taking notes, figuring out where I was and what it still needed. I can't remember the specifics. This was around 2005. After that break, I went back, wrote the rest of the book, and sold it. When that publisher cut this and many other of their yet-to-be-published books, I sold it again.

Other projects, however, I have abandoned probably forever. In the early 90's, I worked on a trilogy of ghost stories, the first book being *Roses Grow.* There was a second book, *Wild Roses,* which I also wrote — so I had two first drafts in my early twenties. Before age 25, I started working on *Winter Rose,* the conclusion of the trilogy. I had an idea of where I was going. I was probably heavily influenced by both Anne Rice and the Dell Abyss books at that time.

It went nowhere. It petered out. It didn't get to where it was going, the rest of life overwhelmed me, and I dropped it in favor of the gargoyle book that became *Sins of Blood and Stone* and my first published novel. But the Roses project, all two and a half novels? Put away. Gone. Forgotten. I still have all the files, but no one's going to see them again.

Sometimes the project just isn't going to work. And if it's not going to work, you at least get the experience of realizing it's not going to work. Failure is vital to our growth as an artist and as a human. I have no problem with ending something that isn't going anywhere. I still learned from the experience, and learned more than that this particular project wasn't worth finishing.

It's always possible to make a wrong turn. A project might continue if you just go back a little bit and excise some of the stuff after it went bad. Maybe a character made a decision that was out of character. Maybe a plot point you introduced led to an inevitable dead-end rather than a satisfying payoff. Maybe something's not working because the story is not being true to itself.

SUSPENSE

Generally, you build suspense by leading your protagonist into a dangerous situation. But how do you effectively make it suspenseful, rather than just a paint by numbers piece? You can find all sorts of lists on the internet – but those feel like numbers to me, and lists can sometimes be limiting. So instead, I'd like to look at what feels suspenseful, and how to create that.

Consider *Psycho*. Not the shower scene, specifically, though that's masterful, but the tension building up to the shower scene. One of the biggest factors is that Janet Leigh's character, Marion Crane, is completely unaware of the danger closing in on her. While she's unaware, the audience is completely aware. There are cues, in the music and the cutting, and we feel uncomfortable because we are essentially voyeurs on her impending doom, and there's nothing we can do to save her.

In fiction, we don't have music, but we do have our word choices, we can use different points of view, and we can employ a variety of forms of foreshadowing.

Look at the suspense built within an action scene. You can examine car chases in a thousand films; the ones that work best are often the ones that show us not just how the characters are reacting, but the dangers they're facing. Let's look at the motorcycle chase on the freeway in *The Matrix Reloaded*.

We don't just see the character and their reactions; we don't just see where Trinity is in relation to the truck, for instance, as the agent takes over the driver. We see the agent try to smash her between the truck and the concrete barrier, and we see her react; it builds tension because the audience doesn't merely react to what's happening but anticipates the dangers. We've already seen the space between the truck and the concrete barricade. We watch Trinity and the Keymaker begin to pass on the inside of the long semi. We see what's ahead – the space the agent's going to use to crush them. We know this is going to happen the moment we see her in the driver's side view mirror. The image cuts to the steering wheel from the driver's perspective just before he's overtaken by the agent. The agent's hands are on the wheel, and we know exactly what he's going to do. We have almost five seconds – a long time in a chase scene – from the moment she starts to pass the truck to the moment the agent turns the wheel.

We're familiar with the geography of the scene – where all the elements and the dangers are located. We've even seen cars shifting lanes ahead of her as she's swerving around everyone. And what happens after this? She turns the bike around to go the wrong way on the freeway – ratcheting up the danger. In the next few seconds, we see a shot of them driving and, in the foreground, cars zooming past in the opposite direction so fast, they're only brief blurs.

Briefly, when she swerves off the shoulder and into traffic, we see what's ahead of her as she swerves. We see all that oncoming traffic. We only get about three seconds of that – watch it, it's harrowing – then she's driving toward us and we're reacting, no longer to the anticipation of danger, but the dangers she's actively avoiding. We see the near misses, as and after she misses, rather than as she's about to miss them. After that, there's a combination of the two viewpoints as another agent shoots at her.

The danger is constantly raised, the threat always increasing, and even if we're confident Trinity's going to survive, maybe we're not so sure about the Keymaker on the bike with her.

The takeaways from this? The geography is important – where is the protagonist compared to the threat, and where are the other obstacles? But also, what threats are closing in on her, what can we see that she doesn't, what do we know is coming? What do we, as an audience, anticipate?

I think you can gain a lot analyzing how others have done something – in this case, building tension – in different genres and in different media – to determine what you can bring to bear on your own work. As a writer, you cannot cut a scene the same way a filmmaker does, but you have methods available to you that a filmmaker doesn't. The way a filmmaker chooses what to show, you get to choose the words you use and what you're describing. The way a filmmaker uses music, you can use mood and atmosphere and word choice.

Sure, you can follow a list that tells you to keep the stakes high and apply pressure to the protagonist and then complicate matters – just as you can use an outline of rising action, climax, denouement. But I don't think you get a lot out of that except the barest bones, and bones that are merely suggestions. If you want to give us a good, suspenseful action scene, you want to build tension and give us meat for those bones – meat that might be horribly mangled if things go awry for our main character – you'd better know more than just the story structure numbers.

SYMBOLISM

I think everything, ultimately, is symbolic of something. A lot of the symbolism I use is incorporated partly by whim and partly by deliberate intention, but a lot of it is actually applied by the reader.

When you write, there are two people involved in the creation of the story: the author and the reader. The reader applies symbolism, or assume symbolism, as they read meaning into something the author didn't necessary intend. This does not make it wrong. Symbolism is an odd thing that can mean one thing to someone but something entirely different to somebody else. It's a problem I have with dream interpretation books. What does it mean to dream of flying? I don't know. Is the dreamer someone who desperately wants to be free of something holding them back or a person deathly phobic of open spaces and afraid of heights?

I don't talk a lot about symbolism in my stories because I think it takes away from the inherent mysteries in what I've written. Symbolism is one of those things you should be able to consider and talk about and think about and understand at a basic level, or at a base level, without needing it to be exposed. If I told you definitely what a particular symbol represents and what it means, it takes away from the other meanings that aren't fully realized until the reader has added their interpretation.

DEADLINES AND ORGANIZATION

Usually, I write to deadlines.

Those deadlines are often self-imposed. Back in college, when I was young, when the Internet was barely a thing and only scientists and educators even knew it existed, when computers were still monochrome and cassettes popular, I started writing a novel. It was my freshman year of college. 1988.

It is definitely not a good book, though I retain the files. It clocked in at 110,000 words and only took me about two years to write. I burned through a variety of outlines and themes. I thought it might be about witches at one point, aliens posing as witches, aliens in human form, or immortals of some sort. In the end, those 110,000 words were earnest and honest and heartfelt and, mostly, wrong. I wasn't skilled yet and didn't know what I was doing. I had an idea but no real ability.

But I did finish it.

I believe the clock – calendar, really – ended at 22 months. That's about 5,000 words a month. Fewer than 200 words per day.

Today, as a full time writer, even if I have a part time day job, I cannot afford to spend most of two years on the first draft of a single novel. So I created a spreadsheet to keep me on track. Sure, it involves spreadsheeting skills – but minimally, really, just a few fancy calculations and a series of lines. I decide on a date I want to finish. Then I draw up a schedule, aiming for a certain word count a day – higher than 200 – and determine if that target date is reasonable. Sometimes, I set that target date after starting the schedule – starting with how many words I expect to write every day. I have daily, weekly, and project goals that way.

It works for me.

I schedule two days of zero words every week – unless I absolutely cannot – because I know things will get in the way. The outside world will interfere. I might get sick or have some other obligations. They're floaters I can use anytime I need them, and I don't have to take them. It's not like an InkStains challenge, where I forced myself to take one day off every month. These are, strictly speaking, a guide.

If I miss my goal for the day, that's fine. It's not a quota. I'm not going to get fired. But I usually try to make it up, either by working one of those zero days or by writing more on any subsequent day. Often, the last few days on a project, I'm compelled to sprint, sometimes doubling my intended word goal and therefore finishing ahead of schedule.

This isn't ideal for everyone's working method, I know that. But it works for me. I created the initial spreadsheet a long time ago. I make adjustments as needed. In this way, I keep myself not just on a schedule, but accountable.

Some deadlines are external. Manuscripts are due by a certain date, stories must be delivered or submission windows will close. (I don't use this structure when working on short stories. Usually, I just write those – and depending on the story, the length, the intention, it can be one or two sittings or days for a first draft.) But it's probably a good idea to track actual external deadlines.

All of this tracks just what I consider the "production" phase of writing. I steal these phases from film. I often do a lot of pre-production before beginning. It's not impossible to write a few thousand words a day if I've already sketched out history and characters and plot points, if I know where the project will end and some of the events that will happen between the start and the finish. None of that gets included in my count or in how long it took to write something, because that pre-production, that gestation phase, can take days or years.

Stories are like that. They roll around in my head like it's a washer/dryer combo, and every once in a while something gets spit out that has been on a spin cycle since college. Or earlier. The original seed for *The Corpse and the Girl from Miami*, published in 2017, goes back to when I was scripting ideas for comic book characters three decades ago in tenth grade. It metamorphosed a long way from its original intentions. But if I were to include that time in my calculations – as well as post-production, which includes the revisions, the editing, the submissions processes, layout and design when appropriate – *The Corpse and the Girl from Miami* was a book that took over thirty years to create.

I can't have a deadline thirty years from now, and I can't wait for a random someone to assign me deadlines, so I assign my own. In the next thirty years, I expect to write more than just one book.

Part of the purpose of a deadline is motivation. It's easy to maintain motivation, but it's also easy to procrastinate, to say I'll get to it later or tomorrow, and tomorrow never comes. It's an endless cycle, and why it took 22 months to write that one novel.

The fastest first draft I ever wrote was eleven days. I was unemployed at the time. During those eleven days, I interviewed for and accepted a job that would be my home for the next three years. I also wrote flat out, morning till night, without real breaks and without coming up for air. The last day was, in fact, the first day of the new job. I averaged almost ten thousand words a day.

It's because of stunts like this that my fingers now hurt all the time.

It's not the best eighty-ish thousand words I ever wrote. They may not be the worst words. It was the beginning of my writing career. I had just sold my first professionally published story, "Portrait in Graphite," and had met a whole new group of friends at my first World Horror Convention in Atlanta. I named a bunch of characters for those new friends, I set it in the town where I did most of my growing up, and it's basically a bloody romp. It was a reaction to reading my first Richard Layman novel. It's vampires – my only vampire novel [Author's note: thus far]. Looking back now, I think it has two saving graces – the opening scene and the conclusion. It would need to be completely re-done. Re-imagined in a way to incorporate myself and those friends, some of whom are names you may know, and make it something new, something more exciting, something unique: a metafictional vampire tale featuring my earliest writer friends, over-the-top in every possible way.

One of those ideas sits five or six projects from *next*, and there it may sit. Other things come up. I have ideas for Midnight books, I have two more *DarkWalker* novels after this one [Author's note: book four], and I'd really like to work on two or three other projects more appropriate to mass market releases. There's also the *Echo* novellas, which together will make a book of some sort, and there's always something new, something old, something ringing in my head and demanding release.

I can't get away from them.

While I spreadsheet about the word counts as I go on my current project, I've never been very good at tracking future projects. They get jumbled in my head, they fight to be king of the mountain, and some – like Medusa – keep rearing their snake-filled heads without making it all the way through. Yes, I put projects aside when they're not working, when I'm stuck, or when they've trapped me. It's worked in the past, it'll probably work in the future – either the novel will be better because of it, or the novel won't be bad because it won't ever get finished.

I have notepads for a bunch of these projects, a stack of them on the shelf behind me in my office. But only one is open on my desk right now – *DarkWalker*. I've kept titles on index cards and posted them on cork boards as a means of keeping track. I've played with the idea of dry erase boards; I know writers who track their upcoming projects that way, but I've never actually made the attempt. I've even tried to track them in a spreadsheet, which, for whatever reason, refuses to work.

Think about how you organize your future projects, those ideas that aren't yet ready for primetime, the thoughts and titles and meanderings that may one day work. Do you have a folder on your computer? A drawer in your desk? Sticky notes? A handmade variation of an abacus to somehow keep things in order?

Do you even make the attempt? I mean, it seems simple enough to write in the moment, to work only on what's prominent in your mind. But there are always other ideas seeping in around the edges, there's always something else that just needs a moment's attention before you get back to what you're doing today. Knowing there's another project on the horizon is one way to fight the fear of running out of ideas. I don't think I ever can run out; every time I pluck an idea from my mind tree, two more sprout to take its place. It's like the mind tree hydra of ideas, always chaotic and twisting and threatening to devour me, and the only way to face such a beast is to try to keep things organized. Pin those heads to their places in the cork board. Combine all the metaphors so *nothing* makes sense anymore. Sometimes, it's really the only way.

CHARACTER NAMES

As I pack to move overseas, I'm forced to restrict the library I bring to almost nothing. I have some 2,000 books in storage, and maybe 200 with me in Richmond – some acquired since I arrived. Many are books I'd like to read sooner rather than later, but I'm a notoriously slow reader. All that I haven't read, with a very few exceptions, must join the library in storage.

My reference library started in my teens with Time-Life's *Enchanted World* and *Mysteries of the Unknown*, but it's grown substantially since then to include books on magic, mythology, the occult, history, archeology, glass, mirrors, the Knights Templar, cookbooks, photography, how to write and how to be creative, and all sorts of other good stuff. Most reference material is in storage. With two exceptions.

The first is a book I picked up as a teenager in the early 80's: *The Best Baby Name Book in the Whole Wide World*. Admittedly, the title is a little over the top. It's a collection of names – western names – and what they mean, divided into boy and girl sections. I can look up John and see that it's Hebrew and means "God is gracious," which also seems hyperbolic but this is the decade that later brought us *The Lost Boys* and *The Adventures of Buckaroo Banzai in the Eighth Dimension*, so it's not my fault.

The other book is also all about names: Yvonne Navarro's *First Name Reverse Dictionary*. I consider Von a friend. Years before we met, I picked up her first novel, *AfterAge,* at a Long Island Borders back when Borders was a pretty new thing. The novel had just come out, and I loved it so much I bought everything else she released after that. I don't have this book because she's a friend. I didn't buy it because I knew her, and I'm not taking it with me because of any connection whatsoever.

I'm taking these two books with me because I consult them frequently. There are always new characters, and I often try to incorporate some sort of meaning into their names. Even the minor characters. Sometimes, characters are named for people I know or have met, who have somehow influenced me or impressed me, but I'm just as likely – maybe more likely – to name someone for a more *substantial* reason, no matter how ridiculous that reason may seem – and sometimes the reason is because I wanted a name that meant *strong*.

First Name Reverse Name Dictionary allows me to look up names by their meanings and see which would be appropriate. If I look up *strong* under male names, it'll give me a list of Celtic, Latin, German, Old English, Irish-Gaelic, Greek-Hebrew, and other assorted western names.

It's a different game when I'm naming someone from somewhere else. When I needed an Australian aboriginal name for *Dark Walker 4*, neither of these dictionaries helped. But both remain great starting places. Searching for names for the main characters in *Echo*, I used these books extensively and discovered all sorts of possibilities. I ended up going to history, though, and naming the primary point of view character for a historical alchemist. It seemed appropriate.

Names are important for different reasons and in different ways, and can tell us much about a character. Sometimes, they're clichés – the big burly biker bouncer dude called Tiny – or iconic – like John Henry. Sometimes, the sound of them tells us something – like Doc Savage. They've even been named for real people. (If you've ever read Brian Keene's *The Rising*, you should know *John of Many Colors* was named for me because one of my earliest chapbooks was *A Game of Colors*.)

Some characters are easy to name. It's not uncommon for one to emerge ready to work, with a name, without any obvious effort.

Other names are meant to evoke a certain feeling or follow a certain rhythm. They must sound right and look right and be right for the character, place, and time. Sometimes, they can transcend places and times, but in those cases, there usually must be a reason – even if you don't reveal that reason to the audience.

Indiana Jones would not work as well if they went with Indiana Smith, and Oklahoma Jones invokes an entirely different kind of character. You can go with "the man with no name," but we can't all be Sergio Leone so we can't always get away with that. (Additionally, it's a wonderful name, and more than appropriate for the character, don't you think?)

You can use names to signify something about the person. You can use the name John – go ahead, you're allowed, even if I'm generally not – to have someone who blends in, someone who maybe doesn't stand out from the crowd – because the name doesn't stand out. Unless of course you're writing in India, when a character John is marked as an outsider, a foreigner, someone who probably doesn't know his surroundings, maybe even someone with a past because he's fled some other place.

When I'm searching for a name, some come immediately – but not always. Jack Harlow, the main character in my *DarkWalker* series, did not come overnight. I wanted a regular, straight forward name that would have some level of distinction but also a hard edge to it, something easy to remember and potentially evocative. I went through several iterations of his first name, and I went through numerous surnames. I considered rhythm, and I considered the names of characters who came before him – not just in my own work but in the fiction and films and plays.

I'm working on a series of novellas right now, and I quickly came up with the name for one of the characters, a woman who is more than she seems, who has a mysterious past and, in fact, a mysterious nature. She was a minor character in the first novella, but the protagonist in the second, and now it's important to find the name of her twin brother. So I needed something that matched hers in terms of meaning – but because of the nature of the story, not necessarily in terms of place. So, if her name was Diane, I wouldn't necessarily feel compelled to name him Jack.

Names don't just belong to characters, though. What about cities, streets, museums, or record shops within the story? You can use actual places, or you can go with someplace fictional. I have a number of clubs strewn throughout my stories called *The Precipice*, because once upon a time, when I was maybe 25, I thought it'd be an excellent name for a bar.

Just like in real life, names can be used to honor someone, or at least acknowledge them. Brian Keene names characters this way all the time. You can see them throughout his books, especially in the minor characters, who share names with his friends and family and literary idols. You can see it in my own stories, too, though not as often, and in sometimes strange places. I don't know a lot about guns, I don't have a history with them, but I have friends who do; so when I want a character using a weapon that isn't, say, a Colt Peacemaker, or an AK-47, or something else iconic and noticeable, they often carry an Oliveri – named for my friend and fellow writer, Mike Oliveri.

With my InkStains stories, I ran into a different problem. I had to name someone new every day, and despite the fact that I do sometimes reuse names in my regular stories and novels, I don't really want to. I try not to. To get around that in the InkStains stories, I decided, sometime in the first year but not before starting, to re-use a single set of names: Jack and Jill. The first time, it was a joke. After that, I realized they were generic enough and could thread through any of the InkStains stories. Not all the characters in those one thousand plus stories are named Jack, Jill, or variations thereof; but when a character in one of these vignettes needs a name and it doesn't have to carry the weight of a James Bond or a Dorothy Gale, Jill and Jack work nicely.

I've found I can get caught up in the naming of a character. There are times when it comes naturally as I write and I don't give it a single thought. In some cases, a little work – consulting Yvonne Navarro's *Reverse Name Dictionary*, or the *Best Baby Name Book*, maybe scrolling through the internet for meanings and mythologies and connotations – will help create someone whose name gives the character a little something before we even get to their introduction.

I've also played with names that aren't names. My novella *Pocketful of Smoke, Fistful of Glass* takes place in a theater in Midnight. A burlesque troupe is performing there, and none of them have names – they are the Gentleman, the Contortionist, the Exhibitionist – while the people in the audience have actual names – like Ann and Bob – which is a reversal of sorts, since the most important characters have titles acting as names.

You can find character names everywhere. Online. At the day job. In the supermarket. On TV. I used to collect names from my days in customer service. It's possibly one of the worst jobs imaginable, in which you're continually subjected to abuse for a pittance, abuse both from customers and management, and the pittance barely pays the rent but only if you've got roommates.

But I collected names. I've always kept sticky notes or something similar at my day job desks. When someone called with an interesting name, a first or last name, I'd write it down. Never both. I always thought that would be untenable if I were caught and accused of wrongdoing. But I wasn't doing wrong, I was only collecting names. It didn't matter if you were calling because you wanted to buy Elton John tickets, or for me to explain why the check you wrote bounced, or to choose a Medicaid insurance provider. The only thing that mattered was, did your name speak to me? I didn't care if you did, or what you said, and I never took out customer service frustrations on callers in my fiction. This wasn't a death list or a list of potential victims. These were potential characters, protagonists or antagonists or supporting characters or throwaway names. These were ingredients into my evocations of stories and plots and places and scenes. Some of these names spoke to me and stayed with me, and some dissipated, even though I'd written them down, because not every name, even if it sounded right once, was actually right to use.

It's also easy enough to go back through your personal history and name characters for people you either liked or didn't like, but I've always felt that leads too much to potential wish fulfillment. When I'm writing, I'm trying to create something more powerful and more substantial than mere wishes. However, my experiences with names and yours might be different, and you might find using names in this manner can be therapeutic. It can also be a way of acknowledging and honoring. It might even keep certain demons at bay. If killing a character named for the cashier at the record shop prevents you from killing the cashier at the record shop – I say keep writing. But also, you might want to talk to someone. I'm not a psychologist. There may be more effective ways to calm those murderous urges.

CHARACTERS

Characters are, arguably, the most important aspect of any story. Story can be defined as the journey of a character from one place to another – physically or emotionally – and their ability or inability to grow and change. The character arc is often the story within our work, while the plot is how they get from the beginning to the end.

So what makes a good, interesting, vital character?

A long time ago, in high school, in my era of *Dungeons & Dragons*, TSR sold character sheets. These yellow pages tracked strength and charisma attributes, hit points, possessions, class, level, everything important to that character. Additionally: in my long ago past, I've had a number of odd and interesting and boring and unimportant day jobs; one time, I worked as a forms designer. Yeah, I designed forms. I know it's not something you even think of as a thing someone does – but I did it, and I did it for over a year. I even knew a forms designer who aspired to cereal boxes.

I used that forms design background, and the software, to create my own character sheets. I still use them today, over twenty years later. If I redesigned these today, they would be different. But I use these sheets to track names, aliases, physical attributes, important relationships, first appearances in a story – especially helpful in a series – important experiences, skills and hobbies, place of birth, all kinds of stuff.

I don't strictly adhere to the labeled boxes, but these character sheets track a lot of information. What do you think would be the most important thing to track?

You don't want to have a character's eyes change from blue to green midway through the book – unless there's a reason for it, which would also be included. I jot down important things they say in spaces devoted to experiences. When and how they die – which may be especially important in the realms of fantasy and horror where death may not be entirely final.

None of these, in my opinion, is the most important thing about a character. That doesn't appear on the sheets at all. These are great guides for who a character is – but to know what they are, to know their soul, you need to be fully and completely aware of something that's not generally included on my character sheets and subject to change.

It doesn't matter if it's a primary point of view character or a major villain or a bit character who only appears in the background for one scene; this most important thing is *motivation.*

Why does a character do the things they do? What informs their decisions and choices along the way? If they make a verifiably stupid decision, is that stupidity justified by their experiences, their intentions, their biases and prejudices, their hopes and dreams and fears? Are they acting, if not in their own self-interest, at least in a way that indicates they believe they are? It's rare for a person, in real life or in fiction, to do something against their interests – even if their self-interest is hidden. Sacrifice, for instance. If a character sacrifices their life to save someone they love, it might be because the life of that other person is more important to them than their own, or because they can't imagine living without that other person; sometimes, it will be a pure, selfless love.

There are television shows where the same characters make the same stupid choices for years, leaving viewers wondering why they don't learn from their mistakes. I think that's a fundamental flaw with a lot of weak episodic television. The motivations that drive a character, the reason they do the things they do – these aren't set in stone. They can shift and change, sometimes drastically, as the character changes and grows over the course of the story.

For example, in my *DarkWalker* series, the main character is Jack Harlow, who walks untouched through the dark. He sees all the ghosts and vampires and everything else, but doesn't care. He just wants to be left alone, he wants to ignore it all and forget it. Then he falls in love with someone very early in the story; as a direct result, his prime motivations change. He wants to stop running, hiding, and pretending he and everything else doesn't exist. He's in a drastically different place by the start of book four. He's seething with anger over some of the events of the previous books and wants revenge. This character starts out very passive but later becomes almost recklessly arrogant in pursuit of his twisted vision of justice. If he was still the same person he was at the beginning of the first book, if he hadn't changed as a *consequence* to the things he'd seen and done, and the things done to him, there's no chance he'd be interesting or compelling, and there'd be no reason for readers to continue reading.

It's not just the main characters who should have motivations. Every character in the story has a reason for the things they do, no matter what it is. Is there a baker who appears in a single scene? You might not need to know everything about him, but maybe you'll want to know if he enjoys what he does, or if he work because of obligations and with a sense of misery and contempt. Does he dream about being the hero of his own story?

Surprise: *he is.* Consider your protagonist and antagonist and their primary supporting cast. This may be their story, but everyone they interact with, every other character they come across – just like every person we run into in real life, at the movie theater, the supermarket, a museum or bar or school, or on the interstate – every single one of them is the hero of their own stories. Even the villains. Dr. Doom thinks the world will be better for everyone under his rule. Darth Vader believes he and his son can overthrow the emperor and end a rebellion that has killed many, many people on both sides. The alien merely wants to eat and survive to protect her young.

Every character, every person, has internal lives. I'm not saying you need to know the deepest depths of every minor character to fill your pages. But I am saying you shouldn't forget they have those depths, which you're perfectly free to hint at without having to fully explore. The intentions and motivations that drive your main characters, or you in real life, also drive every other character inhabiting that world. Especially in longer works, it's nice when you can at least acknowledge that the baker may have a role in their own life other than to make cupcakes for your hero's birthday party.

Writing a Novel

How do you write a novel? The easy answer is: one word at a time. But that's simply not true. When I'm typing, I'm often many words ahead of myself. My fingers fly so fast, I'm not always aware of the words I'm using. "One word at a time" is a smart-ass answer, a cheat, and it's entirely true and completely wrong at the same time.

The scariest truth, actually, is that every novel, every project, will make different demands of you and require different things; therefore, every novel is unique and written in its own unique way. That, also, is completely valid and entirely wrong.

Sometimes, the novel requires research, either in small amounts or metric tons, before you even start. This might depend on the setting, it might depend on the knowledge and experiences of the characters whose stories you're going to tell. So maybe your novel will start with a month or a year of in-depth research on a variety of topics.

Sometimes, the novel starts as a title or a single opening sentence – just don't be tricked into believing you must keep that sentence which started the whole thing. It might be just the kick-start you need to get going. Sometimes, while you're sitting there, an idea creeps into your head and refuses to budge. The only way to exorcise it is to bleed onto paper, and as you're getting it down the concept expands and elicits other ideas and sends you into dizzying possibilities and tangents. In the end, you've got not just the germ of an idea but an entire chapter, two chapters, a whole chunk of novel, and then a whole damn novel.

Other times, you might have to outline the whole thing, exploring every twist and turn, every shred of rising tension, and every opportunity for surprise before you can get started.

The point I'm making – I'm often making a point, even when it doesn't seem like it – there's no one way to write a novel. There's no single path from the blank page to finished book. The path you take to complete one project isn't necessarily going to be the same you follow for another.

I can tell you how I've written books. I can tell you about one I put down for half a year after reaching the halfway mark. I can tell you about the one that came fully formed into my head and took only eleven days to type. I can tell you some books were better than others, some will never be seen by anyone ever, some are now available at bookstores, and some are sitting on the desks of bigtime New York publishers who haven't yet made any real attempt to get it into your hands.

Would any of that help?

Maybe it would be better for me to tell you there's no wrong way to write a novel. Most manuscripts will require a round of revisions. Certain structures work better than others. The tropes of your genre can be limiting or invigorating or both simultaneously.

When someone tells me they want to write a book, someone who's never written one, I ask, "What's stopping you?" I know some answers to that. No time, no energy, no skill, no idea how to start. Anyway, it's impossible to write a four hundred page manuscript, anybody could tell you that – and they'd be telling you the truth. It's impossible to write a four hundred page manuscript. But it *is* possible to break it down and attack it in smaller, more manageable ways. It's possible to write two pages a day – and after a year, whoa, look at that, you've got a whole novel and then some.

I tend to set goals and deadlines for myself because I rarely have them imposed from the outside. Right now, I am contractually obligated to write two novels, but I can't tell you too much because the contract's still in the inking stage and I don't know what external deadlines these will create. In the past, I've typically written on spec – selling novels and stories I'd already written. Even under those circumstances, it helps, or at least it helps me, to have a target date in mind.

I'm always practical and generous but also aggressive with my self-made deadlines. So I plan it out – spreadsheets are great for things like this – and determine I can write this many words a day for this many days a week. Expecting the novel to be X many words, I can estimate finishing by a particular date. I work forward, then backwards, in drafting such a schedule. I build in floating days off because I know it's not realistic to believe the real world won't interfere. I plan for holidays and vacations and obligations that I know will come up.

Maybe you're thinking none of this is about writing a book – but it totally is. It's part of the planning, part of the goal setting, part of the visualization process in which I see – not a book I wish to write – but a book I've written.

The actual writing, of course, will vary.

With the novel *City of Glass,* as yet unsold, I knew the story would take place over 100 days. Multiple story threads would weave through those days, and they would have points of intersection before reaching their various conclusions. I frequently wrote successive days of a single thread, then days for another thread, all out of order because I knew certain things had to happen on particular days. In the end, I had two versions of the book, one that followed a particular set of characters and storyline, jumping from day 7 to 13 to 20 to 25, whatever was required for that thread of the story before jumping to another storyline and moving from day 3 to 10 to 17 to 20. The other version was just the days in order, no matter whose story was being told that day. In the end, structurally, I wasn't sure which was best.

With other novels, with almost all my other novels, I've written linearly, from beginning to middle to end, but that wasn't the right way for this particular novel. So I did something I'd never done before. I did this because the story dictated what was necessary, because the story made demands of me I couldn't ignore, and because it was the right way to write that novel.

How to write a novel, then, isn't the same question as how to *write*; in my mind, it's really about goal setting, working to achieve that goal, being lenient on yourself when something interrupts, and persisting until you reach the end. Do you need an outline? Maybe you do, maybe you don't. Should you thoroughly understand every aspect of the lives of your characters before you write the first word? Possibly, possibly not. Should you have an idea of your target audience? Maybe. I'll say *maybe,* and possibly yes, but probably you shouldn't worry about who will read it – not yet. You should write the book for you, for you and no one else, because even if you're one in a million, and maybe you are, there's some seven *billion* people in the world.

For my methods, I generally find it's good to have an idea of the ending I'm aiming for. I know where the book will, or should, end before I get too much of a start on it. I'm not always right. Sometimes, the ending changes. In the case of my 2006 novel, *Breath of the Moon,* what I thought would be the ending going in actually marked the halfway point.

I think of writing a novel as a process of discovery. I can't possibly know everything that's going to happen before I start because I can't possibly know what's going to influence me during the writing. You cannot write a novel in a single day without experiencing any additional experiences and outside interference. The trick is to use that interference, to learn from what you see.

Part of the novel-writing process is being aware of all the things going on around you, the people on the streets, the everyday drama of friends and family and your own life, and the mysteries and magic you find in the real world.

Of course, that's my process. Yours may be different. Any other writer's may be different. It's not like working an assembly line. We're all going to do things differently, and we're all going to draw upon our unique sets of experiences and knowledge and beliefs and fears and hopes and dreams and everything else we draw from.

Generally, I write with music in the background, typically music I know but not always, typically rock or jazz or blues. Never country simply because I don't appreciate it, and not rap because it's too close to spoken word – voices speaking don't work in the background for me. If the television's on and people are talking, that's a distraction – in exactly the way it's not a distraction when I'm scribbling in my notepad at a café or bar because it's not a single voice in those places but a wall of entirely incoherent background noise.

I know this about myself because I'm thoroughly familiar with my own working habits. I've examined them. I know writers who work with the television on as a kind of background that simply doesn't work for me. I know people who listen to only instrumental music because any words or lyrics get in the way. Other writers want absolute silence when they work. How you're going to write your own novel – is going to be your way, and there's no way I can dictate that to you.

I can, and have, suggested all kinds of exercises with the intention of helping you write better – to use language more effectively to fully elicit the desired response from your readers, to paint more vibrantly with words, to do this whole writing thing better and faster and easier.

NOVELLA CHALLENGE

It seems rather natural to challenge you to write a novel, but perhaps you're not ready. Perhaps you don't have the story yet. Perhaps you're holding off until November and that whole NaNoWriMo thing. Maybe that kind of structure works for you and maybe it doesn't — I don't know, everyone is different, and as I've said repeatedly, no one path will work for everyone every time.

So something shorter. A real, honest, thick challenge: write a novella. Plan it out the way I described: determine how many words you can write in a day and how many days you'll need. I'm not going to dictate a timeframe, but be aggressive. Don't simply set a goal you know you can achieve because it's low and easy. Set a goal that's realistic and challenging. Aim for 15,000 words minimum — much shorter than a novel but longer than a short story. Any genre, any subject, any theme. None of that matters to me. It should matter to you. If you aim for 15 days, make sure you add one or two for days off. You may exceed your goals some days and fall short on others; and on others, you might get no writing done at all because, I don't know, the car won't start and it's snowing and you're trapped in a laundromat with a roll of quarters but nothing to write with. Anything can happen. Be willing to be influenced by the world as you write, be willing to change direction if the story demands it — just because you think you know where you want it to end doesn't mean that's where you'll end. Don't worry too much about quality. This is

ONLY A FIRST DRAFT. YOU'LL PROBABLY GO BACK TO DO REVISIONS LATER, SO YOU CAN FIX ALL THE MISTAKES AND MAKE THE WORDS BETTER AND TIGHTER AND STRONGER AND FASTER AND WHATEVER ELSE IS NECESSARY. YOU HAVE THE TECHNOLOGY.

MOSTLY, ENJOY THE PROCESS, AND BE AWARE OF WHAT DOES AND DOESN'T WORK FOR YOU. DO YOU GET MORE DONE LISTENING TO BARRY MANILOW THAN QUEEN? THEN COPACABANA TO YOUR HEART'S CONTENT. IF YOU PREFER TO WRITE THE FIRST DRAFT BY HAND, I'M NOT GOING TO STOP YOU. IF YOU'D PREFER TO DICTATE IT INTO THE VOICE RECORDER ON YOUR PHONE AND TRANSCRIBE IT LATER — IF THAT WORKS FOR YOU, DO IT.

IF YOU ULTIMATELY DECIDE THE NOVELLA YOU WROTE, OR THE NOVELLA YOU'VE STARTED, ISN'T GOING TO WORK, ISN'T SUCCESSFUL, OR ISN'T WORTH THE TIME IT WOULD TAKE TO FIX — THAT'S OKAY. THOSE WORDS NEEDED TO BE WRITTEN. IF THE WORDS WEREN'T ANY GOOD, NOW THAT THEY'RE OUT OF YOUR HEAD YOU'LL BE ABLE TO MOVE ON TO SOMETHING ELSE.

Writing Short Stories

Let's start by defining it in the simplest terms. A short story is a story that's short. According to the Science Fiction Writer's Association's Nebula awards: a story of less than 7,500 words. After that, you've got novelettes, and when you reach 17,500 words you've got a novella. The novel is a minimum of 40,000 words – although some publishers might not take one that short. [Author's note: these numbers were correct when reported in late 2018.]

Another way to describe a short story is a story that can be read in a single sitting. Often, it can be written in a single sitting, too, depending on your time constraints – but it doesn't have to be. I've written tons of shorts that have taken more than a single day. InkStains stories were written in a single day, usually a single sitting, but you can argue that these are technically some sort of flash fiction.

Flash fiction has been defined as under 1,000 words, under 500 words, under 100 words, or something you can write on a napkin. It's a little bit more nebulous. But for today, for this discussion, let's differentiate between short stories and InkStains stories like this: InkStains are meant to be complete stories, but they're also an exercise, and as such they may focus on a particular aspect of writing – word choice, setting, characterization, point of view, metaphor, symbolism, whatever – and may be successful as InkStains but not as short stories.

I feel like I'm muddying everything up here, and I haven't even managed to define our terms. So it's this: a short story is short, typically read in a single shot. Therefore, the story is much more focused than a novel. There are no digressions, no further explorations, no subplots or side characters, nothing that doesn't directly serve the story.

When I approach a short story, I often know where I want to end, which is important because everything in the story serves the purpose of reaching that end. Everything else is extraneous. Anything extraneous is, well, extra, and unnecessary, and takes away from the story.

Sometimes I'll only have an idea, a concept, a premise, or a character. The writing begins as an exploration – as I've said before, writing is a process of discovery – but that exploration ultimately has a goal. It's like setting off into the woods. It's one thing if you want to discover what's out there, but it's something else entirely if you're searching for the Fountain of Youth.

You might not know what you're searching for until you're part way through the first draft. That's okay. You might fumble about a bit before you really know the essence of the story. You might go on little explorations and tangents, and in the process discovery your story and your character. Then, when you go back to revise, you'll probably remove the stuff that, although it served a purpose in helping you write from beginning to end, doesn't actually serve any purpose for the reader.

When I write a short story – or an InkStains story – I don't always start with a clear idea of where I want to end, but I do know I want to end with a twist or a revelation. A solid statement. A forceful, powerful point at which the story must end. There may be more to tell, but I'm not telling the life story of the characters, and I'm not necessarily exploring the consequences of whatever happened during the story. I'm going in and examining, sometimes in minute detail, a particular incident or occurrence or event. The short story needs to be self-contained, but it's perfectly free to not answer all the questions of what happens next. Unless that's what the story's about. Some stories can sometimes be more meandering, take their time getting to a point, and seem to not have much going on by way of plot – but thematically, if it's well-done, it still moves from beginning to middle to end in a coherent and precise way.

Remember: nothing I say is set in stone. I'm talking about how I do things, and how other writers I know do things, but every writer has their own approach, every writer will have their own beliefs, and every writer will ultimately discovery how they define a short story, how they will write and revise one, and what it means to them.

If I were teaching a course in short story writing, I'd go over particulars of characterization and setting, I'd explore sentence structure and paragraph structure, I'd talk about rhythm. I'd have examples for all the points I was making. But primarily, I'd make you write.

That's what I'd do. I'd make you write the first draft of a story before every class. I wouldn't necessarily grade these based on success, but on effort. I'd make you talk about what you did and why. You included this minor character because they contributed important information about the history of the main character. They served no other purpose, I'd ask. *None.* Couldn't that information have been gotten in some other way? *Not easily.* Couldn't that character be combined with this other character, who does play a role in the story but doesn't have an established backstory? *Maybe I should establish a backstory?* Would it serve the story?

That would be my biggest, most consistent question to you, as the student, as the writer: Does it serve the story? If the answer is no, why is it there? If you don't have a reason, I would suggest removing it.

A WRITER'S TOOLBOX

Part of my job as a writer is to play with words and bend them to my purposes – whether my purposes are evil or benign. To do so, I need to know what words mean, where they come from, how to use them, what other words mean something similar but slightly different. I need to understand those subtle differences. My knowledge of the language will never be complete and all-encompassing, but it needs to be thorough.

Language is just one of the tools in that magical metaphorical writer's toolbox.

I've been called a word-slinger and a wordsmith, but the truth is I've made up words, and not always on purpose; sometimes it's because of my own weaknesses in the language. Since I've lived in places that use American English and also places that use British English – and I currently live in a place that speaks Spanish instead – I don't always know how to spell words like realize; if I should be using an elevator or a lift; or if I live in an apartment, flat, or *apartamento*.

That writer's toolbox is important because it's filled not just with words and phrases and ideas and concepts, it's filled with dictionaries and internets and thesauruses to assist me when my personal knowledge of the language is insufficient. If you don't know whether you should be using lay or lie or lain or laid, if you're not sure you're employing that semi-colon correctly – hint: if you're not sure, you're probably *not* – you have references that will help you.

Observational skills are part of that toolbox. When you enter a room, you notice the color of the wallpaper, the number of bookshelves, and whether the lamps are antiques or modern. You don't always know the specific words that apply to a situation – you might not know the difference between a cellar and a basement, of if those differences even mean anything. The first time you set pen to paper to write something, you might not be sure whether you should be using ground or floor or both interchangeably. These types of things are easy to look up. It's important to remember we live in an age where the Internet knows everything. (Also, the Internet lies. So be wary.)

Observational skills lead straight into deductive reasoning skills, or at least an ability to extrapolate. I'm not saying we're always entirely accurate, or that we have fine enough a nose to distinguish the specific odor of red Georgia clay to determine that the stranger on the train recently committed that sensational murder in Savannah and is now escaping to a safe house in Riva, Maryland. We're not Sherlock Holmes. But we can determine a lot about a person by what they wear and the way they present themselves – and we'll probably be more accurate, at least in the general things, than the average person. This combination of observation and deduction is how we create characters, and how we breathe life into the settings of our stories.

We're also always working. That's the curse of being a writer, of being any kind of artist: we're constantly ingesting experiences, churning the things we see and do and hear in our brains until something comes out – something like a story, a character, a place, a conflict.

A great many of us have enough empathy to understand our characters, and therefore to understand other people in real life, to know why someone might act in a particular way even if we don't share their beliefs or background.

Also, we're extraordinary thieves. We steal from the world around us, from the people we know and the places we go, the songs we hear and the art we see, the films we watch and the books we read. We steal a word here or there, sometimes a turn of phrase, sometimes something somebody says, because we can twist these into our own things and make stories out of them.

We're also alchemists. Not scientists, precisely, not chemists looking to combine elements to catalyze reactions, but alchemists who dabble in a transformative art. We're creating something entirely new out of disparate parts; and like the alchemists of old who wanted to change lead into gold, we're looking to transform all those parts into something greater, something rarer, something unique.

Another thing in our literary toolboxes, of course, is our desire, our aspirations, our intentions, our *drive*. We push ourselves, often until our bodies, psyches, and souls have been ravaged and ravished and decimated.

I don't know about you, but I hope I'm creating something beautiful as I destroy myself.

World Building

Halloween is a season of witchcraft and spookery – is that a word? I don't think that's a word – hauntings and crossings, all kinds of wicked and nasty things, so much so that you can build worlds around it.

But how do you build a world?

The obvious and easy answer is be born a godling and wish it into existence. With a snap of your fingers, you might say. It seems easy, but perhaps that makes for some sloppy world building with many possible unforeseen consequences.

For storytelling, you build a world by making it real – or at least realistic. By establishing rules and sticking to them, and changing them only when it's established you can. You can go all out and get advanced degrees in linguistics and anthropology and history so as to better construct societies with their own working languages, traditions, ways of life, and complete histories and mythologies, a la Tolkien's *Lord of the Rings*. Or you can borrow exclusively from the real world by building a real New York City with the actual Times Square and just change a single thing – perhaps a club at the edge of Broadway that maybe isn't there but could be. Or use a real existing theater, but now you've had the chance to get behind the curtains to see the rafters and dressing rooms and back alleys.

Starting as simply as possible, many fictional worlds are built upon a foundation of the real world, so your world building may not involve much more than creating a single location or two, or borrowing a real apartment and furnishing it in your character's style. I've borrowed plenty of real life locations. In the *DarkWalker* series, for instance, in the first book, Lisa's Orlando apartment overlooking the lake is based on a friend's apartment. Jack goes to Long Island in the second book, to the house where he first saw a ghost – a house I briefly lived in back in the early 90s. In book three, Jack goes to a mine in the Virginia mountains – they really used to mine for silver, among other things. In book four, the Susquehanna River is real, and New York City has actual brownstones, though I borrowed initially from Rex Stout's *Nero Wolfe* before the brownstone's non-Euclidian geometric properties made it more unique. Of course, when they go to Shangri La, I didn't base that on the hotel in Sydney.

All of those settings, up until Shangri La, involved real places, and in many cases those places weren't much changed from reality. They were borrowed wholesale for the books. When building the world for *DarkWalker*, I started with a canvas of the real, of the things you and I can physically find and touch and walk through.

When expanding beyond that, the thing I most tried to keep in mind, the attribute I think most important when you're building your own world – whether it's the wild west or the far reaches of space, an alternative dimension or another version of earth, a real historical place in a steampunk sensibility or a river of gold flowing endlessly toward the sun – whether your world is populated by people like you and me, vampires, ghosts, elves, aliens, interdimensional travelers, gods, dragons, fairies, or sentient telepathic rocks – it must be consistent.

By consistent, I mean once you've establish a certain set of rules, you should stick to those rules. If there comes a time to break those rules – do so intentionally, with forethought rather than carelessness, so you can establish why and how those rules are being broken. In other words, break those rules by following rules already established.

If you're writing about a magical world where spells will cost you physically – the exchange of energy is somewhat consistent with our world – and you later have a magical character stop a world-threatening event by doing something of such enormous proportion that it's impossible, the way you've established the rules – this magical character may be able to do this because of a previously unknown artifact that acts as a power amplifier or pulls energy from the sun, or something other than just using up their own energy.

I hope I'm making sense.

As to how to do this – I start with a notepad for every project, and though I'll scribble about the story and the character and the plot, I'll also keep notes about the place. I'll sometimes draw maps, write out histories, or even – as I did with *Once Upon a Time in Midnight* – write alternative possible histories that have all become something of an urban legend, so that some people can believe this particular place is the highest point in the city, or this other place is the highest point in the city, or this place is – or that the city was founded two hundred years ago when a man sought the most inhospitable place in the world to drink himself to death in – or maybe he did this four hundred years ago – but maybe the catacombs below the city are a thousand years old. All these false histories, legends rather than real histories, become part of the canvas I'm working with, part of the city and therefore part of that world.

I'll track musicians and artists who are named and famous in the city, if appropriate. I'll take notes on climate and special things – for instance, in Midnight, all alcoholic drinks are whiskey or some type of whiskey – one time even including a bourbon-infused wine. I'll repeat certain phrases because they're part of the local dialect. And I'll immerse myself thoroughly in the world, so I can see what the characters see, hear and feel it like they do. I can touch the bricks of the buildings and smell the jasmine in the gardens and feel the claustrophobia induced by tunnels beneath tunnels beneath subways beneath the city.

If I can see and hear and feel all this, if my senses are ignited by what I'm writing, then hopefully, if I've got any skill to apply, my readers can see, hear, and feel all of this too.

One thing to remember: you don't have to tell the reader everything you know about the world you've established. You're allowed to leave room for mystery, for ambiguity, for uncertainty. In the Midnight stories, I never say definitively whether any of those stories about its history are entirely true – because of course none of them are *entirely* true, just as none of them are entirely false – the tellers might just be misinformed.

I set *Stale Reality* in Sydney, Australia. I wrote the book shortly after living in the city for over two years. (I should have stayed longer. Maybe one day I'll go back.) The novel starts, and remains only briefly, in the real world of Sydney, the city you and I know – more precisely, the city I knew in 2005. When all of reality changes and our point of view character wanders the streets, he notices things that have changed – and everything, beyond the reasons for the shift in reality, is governed by the same physics and magic of our world, but I introduce subtle alterations. He looks into shadows he might never have looked into before. This way, he sees all the things we don't see in our world – even though it's still our world.

The world is a big thing. Even in the city where you live, even on your street, there are things you don't know or never really noticed or have only barely noticed but don't know the history of, the reason for, or what role it played in some historically relevant event in the middle of the last century.

I paint in broad strokes, when building my worlds – which is easy to do when the worlds I'm writing about are based on the real world. When we move to someplace else, someplace not based on the real world, those broad strokes might not be enough to create a thorough picture, but such specifics become more necessary.

However, there's an inherent problem in trying to do that. When we describe our own world, we don't usually take time to explain how gravity works, or the internal combustion engine propelling our automobiles down strips of asphalt. We don't dive into the history of Spain when a character from Madrid steps onto our pages. So when the story is set elsewhere, and the point of view character is from that other place, they're not likely to do that sort of thing either.

One common way to resolve this is the fish out of water story, where someone like Alice plunges into Wonderland and can make comparisons between the things we know and the things she's seeing for the first time. When Dorothy arrives in Oz, she can relate it to us because she's from our Kansas. When Bilbo Baggins is introduced in *The Hobbit*, Tolkien's narrative isn't meant for someone from Middle Earth, because if it was we wouldn't need that first paragraph explaining what kind of hole is meant when he says *In a hole in the ground there lived a hobbit.* (He begins establishing his world by telling us what it is not. *Not a nasty, dirty, wet hole, filled with the ends of worms and an oozy smell.*) Once he establishes exactly what kind of world Bilbo lives in, with all the other hobbits and, as Tolkien says, a great deal of *comfort*, then Bilbo becomes our fish out of water character as he's thrust into the greater, wider and wilder world of dwarves, trolls, orcs, and dragons.

ENDINGS

Endings are where we, as writers, aim for when we set out on our literary adventures. After the story and the plot have to come to a satisfying conclusion, we have to wrap up the rest of everything as quickly as we can and get out, leaving our readers on a strong note.

I generally have an idea of the ending when I start. Other people work differently. Some people plot out every twist and turn and event in great detail before starting – and maybe that counts as starting, I don't know. I have an idea of where I want to end; and especially in a short story, but also in a novel or any other narrative, everything has to lead to that ending.

Of course, you can have happy endings or nihilistic endings, or you can end on a note of ambiguity – think Stockton's *The Lady, or the Tiger?* That story ends with a question: which door is our protagonist about to open? Our individual answers probably reveal a lot about us – are we cynical, do we believe in love, do we believe in a love without jealousy or need? It's a powerful question, and over the course of our lives we might re-think the answer and re-consider how it ends, or how we've always believed it to end.

What I'm saying is: a strong ending will stay with you long after you've finished reading.

But endings can be complicated. How many endings are there to *The Lord of the Rings?* Spoiler alert: they defeat Sauron, and there's still hundreds of pages to go – because while that seemed to be the plot of the book, the story was not how they defeated Sauron, it was about Frodo Baggins and his journey. The book cannot end until his story comes to an end, even if the primary plot, the events that drove much of the trilogy, has already come to an end.

Often, the endings of the plot and story happen together, simultaneously, in one moment, but that's not necessary.

So, what makes a good ending?

Inevitability.

Even if there's a surprise, even if there's a twist, my favorite endings are the ones where you look back and see how it was all set up so no other ending would have worked. No matter how out-of-left-field it may seem, the ending also feels like it had to happen. "I can't believe I didn't see that, it was all right there," is a much better ending than, "Oh, and suddenly the cavalry arrives to save the day? Yay."

Surprise endings are wonderful, but not required. But even a surprise ending ought to be inevitable.

And everything on the way – from the very beginning – should lead to that end. Remember back in high school when they made us write essays and told us the conclusions of ought to tie back to the thesis in our opening paragraph? The same thing still holds true, although I think we can apply a bit more artistry now. We're no longer trying to piece together the bits and pieces we've awkwardly wrapped with a single bow in an effort to get a passing grade on a subject we're maybe not at all interested in. Now we're writing stories – something close to our heart, revealing a piece of who we are and how we see the world; we no longer have to fumble in the dark searching for substance that doesn't exist. We create the substance.

Ultimately, our stories are a clear line from beginning to unavoidable conclusion. The line doesn't have to be straight. There can be subplots and diversions, still reaching for that same strong, solid, memorable end.

PART THREE
EVERYTHING ELSE

WORDPLAY

I read a lot of books about writing and creativity, and about words and wordplay. Recently, I read a book by Mark Forsyth called *The Elements of Eloquence: Secrets of the Perfect Turn of Phrase.* It goes through a number of rhetorical devices that are just fun to play with. It includes things you're probably familiar with, like alliteration and synesthesia. And then it goes through things you're probably familiar with but have never heard the terms. For example: when James Bond says his name is "Bond, James Bond," that is a diacope. I didn't know the term, I probably won't know the term forever, but that's what it is.

I read those types of books all the time. I recommend this one because it's fun and nicely written. It's got short little sections on each of these different things, so I played with some of them. I didn't try to write something using each of these, but I found I was starting to incorporate many of those types of devices intentionally into some of the InkStains stories. I was doing it with more knowledge, but I don't know that I was doing it with more frequency, because these are the types of things you're already doing as a writer. I was just having fun.

So when I post onto my personal Facebook page that I have been breaking rules and hearts since 1970, I'm doing a few things. First of all, I'm probably exaggerating, I probably haven't broken all that many hearts. I probably haven't broken all that many rules, either. But I am using a rhetorical device in which I'm applying that one verb, *breaking,* to both nouns – *hearts* and *rules* – I am breaking both at the same time. I am not breaking rules and breaking hearts, I'm just breaking rules and hearts. I am not picking pockets and picking locks, I am picking locks and pockets. I'm probably lying to you. Maybe on all accounts.

HARDSHIPS

Life can be hard. Disappointing. Cruel. Even nasty. Sometimes, life throws a curveball (yes, it's a weak metaphor) that simply cannot be avoided. It disrupts everything. It maybe changes everything. Someone asked me how to deal with one these when they were thrown, how to keep on being creative in the face of incredible personal calamity.

Essentially life, or the universe, said, "I am not allowing you to do this right now."

This is a point where life takes over. There are going to be times when you can't do the project. I'll use myself as an example, and a situation I hope doesn't happen. Let's say I get into a car accident tomorrow. I'm fairly certain I will be unable to write for a while if I end up in a coma or something like that. That is obviously an extreme example, but many of the worst things we face are extreme. [Author's Note: this is a blatant and terrible example of a physical incident, and cannot possible illustrate the full range of emotional, psychological, financial, and other kinds of setbacks we're all at risk of every day.]

You can't beat yourself up over being unable to create at such a time, though I know people who might consider this some kind of failure. One of the most important things to remember about a project like InkStains: there is no losing. There is no failure here. If you're unable to get through the project because something happens, something out of your control interferes – well, something interfered. Start again when you're able. Next week or next month or next year. In the end, it's not a matter of whether or not you're able to complete it; what's most important is your intention and your follow-through. If you didn't finish, that doesn't mean you didn't make a valiant attempt. The attempt is more important.

I hope you're able, first, to get through what you're having to deal with. I know it can be rough, it can be challenging, it can be frightening. Life can be that way and often is. There are so many things out of our control, so many unknowns, so much that can happen that can shatter any attempt at artistic pursuit. Art may be life, and I believe it is, but there are times where art is overcome by things you must deal with in order to continue to survive and thrive – and that is definitely more important.

We all go through rough patches. Life goes in entirely different directions than we want. Sometimes, our hearts get broken. Sometimes, life throws a "curveball" that's more like a locomotive and it shatters us and scatters our remains across the countryside. It can be hard to get up from that.

How do you get up from that?

For the most part – this is tough – it's time. Time is what it takes to get past some of the roughest, harshest things that happen to us. I'm never going to suggest that it's easy. I know it's not. If your heart has been broken, it's no different than the whole world simply crashing to an end. If you've been out of work and can't find a path forward, I know how crushing that can be, how devastating to your soul and your heart. It takes a physical toll as well. I'm not going to try suggesting you work your way through this and write with it, or make music with it, or act with it.

But. You can. If you're able, channel all of that negative energy into something that's positive, channel it into something that will give you more strength, more confidence, and the ability to get beyond it. If you don't have that ability yet, if you're unable to overcome that even for a few minutes in order to do this, remember that time, ultimately, is on your side. This will end. Whatever you're going through, the emotions dragging you down or slowing you up or breaking everything apart and making the world so dark a place as it seems – there is a light at the end of that tunnel, there is an other side, and you will get through. If you can't use it to fuel your creativity in the moment, if it's too much, if you can't utilize it as a tool to break free, know that you *will* be able to. Eventually.

That's really not encouraging, is it? In the end, you're going to have to go through heartbreaks, you're going to have to go through illness and unemployment and everything else. It's all out there, and it can all come your way anytime. There's never any warning. I don't have an easy answer on how to get through any of that. The only thing I can suggest is there will be a path forward, there is a way through, there will be a solution. It might not come how you expect. It might be as "simple" as distance. With heartbreak, for instance, distance gives perspective; you can remember what you loved and why it failed, why it didn't work, why it didn't go the way you wanted it to go.

Answering some of those questions can do a couple of things. It might be totally the fault of the other person – in most cases it is. It can also be you had something to learn. You might look back later and say, I should have seen this coming because there were warning signs. Then you can use that, not just to make your own life better, but to improve your creative expression. You can utilize all of that – there's a lot of fiction out there, and a lot of music out there, entire genres of music – the blues and country both seem to focus on either the things you never had or things you've lost. We all lose things, we all are always going to lose things. In the end, we're all going to lose our lives. This is a limited run. Make the best of it. Find your way through. Find your way out of whatever quagmire has got you so bogged down, and try to find a way to make it useful to you – it not immediately, then sometime in the future.

I know writers who are still, to this day, even in their 50s and 60s, writing about things that affected them as teenagers, often with honesty and with such perspective it's impossible for a reader to not empathize. If their readers didn't experience the same thing, they have experienced something similar. That shared experience is what makes us all human. It allows our creative expressions to reach other people and be meaningful. Not everything you do as a creative person is necessarily for an audience. Plenty of people write on a daily basis in journals no one's ever going to see. It would not be a horrible thing to write a page every day and throw it in a fire, let it burn with the certainty it'll never be seen by anyone outside of you. If that's how you want to express yourself, that's the way you do it. I have every confidence you'll find the path that's right for you to achieve whatever you're wanting to achieve. The expression has many different possible outcomes. You may be looking for an audience, a wide audience, a broad audience – or you may have a specific intended audience – these handwritten letters are only for your lover – and that is beautiful. I encourage you to find a way to make those things happen.

STEPS ON A JOURNEY

There comes a point during this project where I reach the end. On December 31st, I write the final InkStains story for the year and take the next off for other projects. There's a degree of completion, of achievement: something to be proud of, a chance to say I've completed something I've begun. Not everybody finishes, and I don't expect to finish everything I start. But that achievement is extraordinarily important. Powerful. It can drive future attempts, future artistic endeavors. It can fuel your soul, your hands, your eyes, your mind. It can fuel your creativity and get you started on other projects.

In fact, some projects lead directly into others. I'll use an example from real life. Somebody I know, someone I love, spent a great many years educating herself. I don't mean she was reading up on things in her spare time; she was pursuing higher education, thoroughly higher education. She'd gotten a master's degree and finally, in the very recent past (as we're recording this, less than a week ago), she defended her dissertation to earn her doctorate. The day she successfully defended, she completed a long term project. There's still paperwork to file, there's the whole walking and physically receiving her doctorate, but she's basically finished the final phase of a long term project. She didn't go to school just to learn something; she went to learn something with the intention to apply going forward. She has a next step planned. She's going to use the credentials she's just earned to further another project, a longer term project, a book project based in large part on what she's studied. These newly earned credentials will give it weight.

Earning a doctorate degree is a long term project, something most people don't do. I'm extraordinarily proud, and I know she is as well. And that's just one step, because now there's going to be another project. She'll take the tools and experiences and education of the past many years into her future.

A lot of projects are like that. Projects begin as long term endeavors and end – only to have another project follow immediately after.

If you're studying martial arts, when you've studied long enough to earn a black belt or equivalent, that's when you discover you've actually just spent all that time preparing to begin learning, albeit in more detail and greater depth.

The trick on these longer term goals is not to forget that you do, in fact, have a long term goal. That doctorate degree involved many, many steps; she had several years of classwork after earning the Master's, comprehensive exams to pass, and a dissertation topic to get approved. Her chairman approved every chapter as she wrote it before ultimately facing a committee that would determine her fate. Each of those little goals along the way, each of those classes and exams, was in fact a goal as well – a short term goal that served as a component to the long term goal. Even the long term goal has a longer, deeper goal after that.

It's like they just keep going. It's never ending. It's one of those snakes that eats themselves. You find there's more forward movement ahead. You're not done just because you've reached what you considered to be the end of a project. When you write a novel, there is an amazing sense of achievement after finishing the first draft, but then you have to do all the revisions. Then you have to sell it to a publisher or go the publishing route on your own. Then you've got to reach your audience. There's always another level – basically, another project that needs doing.

Need might be too strong a word, because you don't necessarily have to go further than that first draft. It might be that it was a learning experience and you've gotten everything you needed out of it, which is great and fantastic – congratulations, I'm extraordinarily pleased to hear it. But even then, it sounds like just another step on a longer journey.

THE STORY OF THE CORPSE AND THE GIRL FROM MIAMI

Today I'm going to tell you a story about a story – a story that began as an InkStains before there was an InkStains.

Prior to the InkStains, in 2010, before I'd come up with the idea of doing an InkStains for a year, I had already been doing other such projects. I called them 7-in-7s, wherein I would write seven stories in seven days. This began with the IMPs (I don't remember what that acronym stood for), a writers group on Compuserve, a bunch of fantasy and science fiction writers got together and supported each other back in the early 90s. These were the young days of the Internet before AOL started sending everyone CDs. Sometime around 1996, the first 7-in-7 challenge happened. More than one of us participated. I don't know who originated the concept, but I ran with it. I didn't do the 7-in-7 just that once, but over and over again, without any particular pattern. I would simply decide *now* is a good time to start another. Now flash forward to April 2010, when I decided to try something bigger – the 30 Days in April, where I would write a story every day for the month.

During that April, I wrote 30 stories. Some are objectively terrible, and some maybe decent. One, I developed into a novel. The original story was called "Armando Luiz Salazar." The story had an ending that demanded more, and a lot of things – including characters – changed from that original story for the novel.

I started writing the novel in October 2010. I wrote about a quarter of it before the summer of 2011, not a particularly rapid pace. Then I attended an artist retreat in Maine – the Golden Apple Art Residency. I spent two weeks isolated on the outskirts of a town with a population of fewer than one thousand people. The food was great. The people were great. There were four artists total, plus Greg and Shelley – who owned and ran the place, provided us with food, and took the artists out for day trips. We were free to wander and do whatever we wanted. We each had a private cottage, and we each had a studio. During that two weeks, I wrote the middle half of that book – and the last quarter over the following six months.

That same trip, I spent a few nights in Boston because the book took place there and I needed a better feel for that city. I had some idea, but I wanted to make sure I had everything right. It was a very helpful trip and reminded me of a couple of things. For example, Boston is a brown city.

Other cities are different colors. New York tends to be gray, Sydney blue. Boston was brown – primarily in the bricks of its skyline. It was also important to see the fire escapes, the graveyards, and the history. Witnessing firsthand the way the city existed around itself was an important part of what I was doing with that story. It wasn't necessarily vital. I might've been able to research this some other way. But on the ground research can be extraordinarily valuable.

By April 2017, almost seven years to the day from writing the original story (April 18, 2010), "Armando Luis Salazar" has changed in some very major ways. One of the characters is completely different. I replaced her with somebody else. The book, the way it developed, is called *The Corpse and the Girl from Miami.* One part crime noir, one part horror, one part magic, pure pulp.

This attempt at a pulp novel began as a short story, part of a predecessor to the InkStains challenge; and other InkStains have demanded that they, too, become novels. I've already written the first draft of one of them.

LET ME ENCOURAGE YOU

I recently attended a convention in California. StokerCon is the awards banquet for the Stoker Awards, the horror version of the Oscars. There was a lot going on, as there are at most conventions. Panels and readings. An educational track. I got to see a lot of old friends and make some new ones.

One reasons to go to conventions is to meet friends, make connections, network, and hang out with like-minded people. For me, that's a big part of it. It's getting away from where I am now, where there aren't a lot of people with similar interests or similar artistic journeys and therefore not a lot of people I can talk with about this type of stuff.

When I go to these conventions, I get a chance to see people who do the same type of thing I do, who read and enjoy and write the same types of thing. Writing is often described as a solitary art. There's a reason for that. When you're writing, it's just you and the pen and the ink, or you and that computer and blank screen. It's you against yourself. It can be hard to do.

Going to the convention is a great opportunity to get some recharge going on, a revitalization of your passions – a renewal if you might. It's fantastic to be able to do that.

In the age of the Internet, you don't necessarily have to be alone all the time, but it's still good to make that physical contact – that real life connection with other people who are like-minded, who have the same ideas, the same thoughts, the same passions, the same or similar artistic paths and journeys ahead of them. Sometimes, you go just for a little bit of encouragement.

That encouragement doesn't always have to be somebody saying, hey, I encourage you to do this. But in real life, especially in geographically isolated places where you can't find a lot of people doing the same type of thing, encouragement can be hard to find. Not everybody's family is encouraging. Some parents have very specific ideas of what they want their children to do. I don't have that issue, exactly, but a lot of people do and it might be you.

So what I want to tell you right now is, if you're lacking encouragement – first of all, you shouldn't *require* encouragement to continue, but there are times when it helps, just as discouragement, whether active or passive, hinders. Encouragement can come in a lot of different ways. It comes in the form of people buying your books. It comes when strangers send e-mails proclaiming how much you have affected their lives. Sometimes, it comes in the form of somebody simply believing in you. But it can be difficult to find. It doesn't always come freely. And it's not something you can ask for. You can't go to somebody and say, hey, you, please, give me some encouragement over here, c'mon, I'm a little bit lacking. It's not like you can find a street-corner dealer in encouragement.

So let me be your dealer today.

If you feel in any way you are lacking encouragement, I am here to encourage you. I mean, the InkStains project, in a very real sense, was a way of providing my own encouragement – the idea that I can sit down to write a story every day for a year is not merely insane, it's inspiring.

While there are people who have told me InkStains has inspired them, it's also inspired me. I know I'm able to do this. I've done it twice already. I'm on my third year right now. [Author's note: the third year was 2017 and is now complete.] I know I'm capable. I know I've improved as I've progressed – my writing style, my word choice, my phraseology, my character development, my sense of place – all of this has benefited from having attacked stories in this way.

In a very real way, it's self-encouragement of the strangest kind.

Today, though, let me encourage you. If you can't find it elsewhere, I can be the source of your encouragement. Because I believe you're capable of pursuing your thoughts, much like dreams, and discovering what's inside you to be discovered. I believe you have the strength and the doggedness to continue even when faced with obstacles and adversaries. I also believe you'll know when the path you've chosen has gone wrong and it's time to shift direction and focus. I have faith in your ability to know what's best for you and to chase after it.

Now: take a moment to encourage somebody else. Someone out there needs encouragement, somebody you know or love or admire, somebody maybe you've never talked to, maybe somebody whose books you've read or music you've listened to. Go out and encourage them, or at least tell them you appreciate what they've done. Write a review on Amazon, or send them a letter, or stop them in the hall at work if this is somebody at your day job. Tell them after their performance in a bar, tell the bar, send a note backstage at the play, tell somebody you understand where they're coming from, you believe in them and you believe they are, in fact, succeeding on whatever step of their journey they're at, and you found it to be inspiring or encouraging yourself.

Lend that encouragement to somebody else, just for a little bit, without any expectation of response. It's amazing, the way that you don't lose anything when you spread this kind of encouragement. Like love – you aren't loved less because you love somebody else. Generally, you are loved more.

This is my InkStains challenge for you this week.

JURY SUMMONS

I received a jury summons. A lot of people don't like getting jury summons and have no desire to go. As a writer, as an artistic person, I know every experience feeds that artistic beast inside me. Everything that happens can end up in a book. I tell everybody I know that any word they say, anything they do, possibly and probably almost definitely will end up in a book. So I thought jury duty might be a good thing.

This was the first time I'd been called in approximately 15 years or more. I was told to phone in the night before, after 5:30pm, to find out if I was still required. I called in shortly after 5:30pm and learned I was not still required. I was dismissed. I was informed I was free to go about my regular business, which meant I had to go to the day job – which is what I did.

Then I wrote a story about jury duty anyway.

QUESTION: IS REREADING INKSTAINS LIKE LOOKING THROUGH OLD PHOTOS?

Of course I look back at the previous InkStains stories, if for no other reason, to rea them on the podcast. I have to pick the ones I like best – the ones I like best *now*, that I think would translate well to being read – and that may be very different from what I liked best *then*. I read some of these stories and have no idea where they're going. I have no memory of writing them. Over the course of three years of daily InkStains stories, I have written more than a thousand. Some are blatantly forgettable. A few are tied to a place or an image. Some, I remember quite distinctly – like the egg thief or the woman with the map tattooed on her flesh. Reading them can pull me back to the moment of writing. I am, physically, miles and years from where I wrote the first series, but I can still picture my office the night I wrote about that magic box. I return to the stone table and bench outside my last day job anytime I read the story about the oak trees. They might not be good stories, they might not actually work, not all of them, but they evoke in me an image and a memory. In that way, they can be exactly like a photo album. But not all of them. Unfortunately, some have become anonymous tales that once upon a time I probably wrote. That doesn't make them better or worse as stories. It doesn't matter, in the end, if the story evokes a memory in me – although that was the question – what matters is what the story evokes from the reader.

Take Notes Challenge

My InkStains challenge for you today is not to write a story, necessarily, or write a song or cook a meal or create a dance. It's not to practice or anything like that.

It's to take some notes.

What I mean is start carrying a notepad, something small enough for your pocket. If you don't have one handy, go online and find one. Moleskine sells them, other places sell them, and you can possibly find something appropriate at the grocery story. Just something you can carry in a pocket or a purse. Take notes. Take note of things that inspire you during everyday life. Maybe you hear song lyrics that resonate. You might overhear snippets of a conversation. Remember, as artistic types we are always watching and observing, to see how everybody else lives. It doesn't matter if they're your type or another type, and it doesn't matter if they're artistic. Being artistic, being observant, is a little bit like being voyeuristic. When you hear that snippet of conversation, think of it not in terms of gossip but in terms of character building, in terms of plot development. How can you use that type of thing?

Record your stray thoughts, the random things that pop through your head. You have them, I have them, everybody does. Sometimes they're meaningless and pointless; you don't have to record every single one. But once in a while, I put down words that almost mean nothing during the day, and I later look at it again and think this might be the title for a story or for a book. Or maybe a series of

BOOKS, WHO KNOWS? IT COULD BE BIGGER THAN THAT. MAYBE IT'S THE TITLE FOR A NEW HBO MINISERIES, AND IT COULD BE A COMIC BOOK SERIES AS WELL, A BUNCH OF BOOKS WRITTEN BY A THOUSAND DIFFERENT AUTHORS THAT WILL REACH OUT TO THE COSMOS. IT COULD BE THE NEXT BIGGEST THING EVER.

AND IT STARTS WITH JUST A COUPLE OF WORDS SCRIBBLED ON A SHEET OF PAPER IN THE NOTEPAD I CARRY IN MY POCKET. IT COULD BE A NOTEPAD YOU CARRY IN YOURS.

CARRY A NOTEPAD OF SOME SORT, A PEN OR PENCIL, SOMETHING TO WRITE WITH. IT DOESN'T HAVE TO BE SPECIAL. YOU DON'T HAVE TO SPEND A THOUSAND SOMETHING DOLLARS ON A MONT BLANC PEN. YOU CAN SPEND 97 CENTS ON A BIC AND THAT WILL WORK JUST AS WELL. STEAL ONE FROM THE OFFICE, THAT WILL ALSO WORK, I DON'T CARE. THE POINT IS TO LUBRICATE THOSE THOUGHT PROCESSES, GET THEM GOING, MAKE THEM WORK A LITTLE BIT. THE MORE YOU OBSERVE, THE MORE YOU PAY ATTENTION, AND THE MORE YOU NOTICE THINGS, THE MORE YOU WILL NOTICE THINGS AND PAY ATTENTION AND OBSERVE, AND THE DEEPER YOUR UNDERSTANDING OF THIS HUMAN EXPERIENCE WILL GO. THE BETTER YOU UNDERSTAND PEOPLE, THE BETTER YOU CAN SPEAK TO THEM, NO MATTER WHAT FORM OF ART YOU PARTAKE IN.

MYSTERIES OF THE UNKNOWN

Do you remember the 80s commercial for Time-Life's *Mysteries of the Unknown*? It's two minutes long and can be found on YouTube. The voiceover is phenomenal. Chance? Coincidence? Imagination? When I was in college, someone at our radio station, not me, parodied it. It went something like this: at one moment, 15 year old Bobby swings his fist. At the precise next moment, his little brother feels pain in his face. Coincidence?

I don't think they sell these anymore, and maybe they haven't sold these books in decades, but you can find them in used bookstores and on e-bay, and you can find them on my bookshelves. The complete set. Also their *Enchanted World* books, which started with a red book about *Wizards and Witches* well before the age of Harry Potter.

Since these books are decades old, the information in them may not be the most up-to-date. You've got shows on History channel like *Ancient Aliens*, for whatever reason, where of course everything is because why not aliens, but at least they've got stuff more recent than 1983.

When I was young, I bought these because I wanted to know more about unknown sciences and myths. I wanted to know about ESP and UFOs. I wanted to read about ogres and dragons. Apparently, this has always been an area of interest for me. These books were condensers of information. Like Wikipedia today, they contain bits and pieces from a variety of sources, and maybe some of those sources are questionable.

I continue, even today, to buy such useful reference books. Not because they have the answers, but because they pose questions. And they present possible solutions. I don't need to believe aliens came from a distant star system and helped build the pyramids. I have absolutely zero reason to. However, there's also zero reason why I shouldn't use that as a jumping off point for a story.

I get books with maps of places that never were, and also histories of places and people that do (or did) exist. These types of overviews are a rough start, not specialized in-depth information. They're the surface. When I start working on a project, I tend to go deeper. So books like *Mysteries of the Unknown* may spark my imagination and may set me on a course, but they're really only a start.

I find books on glassmaking, for instance, and on mirrors, on astronomy and the constellations, if I want to write about a man building his own telescope. I haven't written that story yet, but maybe now I will – that's how ideas are born. You pull various bits and pieces from all sorts of places.

Those Time-Life books served, for me, as a kind of imagination foundation. They fed my need for mythology and parapsychology that had previously been aroused by *Star Wars* and *The Lord of the Rings*.

I also played *Dungeons & Dragons*. Some of my earliest stories were bad D&D plotlines. When I was first submitting stories, it wasn't uncommon to see guidelines specifically saying they didn't want your D&D campaigns. Yes, some of the first fantasy novels I read weren't merely bad rehashes of *Lord of the Rings* and *Dungeons & Dragons*, they were actually set in D&D scenarios and officially licensed. Some of those weren't bad.

The more I read, though, the more I wanted. The more I devoured. I've gone well beyond scripting bad D&D plots and reading *Ravenloft* novels.

I started at the surface because it itched. I scratched and went deeper, learned more, developed my skills, and heightened my own psychic powers to the point that I can now put images directly into your mind – with the power of language.

Coincidence?

RESEARCH

Research allows you to get deep into the guts of a subject, and it means many different things. You can read about the topic. You can talk with experts. I used to do something I called easy research, which was basically going to a person who played the piano to ask, "What kind of piano would a wealthy man buy in the 1800s?" It didn't give me real knowledge, but it gave me something to start with – it gave the surface of a fact, you might say.

When I started writing a book I called *The Boston Book*, because it was set in Boston, I got one quarter of the way through based on things I read, things I saw on television, and friends who either had lived there or lived there currently. But that wasn't enough. In the end, I took a research trip. I visited Boston to get a better grasp of what the city was like. I wandered aimlessly. I took in sights. I ate their pizza. I loved their pizza. There's a place in the North End – I think it was the best pizza I've ever eaten – and I was born in Manhattan.

I'm getting sidetracked. I went to Boston, and I learned some very necessary things about the city, small things that would be difficult to explain. I was reminded, for instance, of fire escapes, since the city I live in now doesn't have buildings and, apparently, doesn't have fires, so no one ever needs to escape them. And I learned that Boston was brown. I mean, when you look at the skyline from Piers Park, the city has a distinct brown shade.

Sometimes the necessary research involves going someplace other than a library.

The world is different now than it used to be. Perhaps we don't need those Time-Life books to kick start a fragment of an idea in our heads because we now have *Atlas Obscura* and *Roadside America*, both online, to give us some broad sense of knowledge about new places. Still, there is something to be said for getting right there, breathing the air, feeling the heartbeat.

That Boston book ended up being called *The Corpse and the Girl from Miami*, because the two main characters are those title characters. It benefited greatly from my brief visit. Just as my novella, *Necropolis*, benefited from my taking a day and a camera to Lidcombe, outside of Sydney, to visit the Rookwood Necropolis.

That kind of hands-on research gives you a sense of atmosphere and ambience, while the books I read as a teenager gave me a basic foundational knowledge of things creepy and absurd. Two very different kinds of research, and not the only two.

There's a thing called Expository Writing, in which you don't do any outside research. You work with what you know. I took an expository writing class in college. One day, topic was to write about your earliest childhood memory. I did this, yes, but not before deciding I'd rather do something else. So I wrote about wandering the streets of New York City without memory and being adopted into the Urbancik family – all a fabrication. Maybe because I preferred to write fiction? Because I have a psychological barrier preventing me from recalling my earliest childhood memories? Maybe I'm just contrary. I ended up giving the teacher both versions, the made up version and the actual. All these years later, I don't remember what earliest memory I wrote about. I'm decades older, now. I bet some of those childhood memories have changed. Time has a way of doing that.

[Author's Note: I think I wrote about Ferris wheels on the back of trucks in Queens.]

Books About Creativity

I have a lot of books about writing, a lot of books about photography, and a lot of books about creativity. It's like I have a passion for these things. Beyond the reference material I've got on ghosts, ESP, aliens, pyramids, crystal skulls, and the Knights Templar, I have books on the art and the craft and the business. I'm fascinated by some of these approaches toward creativity.

I have read books by writers, dancers, and magicians which, at their best, don't try to teach the reader how to be creative but share how they, personally, approach their arts, and encourage you to be equally bold. At their best, they inspire, and sometimes offer excellent suggestions that may help you through rough spots in your personal creative journeys.

Sometimes, it's important just to know you're not the only one. Even in groups of people who are supposedly like-minded, I still find myself at the edges, almost on the outside. I think too much, and I think constantly, and no amount of bourbon will stop me. It helps, knowing I'm on the same outside as other artists pursuing other goals.

Phillip Petit has a great book called *Creativity*. He's a juggler and a tight-rope walker. Author Jeff Vandermeer has his *Wonderbook*. Johnette Napolitano, singer and bassist for Concrete Blonde, has a short book called *Rough Mix* that somehow fits into this same category without even being about the creative process. *I Am Iman* is extraordinary, and also filled with photos.

WE ARE NOT ALONE IN OUR ALONENESS. THERE ARE OTHER LIGHTS OUT THERE SHINING THROUGH THE SAME DARKNESS, AND THERE ARE PEOPLE WHO ARE NOT JUST TELLING THE STORIES AND SINGING THE SONGS AND MAKING THE ART, BUT THEY'RE TELLING US ABOUT THOSE JOURNEYS, THEIR STRUGGLES, THE TRIALS AND FAILURES AND OBSTACLES AND DEAD-ENDS ON THE WAY TO THEIR SUCCESSES.

I DON'T WANT TO TELL YOU HOW TO DO ANYTHING, HOW TO WRITE OR TAKE PHOTOGRAPHS. I DON'T WANT TO LEAD YOUR INTO THEMES OR SUBJECTS, AND I CERTAINLY DON'T WANT TO DICTATE THE ANGLES FROM WHICH YOU APPROACH THEM. I WANT TO INSPIRE, ENCOURAGE, AND ALSO CHALLENGE YOU.

FOR THIS WEEK'S INKSTAINS CHALLENGE, I WANT YOU TO FIND SOMEONE WHO CAN INSPIRE, ENCOURAGE, AND CHALLENGE YOU. I WANT YOU TO FIND A BOOK, NO MATTER THE SIZE, OR EVEN A PODCAST OR VIDEO THAT DOESN'T SET OUT TO TEACH YOU HOW TO DO SOMETHING, AND DOESN'T ATTEMPT TO ANSWER WHY YOU SHOULD DO SOMETHING, BUT SIMPLY INCITES YOU TO DO IT.

The Room that Moved

I recently broke out the remnants of a long neglected project. For three years, the file languished on my hard drive. Its notepad, in which I track everything and ask questions that need answering and remind myself of all the little loose ends that will eventually be tied up or purposefully ignored, was in a pile with all the others.

I recently moved. I'm still in boxes, not because you always end up leaving a few boxes undone when you move, but because things are still jostling for a home in the new space. I've got about 70 books unpacked. The rest are in storage. I have blank notepads, of course, and my InkStains notebooks, and a variety of other blank paper stuff and pens.

I have a lot of pens.

I have little notebooks – they're Moleskines, not the hardcover ones but the smaller – Cahiers, I think they're called – each devoted to one of the projects I'm working on or planning to work on. I have no shortage of ideas. Some are ready to run with, some are barely anything more than a title or concept.

Once Upon a Time in Midnight and *Stale Reality*, two of my novels, started as titles. In both cases, it was years before I had anything more than that. The same is still true. I have tentative titles. In many cases, tentative titles do not remain. *The Boston Book*, when finally released, was called *The Corpse and The Girl from Miami*.

Even the projects I'm not currently working on, the projects I want to tackle in the future, get to live somewhere. And I scribble all these notes, these ideas and possible scenes and reminders and questions, by hand. Because that's how I work.

I have a number of these notepads. When one of these projects begs to be released from my skull, I flip through the notepad and review the notes I've already made. Even if I'm not going to use them all. Like an outline, notes for things that may happen tend to change.

Notepads aren't the only tool I use when working on a larger project. There's a lot to keep track of, and I've never attempted to use software like Scrivener. I keep Character Sheets, where I track all the necessary physical traits, like eye and hair color, actual and apparent age, stuff like that. I track important relationships, parents and spouses and such, even the ones that are only mentioned one time during the manuscript. Because these are the types of things I don't want to get wrong.

One time, back in the early 90s, I wrote a novel called *Roses Grow*. Yes, that's the title from a Concrete Blonde song. No, it was not the title I started with. It was a ghost story, and partway through someone asks the ghost, "What about the roses?" The ghost responds, "Roses grow," which I thought was fun.

This is not, by the way, a novel you will ever find. Maybe a dozen people have ever seen it, and though some of loved it, it's neither my strongest nor most effective effort. It's what you might call a *trunk novel*, and will likely never emerge from the trunk.

Early in this manuscript, I described a room on the second floor of a mansion. It was an important room, and an unusual room. In the end, when the main character set fire to the mansion – sure, I'm spoiling it, but you'll never read it – that room is on the first floor across from the dining room. Which is totally, completely, and one hundred percent wrong. And bad. Not a minor mistake at all. Because I didn't yet know how to have a system in place to track important details. I relied on my memory. My head. Which should never have been considered trustworthy.

I fixed it. I eventually trunked the novel for entirely other reasons. And now, I have notepads.

You probably should devise a system that works for you, especially on those longer projects, because it's always possible you'll be sidetracked, or the story will hit a brick wall, and a year later you'll return to it. Keep those notes, keep those character sheets, use index cards, sticky notes, spreadsheets, colored pens and highlighters – whatever you need to make sure you don't move important rooms to entirely different floors of the house, and to make sure you keep those characters' brown eyes from turning blue.

CHOOSING PROJECTS

I am an idea factory.

I have hundreds of little ones dancing in my head. The noise can sometimes be deafening. If I selected projects based on potential profit, I'd be a rich man. And as you know, I rely on someone out there buying one of my books every day just so I can eat breakfast.

Deadlines are, in fact, wonderful motivators, which is why, when I don't have externally applied deadlines looming, I build my own. The InkStains had a daily deadline. There's a reason for that. No deadline at all means it doesn't matter when I finish, and that's not conducive to productivity. I aim to be productive. I intend to create good, quality stories. That includes finishing them and moving on to the next.

So, when those considerations are behind me, how do I decide what to work on next? Some of those hundreds of ideas dancing in my head are prima ballerinas. Stars. They shine more brightly than others, but they're also vicious little things and sometimes devour lesser ideas. (Yes, the resultant amalgamations generally create more intricate and powerful stories.) Some ideas live there for a long time. *Once Upon a Time in Midnight* and *Stale Reality*, two of my novels, started as fledgling ideas that needed time to develop and mature before becoming something substantial enough to carry an entire novel.

Some smaller ideas, often only needing a few pages, demand attention. They're the class clowns. They don't always have a lot of depth. Occasionally, I have to write out one of those just to excise it from my head, or to prove they aren't worth the effort yet.

Sometimes, however, a little thing becomes something bigger. In one of my first year's InkStains stories, I wrote about a man trying to demonstrate how much he loved someone. He used a variety of methods. One day, he did something – I won't say exactly what, you'll have to wait for it – but it failed to impress the character he was trying to impress.

However, that single paragraph stuck with me. It had barely been an idea, less than a scene in the overall structure of a five page story. It stuck inside my head, like a seed, a ballerina seed, and it grew. It grew out of control: in the background, in the foreground, everywhere, until finally, a few years later, I had no choice but to write the novel. I incorporated other ideas, and a whole new set of characters, and it's in my agents hands right now. Hopefully it'll soon be in your hands, and then I can buy another breakfast.

Talent And Skill

This is personal opinion, and isn't necessarily how everyone else divides these things, but I think of talent as something you nurture and skill as something you develop. Either can bring you success in your art. The combination, I think, is what leads you to being exceptional.

The dividing line is rather fine, and not often easy to see. I don't want to call anyone out, but I can look at some books, some very successful books, where the writer was obviously talented but the skills were lacking. You can watch those skills develop in their future work. In that case, talent was the driver, and that doesn't take anything away from the final product.

Talent, I think, is what you're born with, and skill is what you learn. The thing is, I also believe everyone is born with a creative side, and what we really need to do, while learning the skills involved in our art, is tease out and nurture those inborn talents.

BOOK FLOOD

I don't know if this is an InkStains challenge or something else, but next year, I want more books – not just for me, but for everyone everywhere. I want to return to the glory days of Book Row in Manhattan. I want a hundred publishers putting out powerful, educational, entertaining, massive, and miniscule texts of all sorts. It'll take more than a year to accomplish this. I think there's five publishers in New York now? There were dozens when I was born.

The world has changed. We have changed. I'd love to see a return to the days when everyone read, but I don't even know if such days ever existed. I'm reading *The Man Who Invented Christmas* right now, about how Charles Dickens came to write *A Christmas Carol*, and it's a reminder of a day when a frighteningly small percentage of people *could* read, and a frighteningly small percentage of people had any formal education at all.

Today, apparently, they publish more books per capita in Iceland than anywhere else in the world. At the end of the year, attached to the Christmas season but I don't think it needs to be, they have their Christmas Book Flood. Reykjavik is, in fact, recognized as a UNESCO City of Literature. I don't even know what that is. It sounds amazing to me. Every year, starting with a mail-order catalog delivered by post – a catalog of books – they have their annual Book Flood.

That's what I want.

A flood of books. I want to have a Book Flood Party next year. I don't know what that's going to look like or how that's going to work, I don't know who will be there or even where there will be. But it will be a book thing. And you can join me.

There's no need to wait until next year, either. Go buy yourself a book now. Buy one for a friend. It doesn't have to be one of mine. Anything you find interesting, even if you've already read it. Buy a throwaway paperback, a dime store pulp, a thick biography, something classic, something literary, something filled with pictures. Buy a book, see how it feels, how it smells, how it tastes – well, maybe not that far.

DO SOMETHING CHALLENGE

FOR THE NEXT MONTH, ONCE A WEEK, FOUR OR FIVE WEEKS IN A ROW, THOUGH NOT NECESSARILY THE SAME DAY OR NIGHT EACH WEEK, GO APPRECIATE SOME ART. ESPECIALLY IF IT'S OUTSIDE THE FORM YOU WORK IN. AS A WRITER, I FIND I'M OFTEN INSPIRED BY MUSIC AND PAINTINGS AND FILM.

SO GO TO A MUSEUM. GO TO A GALLERY OPENING. GO TO A JAZZ CLUB. IT SHOULDN'T BE THE SAME THING EVERY WEEK. THIS WORKS BEST IF IT'S ALWAYS SOMETHING DIFFERENT. EXPLORE THE WORLD OUTSIDE OF YOU, THE OTHER ARTS AND ARTISTS. FIND A POETRY OPEN MIC NIGHT, ATTEND A LECTURE ON DADAISM AND THE SURREAL, TRY A NEW RESTAURANT, SEE AN ART HOUSE MOVIE.

DON'T DO THIS AS AN ASSIGNMENT. I'M NOT GRADING YOU. DO THIS AS A MEANS OF RECHARGING YOUR CREATIVE BATTERIES. OF EXPANDING YOUR LEVELS OF AWARENESS. OF MEETING NEW AND INTERESTING PEOPLE WHO DO THINGS LIKE YOU BUT NOT LIKE YOU.

SET OUT ON AN ADVENTURE OF DISCOVERY.

Maps

At a signing event, I had a conversation with an artist, Cat Scully, who makes maps. I've always been fascinated, in some minor way, with maps. I say a minor way because I've not become a professional cartographer, I don't know the names of famous mapmakers from history, and I don't have a full size map of a world – ours or any other – on the wall over my desk – which, now that I say this, is surely a failing on my part. But I've always loved maps, and I've written a number of stories, a number of InkStains stories, in which maps featured prominently.

I'm working on a novella right now, in addition to my daily InkStains stories, and there are two scenes which feature maps in important ways. I can't discuss it any detail except to say the maps are important, and I've already said that. [Author's Note: the novella is *Echo*, due out from Eraserhead Books in early 2020.]

All this map talk has reinvigorated my fascination with maps, so I found one of my notepads, a special one I had labeled *Atlas*, in which I'd already sketched a half dozen maps. They're mostly terrible. Some are worse. The first one, I think, might be the best. It's mostly empty on the inside, with a sketch of a rose compass; around the edges, at the furthest reaches of the map, I wrote the word dragon in every language I know, and in quite a few I don't. It is a map of the edges of the map, and there, as you know, be dragons.

The Atlas was one of my sidelined projects. I was just playing with maps, despite having zero skills in that area, and I let it drop aside. I moved on. I did other things. But maps, in general, never strayed far from my mind. Thanks in large part to artist and mapmaker Cat Scully, I have broken out a set of Prismacolor pens in varying widths and begun again. I watched YouTube videos on how to make maps – which were not always helpful – and I drew a few terrible, terrible maps.

But then I did something I thought was extraordinary. I mapped the novella I'm working on. Not a map of its streets and alleys, its apartments, and its theaters – all of which are important – but a map of the story itself, the connections between the characters, the essence of each character and their secrets, and I put the theater at the center because it seemed to be central to the story. I also have a second, prominent center that's not merely vital but dominant. It's a map maybe only I can read, and maybe it serves no purpose other than to give me a moment of fun.

URBANCIK PRONUNCIATION GUIDE

A question I'm asked a lot is how to pronounce my last name. Which isn't fair, because there's another dozen people in the United States who have the same last name and some of them, even some I'm directly related to, pronounce it differently. I say Urban*cik*. My mom says Ur*ban*cik. (I figure it's mine by blood and hers only by marriage, so mine is more correct. Yet still Americanized.) I believe in The Czech Republic, they would likely roll their R's, and pronounce the C like a CH. In the end, no matter how you say it, I can be fairly sure you're talking to me. It's rather uncommon.

I saw a list somewhere of the 50,000 most common last names in the United States. My name was not on that list. Probably a lot of people who arrived in the U.S. in the late 1800s and early 1900s, if they shared my name, dropped the suffix. Someone with the last name Urban might be a distant relative. But the suffix places the name, geographically, and I appreciate having that kind of heritage to look back on, even if I know next to nothing about my ancestors. What I do know is this: my name came to the U.S. from the Austro-Hungarian Empire in 1902, and I am the fourth in a line. I should have a vast estate and fortune somewhere, but someone forgot to tell me about it.

LINKED STORIES AND SIGIL MAGIC

A musician we've seen in some of my stories is a recurring character. Not many stories. Mostly, they're unpublished, so when I say we've seen him, I mean I've seen him. He's the Master of Winds. He plays all the wind instruments. He first appeared with a flute in the novella *Necropolis*. He appears in a Midnight novel I haven't yet finished. He's a force of nature, in a way, and I don't think I'll ever completely explore him.

I did, for one month, write a series of InkStains stories featuring the Master of Winds. I found it wasn't as much fun to write about him, directly, as it was to write about someone encountering him. I didn't want to spoil the mystery by explaining or defining him. Depending on the nature of the story, and the nature of the character, you can get away with leaving some mystery. By incorporating a bit of that same mystery elsewhere, you'll start to create a depth to your worlds, a thread that links the stories, like what Stephen King did – all those stories of Castle Rock and Derry – linking them to other places that are real, then linking them to other fictional places, even fictions outside his own, so that ultimately, by the time the *Dark Tower* is finished, all stories everywhere are part of his world.

It's the same in comics. In DC Comics, all the various universes belong to the same multiverse, which is to say even different versions of earth share the same existence. It's difficult to explain in just a few words, so I won't try. Let's just say there's more than one Batman because there's more than one earth, and all of those earths exist simultaneously.

Years ago, at a convention in Atlanta, I met Clive Barker. Literally bumped into him at a bar. We talked for a while. He probably doesn't remember it, because I was one of the masses who shared a few minutes and words with him. One thing he said that weekend, which I think he's repeated since, is that the novella is the perfect length for horror. Not too short, not too long. Get in, get terrified, and get out.

I tend to like the novella as well, and I recently finished the first draft of a new one. The writing of a novella, like the reading, is a quick thing – in and out. It took only eleven days to write the first draft, though the first day was a week or a month before the second, and on one of those other ten days I wrote nothing. But the story did not develop, begin to end, during those eleven days.

No, it was born months ago, while I was trapped in a phone meeting at the day job, talking not just about something boring, but about something only tangentially related to what I did. I was there, mostly, in case I was needed. I often wasn't. Sometimes I was – and when I made a difference, it mattered. But for those days when I wasn't, I kept a stack of sticky notes at my desk.

I never wrote at the day job (lunch hour, however, was not on the clock). I always divided those two things. But I find the physical act of writing, putting words onto paper, relaxing. So I would write random words, often words from the phone call, on a sticky note. Never anything that required thought. After all, I was pre-occupied, and I've never found it conducive to either activity to split my attention. But I often, on those sticky notes, wrote a few words completely unrelated to those meetings.

One of those words, *Echo*, became the title of the novella. It was born that day as only a title, a word, a word that anyone can use to create an entirely different story than the one I eventually created.

I scribbled that word over and over during a number of phone meetings, and sometimes when I was just bored, at the day job or not. I developed a way of writing it, crafting the letters individually into a kind of logo for the unwritten story, eventually creating what someone suggested was a form of sigil magic. It was unintentional, yet there I was: invoking a story, drawing it into and out of my head. I thought about it some, turned over a few ideas, rejected others, and realized, eventually, it didn't involve the Echo of Greek mythology. I kept it alive, as I keep a number of titles and ideas. At some point, I wrote a couple hundred words, what I thought might be the beginning of this story.

A week or a month later, I realized those words were not right. I couldn't go forward from there because the tone was wrong. The voice was wrong. I mean, of course it's my voice, but my voice doesn't sing in just one key. I reworked those words, then aimed for 2,000 new words a day and set forth. I didn't know when it would end. I didn't know if I would reach my goal every day. I didn't know where the story would go, not right away. I set out knowing only how it began and who it involved and how the title could be written.

A week or so later, on Halloween, I took a day off. It was important to see the decorations, share wine with friends and neighbors, and maybe eat some candy. I don't remember. It was a week ago. I had missed my goal only one day.

What did I do when I missed my goal that day? I shrugged it off, attacked the next day fresh, and didn't worry about those words I'd missed. In the end, all the necessary words would make it into the story.

Two days after Halloween, I did a double session, hurting my fingers to do so, and completed the first draft. I took the next day off as a means of relaxing, of letting my fingers rest, of recharging. But by the middle of the day, I felt myself slipping into a post-story melancholia, a kind of blues unique to writers, possibly akin to postpartum depression. I was able to recognize and do something about it. I designed a possible cover for *Echo*.

[Author's Note: the novella, *Echo*, due from Eraserhead Press in early 2020. My cover design will not be used.]

STUDY CHALLENGE

STUDY SOME ASPECT OF ART YOU'VE NEVER LOOKED AT BEFORE, WHETHER IT'S YOUR PRIMARY ART OR NOT. YOU'RE A PHOTOGRAPHER? READ POE'S ESSAY ON DAGUERREOTYPES IN WHICH HE CALLS PHOTOGRAPHY "THE MOST EXTRAORDINARY TRIUMPH OF MODERN SCIENCE." YOU'RE A PAINTER? EXAMINE THE STYLES OF A CULTURE YOU'RE NOT FAMILIAR WITH. YOU WRITE ABOUT VAMPIRES BUT HAVE NEVER READ ANYTHING BUT *INTERVIEW WITH THE VAMPIRE*? READ *VARNEY THE VAMPIRE* OR *CARMILLA*.

SPEND A DAY AT THE MUSEUM, OR PORING THROUGH CURIOUS AND FORGOTTEN LORE. (YES, SORRY, I WAS RECENTLY AT THE POE MUSEUM IN RICHMOND AGAIN.)

SPEND TIME AND ENERGY AND, IF APPROPRIATE, MONEY, ON WHAT CAME BEFORE. READ *THE BEST SCIENCE FICTION STORIES OF THE 1950S*. READ AN ART HISTORICAL TREATISE ON VAN GOGH AND JAPANESE PRINTS. LOOK THROUGH THE FASHION PHOTOGRAPHY OF EDWARD STEICHEN.

IN FACT, STEICHEN IS A GOOD EXAMPLE OF SOMEONE WHO'S DONE JUST THIS. HE TRAINED AS A PAINTER IN THE EARLY 20TH CENTURY, THEN WENT ON TO DEFINE FASHION PHOTOGRAPHY FOREVER, IN PART BY POSING HIS MODELS IN THE WAYS THEY MIGHT HAVE POSED FOR THE PAINTINGS OF PREVIOUS CENTURIES.

STUDY SOMETHING RELATED, DIRECTLY, INDIRECTLY, TANGENTIALLY, OR MERELY THEMATICALLY, TO YOUR OWN ART. FIND THOSE CONNECTIONS. EXPLORE WHERE YOU WANT TO GO WITH YOUR ART BY KNOWING WHERE ART HAS ALREADY BEEN. DISCOVER SOMETHING.

Stars Wars and Me

Let's go back in time to the very beginning, the first movie, known only as *Star Wars*. I was young, very young – only six when the film came out. My mom and someone else's mom took all of us – in my memory there must've been a hundred of us. We went to a theater somewhere in New York City. I couldn't tell you where or which, I can only say the place was huge, and even in the 70s it had three screens. There was a lobby the size of an airport hangar, and the screen was a thousand feet wide.

In contrast, the screen I saw *The Last Jedi* on was barely bigger than some televisions.

The thing I remember most was the enormity of it all. This was not the first time I'd ever been to a theater. This was not the first movie I'd ever seen. But it is the first I remember.

It wasn't story or character or plot or movie making finesse that impressed me. *Star Wars* reached into my head and ignited my imagination like nothing ever before. It was my first fire.

That winter, I remember playing *Star Wars*. I always wanted to be Luke Skywalker because, well, he could walk through the sky. Was I taking things literally? I was seven that winter, so yeah, I probably was.

The Force was my introduction to the supernatural and the paranormal, though I didn't know either word then. Later, I would read Arthur C Clark's *Mysterious Worlds* and subscribe to Time-Life's *Mysteries of the Unknown* and *Enchanted World*.

I refer to *Star Wars* as one of my foundational influences. To be honest, it's probably the first and biggest of them all. *Batman* didn't hit me until later, even if I had been tuning in at the same Bat Time every day. Neither *Lord of the Rings* nor *Dungeons and Dragons* reached me until a few years later – at around age 12 or 13. *Star Wars* hit me in the right way at the right time to fire all cylinders. I had the action figures. The first two I remember were Luke and Vader. I would make them duel long before we ever saw it happen on the screen.

The action figures contributed to this, without doubt. The movie kick-started my imagination, but the toys allowed me to exercise it. Over the next few years, I got a lot of them. It wasn't a collection. You would never have called it that in the 70s and 80s. They were just toys. At some point, later, I gave them all away – very possibly in an effort to ignite someone else's imagination.

Looking at it objectively, there are all sorts of problems with *Star Wars*, with all the *Star Wars* movies. The dialogue reads straight out of a comic book – and I mean that in a bad way. There are contradictions within the plot. But there are moments of brilliance, even simple moments understandable at the age of six.

Back to those action figures for a minute. You know why Boba Fett became such a favorite character, right? Because of the action figures. Mail in five proofs of purchase, and six months before *Empire Strikes Back* came out, Kenner sent you a free action figure from the upcoming movie. We all had him. We had months and months to play with him, and to make up our own stories, before the movie even came out. We made him a badass, of course, because he wore a jetpack, and there was nothing more badass than flying around with a jetpack blasting your enemies.

When I say *Star Wars* is my favorite movie of all time, it's not because the movie is great, though I think there's much greatness to be found there. And it's not because the characters spoke to us, though of course everyone has their favorite. It's certainly not because the dialogue was realistic, or because we understood its hokey religion. It's not because this movie defined my childhood.

No, it's because, in a very real way, *Star Wars* charted the course of my life.

GUILLERMO DEL TORO

I've been reading Guillermo del Toro's *The Cabinet of Curiosities.* I didn't know exactly what it was when I got it, so I'll be vague in describing now. It's a collection of photos from his personal collection of the macabre, from his films and all of filmic history. It's a collection of his notepads, which of course speaks to me because I have a dozen on my desk right now. It's a collection of essays, some biographical, and some transcriptions of interviews, and some about the things that have inspired del Toro. It's also a collection of his thoughts on writing and creativity and filmmaking and legacy.

It's a coffee table book with cool pictures and a good bit of rich, and varied, things to read, and I'm enjoying it a lot. So this week, as I'm reading this, I start seeing people post their pictures online from the travelling art exhibit of del Toro's memorabilia and treasures, which concluded this week in Toronto and, to the best of my knowledge, is done. I didn't even know it was happening until it was too late.

Also this week, I saw *The Shape of Water.* The book pre-dates the movie, but I see hints of the film inside, in his collection and in his inspirations. He says right from the start *The Creature from the Black Lagoon* was what I call a foundational influence on him – one of those things that got him at an early age and ignited his imagination. The book is, essentially, an illustration of imagination, of course tinted for fans of del Toro's work, horror, and fantasy. I think it also shows how much he loves what he does, how much a part of him this whole creative process is.

I feel, in a very real way, like I've just discovered a fellow traveler on the same road I travel – through the dark and the fantastic, through the fires of imagination and creativity. I would not say we tell the same stories or that we approach the same themes. But I see similarities. I find the exuberance displayed in this book, and the lovingness that's so obvious in his films, to be – *contagious* is the wrong word, because I've already caught it – to be familiar.

Did I love *The Shape of Water?* A little bit. Not a lot. There were things about it I really liked, and it would be hard for me to point to things I disliked. I wasn't surprised by the ending. I won't spoil it for you if you haven't seen it, but I knew from very early on how it was going to end. Of course, I often know that about my own stories, too. And just like with the stories I write, I didn't know how we were going to get from where it started to where it would, inevitably, conclude.

I intend to re-watch a few of his films. I haven't seen either of the *Hellboy* movies since they were in the theater, and *Pan's Labyrinth* in at least as long. I've never seen some of his others, and I now realize that's a mistake. For me.

I mentioned Guillermo del Toro's notebooks, and I mentioned my own. I have a lot of them. I've used them for writing the InkStains stories. I have little ones that fit in my pocket, and I never leave the house without one. I have small books devoted to particular projects, and keep a bunch of those in an orange sack that have cover images I've stolen from the Internet that are only meant for me. When I had a day job, I kept a notepad at my desk to scribble in, just so I could feel the ink flow. I started back in college, forever ago, in the same cheap notebooks anyone would use to take notes in math class. Over time, I experimented. I went through a phase of writing with silver and gold pens. I've used the books as diaries, a little bit, but primarily as sketchpads. I'm a writer, so my sketches involve words. I recorded things I'd heard or read, I quoted songs and movies, I wrote out possible future scenes. They're random and, when I look back, a little bit fascinating. It's like exploring someone else's past life, because there are so many things I simply don't remember. It's also amazing, sometimes, seeing the seeds that eventually became real projects, and being reminded of the seeds I haven't yet tended.

Your Cabinet of Curiosities

You might have someone else with whom you feel this same strange, inexplicable companionship — no, that's not exactly right — *comradery* maybe? Someone who speaks to you beyond just the measure of their films, their music, their books. I challenge you to find such a person, whatever your art and whatever their art — they do not have to do what you do — and learn more about that person. Read something about them, not merely an interview in *People* magazine. Find out what makes them tick. What songs they listen to when the lights are dim. The flavors flowing through their blood. Read a biography, or something like *Cabinet of Curiosities*, an exploration into what makes them tick.

EDGAR ALLAN POE

Memory is a freaky thing. You remember some conversations verbatim years after the fact, but you can't remember why you went to the grocery store. If my memory can be trusted, which is to say if I'm not overly mad or given to exaggerations and falsehoods, if I can be trusted to be seeing the truth when I call upon my memory, I was officially introduced to Edgar Allan Poe in a class of some sort, in Middle School, at approximately the age of twelve, by a record.

This was the early 80's, so I mean a vinyl record and an old school record player. I can't say for certain who the narrator was; in my memory, it was Vincent Price. Who better? It's entirely possible, because I still remember listening to it. I was sitting in one of those little school desks and the lights were as low as they got. It was a relatively open area being used as a classroom, but I don't remember if it was English class or something else. [Author's note: based on things I know now, it seems more likely it was Basil Rathbone.]

They put on the records and we listened. I distinctly remember hearing "The Black Cat", and seeing it in my head, seeing every little bit of it. We listened to "The Cask of the Amontillado" too, and "The Pit and the Pendulum."

And here, I'm forced to interrupt myself. Because I met "The Pit and the Pendulum" much earlier than that. It was Atlantic City, sometime in the mid-70s, somewhere off the boardwalk, and my godmother and her sisters and I, and who can say who else, were going through a haunted house of some sort. Maybe my first ever haunted house. We walked through a hall past scenes behind glass. I don't remember any of the scenes except that pendulum. It was there, at least in my memory of it, that a door burst open in the darkness and a voice commanded, "Move along!" It scared the hell out of me. I was what, five years old? Easily frightened? Maybe that was the first scare of my life, the moment that led me to who I am today, writer of fantasy, dark fantasy, and horror. [Author's note: probably not Atlantic City but maybe Seaside Heights.]

Such memories are inconsistent, easy to refute and poke holes at, easy to categorically deny. Doesn't matter. I remember Edgar Allan Poe and his stories before almost any other.

I do know, without doubt, I took a speech class my first year of college, and I took writing courses of all types. Somewhere along the line, we recited poetry, as a class, one line at a time, going round the room in a circle, and I memorized Poe's poem "Eldorado." Maybe it's not his most famous or best known. It's not

ONCE UPON A MIDNIGHT DREARY, WHILE I PONDERED, WEAK AND WEARY,

OVER MANY A QUAINT AND CURIOUS VOLUME OF FORGOTTEN LORE—

which makes me wonder, really. What was the narrator reading? Has anyone done a study of that? I'd be extraordinarily curious.

Edgar Allan Poe was born 19 January 1809 in Boston, Massachusetts, and the world, fortunately, has not been the same since. From when I record this, we will celebrate his birthday in just a few days, but I want to start earlier. So here we are.

I never considered Poe a foundational inspiration. I never thought of him as one of the reasons I do this. I probably should. Because I most certainly have been influenced by the tapestry of Poe's work. I find it rich and provocative and superb. But I have also been influenced by writers who have been influenced by Poe, and writers whose influences were influenced by Poe, and writers who were influenced by writers who were influenced by...all the way back for almost two hundred years.

I could go on for pages talking about the influence Edgar Allan Poe has had on literature and culture. I could quote Jules Verne or Arthur Conan Doyle or HG Wells or Stephen King in trying to convey this. But the sad truth is, I have not read everything he's written. I almost think it's impossible unless you can get a hold of letters and such that were never published – I'm sure the museums have some. There's such a museum here, the Edgar Allan Poe Museum in Richmond, Virginia. There's another in Baltimore, and I think one in Boston, as well, and others.

I have no good reason to not have read everything by now. I'm old enough, aren't I? I've read enough, haven't I? I try to read broadly, but I'm a slow reader, so I can never read everything I want. I have hundreds of books on my shelves that I've read, yes, but also hundreds I haven't gotten to yet.

And more than one of them contains Poe. More than one is exclusively Poe. More than one, in fact, is a complete collection of his fiction and poetry.

ROMANCE

Valentine's is a celebration of romance. It's a day we're supposed to shower our partners with gifts that show the depth of our love. And while it's a manufactured excuse to do this, while it's a once-yearly reminder to most men and some women to search for some sort of romance inside their hearts, I do not believe romance should be relegated to a single day every year.

I once defined romance, in as scientific and contradictory a way as I could, as one part spontaneity, one part forethought. I know those don't seem to make sense. It's the ability to see something and know enough about the person you're with to recognize this is the right thing. I know a woman who would go crazy for a Hello Kitty handbag. I know I, personally, have an absurd and unexplored love of artistically-designed playing cards.

Romance is a genre in fiction, but it's also a component of many stories. Even some of the older ones. Remember Orpheus, going to Hades, confronting the god of the underworld to rescue his wife, Eurydice? His music was so powerful, so enchanting, even the god of death said yes, take her. That required no forethought and no spontaneity, but determination and courage. Maybe my definition of romance is too narrow.

Maybe that's a bad example of romance outside the romance genre. What about Han and Leia in *The Empire Strikes Back*? What about *The Princess Bride*? Is that a romance or an adventure story?

I've always believed the genres are a little mixed up, anyway. Romance and horror were never more than a hair's breadth away from each other. Don't forget all those movies with a romantic lead opposite the hero or heroine.

I say heroine knowing full well that most, so high a percentage it's practically 100%, love interests play opposite a male hero. I think that's limiting. The romantic interest for the woman is usually the hero, sure, and sometimes the romantic interest for the man is the heroine – but even that is limited to heterosexual relationships, which of course is nearly 100% of what comes out of Hollywood.

Maybe it's because the Hollywood definition of romance is skewed.

It's easy to illustrate that. In the early days of Hollywood, when the studios came into existence, the money men were in charge of everything – and that's never changed. Hollywood is a game of money, and the people spending the money, rightfully or not, think they're only going to make a return by repeating the same stories with the same kinds of characters over and over again. There's some experimentation, but not a lot. The biggest recent step outside of this, in a major Hollywood film, was the romance in del Toro's *The Shape of Water*. [Author's Note: this was written in late 2017.]

Relationships, romantic and otherwise, come in all shapes and sizes. Our art and poetry and music and stories have, throughout history, been attempts at expressing the depths and heights of our loves.

The truth – I'm going to be a bit sentimental here – I believe we are all capable of limitless love, just as we're all capable of limitless art. Am I saying love and art are the same thing? No. Love is too big to be captured by art alone. And art is too big to reflect only romance.

But art and romance are often intertwined. One reflects the other. So show your love, or explore your love, or hide your love in your art. Revisit lost loves or unrequited loves. Explore them in your art, whatever your art is, and if you're willing, share it – with the world or even the person you love.

Yes, I'm fully aware there's a lot more to love than romantic love. But this episode is airing on Valentine's Day. Anyway, I don't believe romantic gestures must be limited to romantic partners. Certain types, sure. You don't want to buy a bunch of stuff from Subculture Corsets and bring that to a coworker unless you've established some sort of relationship that permits this. However, I remember one year in particular, I worked in an office dominated by women. On the way in I stopped at a florist and picked up a dozen roses so I could give one to everyone I worked with. A romantic gesture for people who were not my romantic partners – and I did this with my romantic partner's knowledge. Romance isn't about buying chocolates or flowers, it's about acknowledging the people you care about.

THE HORRORS OF MOVING

The process of moving is terrible and terrifying. You start with all the things you own, the good things and the bad things, the mistakes, the mementos, the books, and the furniture. Then you get a bunch of empty boxes and hide everything inside them. Label the boxes if you can, though of course by then end they're all miscellaneous boxes and you're just shoving in anything and everything that's left. Tape them up, load them into a truck – or get friends or movers to load the truck with you – then ship them to wherever you're going. I once moved 10,000 miles. This week, I moved only two. The process is identical.

After you get all those boxes, or at least most of those boxes, into a single place, it's time to unpack and sort and re-prioritize all the material things of your life. Unpack the most important stuff first, the second most important things second, and after that it's just a free for all of random boxes and packing paper and balls of tape your cat can chase under the freshly moved couch where you'll find them the next time you move.

There's a nostalgic factor to moving, to the packing and unpacking, when you open something you haven't opened in a while and look at pictures you'd forgotten existed and see faces you haven't seen in years. There's questions of importance: do I really need to keep this jar of marbles? What do they mean? What did they mean to me when I got them? When the hell was that, anyway? Who was I with? Oh. *Her.*

And then you toss the jar of marbles.

Inevitably, you lose things. A few moves ago, I think I lost some boxes of books. All my Ray Bradbury books, for instance. And a few other things, like a *Starry Night* scarf and my first fountain pen. The moving gods, or the moving gremlins, take their toll, and you never know which box it will be. Never the most important, never the one with the bills that still need to be paid or the things that go first on top of your desk. But never the least important, either. Never the box filled with jars of marbles and other memorials to events, places, and people you don't even want to remember.

Moving gives you a chance to realize what is and isn't important, what matters to you, what's always mattered to you. You'll rediscover your earliest pieces of art, and you'll realize the things that inspired you then and the things that inspire you now are not all that different. The themes may vary and shift, but the central point of all your art, all your paintings and stories and songs, remains the same: you.

You are the central theme to your artwork. You draw from your experiences, you expose your emotions, you peel back your fears and hopes and put them on display. And you'll discover that, among those things you haven't gotten rid of, those jars of marbles following you from one city to another – you'll find echoes of your artistic themes. Layers of what you've done and what you've seen. The process of moving shuffles all of these pasts and keeps them fresh. Stay in one place too long, you might become stagnant.

That's one way to look at it. If you stay in one place, you might also develop roots, you might deepen your themes and experiences rather than broaden them. Statistically, most people live and die within a very short distance of where they were born. There's nothing wrong with either path. There's nothing inherently good or evil, right or wrong. These are just choices we've made, reactions to circumstances, leaps of faith. Whether you move near or far or not at all, it's good to sometimes explore the recurrent themes in your art, the ideas and concepts you've been returning to, and ask some questions:

Have I learned something? Or taught something? Have I moved beyond my initial themes and questions and ideas, or am I just making the same things over and over again? Is that wrong? Have the things I kept close to me been important? Have I developed, either in depth or breadth or clarity or intention? Do I know what I'm doing? Do I know why?

I'm not saying you have to answer all of these questions here and now, and you certainly don't owe me any answers. But these are questions, as an artist, I ask of myself every once in a while. I don't just bury myself in my work and plunge forward like an out of control bobsled down a hill, though there are times when that's exactly what I do. There are also times when you look up and see what's around you. You look beneath your feet at where you're standing, and you can ask how you got here, why you got here, where do you go next.

Me? I moved two miles this past week. My muscles ache and my focus has been rattled, but I timed it perfectly. I finished a project one day, packed the next. If only art was always that predictable.

SLICED BREAD: THE BEST THINGS SINCE...

There was a day, long ago, prior to recorded history, when someone with a knife realized something could be done. They used that knife, thoroughly and viscously, on a loaf of bread. Now everyone compares every new invention to sliced bread.

Actually, it wasn't so very long ago, and there's a man credited with that creation. Otto Frederick Rohwedder invented the machine that sliced a whole loaf of bread at one time. The Chillicothe Baking Company in Missouri used it, and on 7 July, 1928, sold the first "Kleen Maid Sliced Bread."

And what did they compare this to, you might ask? There's a movie or something that has someone saying, "It's the best thing since – ever," which is great, and fun, and funny the first time but not the fiftieth time you hear it. Sliced bread was advertised as "the greatest forward step in the baking industry since bread was wrapped."

Which is a strange way of saying there has always been something before us. I'm sure there was a first human being to do a first thing at some point, but even that was predicated on the accomplishments of other animals – or perhaps aliens. [Author's Note: This is a joke.]

Invention is rarely a whole cloth creation. Instead, it is another step forward – like sliced bread was better than merely wrapped bread. Or invention borrows something from another industry and uses it in a way that's never been done before.

Gutenberg didn't invent the printing press out of nothing. He adapted existing tools and devices, and made a few additions of his own, to processes like woodblock printing, which had already existed for a long time in China.

I don't mean to lessen his accomplishment. I just mean to borrow from Isaac Newton, who said, "If I have seen further, it is by standing on the shoulders of giants." This, of course, borrows from Bernard of Chartres, who essentially said scholars of his day were dwarves on the shoulders of giants. They didn't have keener vision or greater height, they were lifted up by the accomplishments of those who came before.

As artists, one of the greatest resources is all the art that came before us. The stories we write today are born within our own heads, but it's undeniable that the forms and structures and fillings, the fountains for those stories, predate us. While you don't need to be thoroughly versed in the histories of your art or genre, you probably already have a basic understanding of things that came before.

It never hurts to broaden your horizons, to dig deeper, to go further than you've gone. While mere hacks might simply regurgitate what they find, true artists rephrase and reshape former glories in entirely new glorious ways. Film started by recreating what we already saw on the stage. Over the course of time, artists like Georges Méliès and Lotte Reniger and DW Griffith pushed their art further, eventually leading to today's Avengers movies. But to get there, we had to invent lenses, play with shadow puppets, build zoetropes, draw flipbooks, and take photographs. We had to unify sciences and arts to command lighting and understand how to create the illusion of life. When films were on film, every second was typically made up of twenty-four frames as a means of tricking the human eye into believing there was movement. There is no movement in film. It is a the high-speed progression of still frames fooling your mind. Film was, in the earliest days, a trick of magicians.

We, as artists, are the magicians, whether your art is film or story or paint or magic. There's a history, a progression of human accomplishment, that has created the tools we use as well as the images we reference and allude to. We, as artists, must do more than merely see what those giants saw before us. We must climb onto their shoulders and look further, look farther, look deeper, and somehow find the next best thing since sliced bread.

LEGACIES, AND CLICKERS FOREVER

Right now – this is a cheat – I'm reading *Clickers Forever*, the tribute anthology to JF Gonzalez. I didn't know him as well as many of the other contributing authors. In addition to my short story and other fiction, I'm finding a lot of personal reminiscences and metafictional elements. Overall, it's not what I expected. The table of contents is a who's who of horror, and I believe paperback copies are available. In a very real way, this is a symbol of Jesus's legacy.

It reminds me, though, that we all have an impact on the world, on other people, whether those be big or small impacts, whether they be positive or negative. There are opportunities for all of us to be a positive force in someone's life, to give that little bit of encouragement someone may need, to collaborate with them on our various little mischiefs, to provide fodder for their muse, to give advice or a shoulder to cry on.

I've gotten to where I am by making a series of mistakes. Big mistakes and small. I've had successes, too, and I'm not really interested in listing off the stupidest things I've done. That's why we have the internet. Find the pictures yourself. I'm also where I am – and I have no illusions as to where I am, I'm a struggling author attempting to find an audience and survive in a world that doesn't necessarily strictly forbid such a thing but certainly discourages it – but I do have a roof over my head, which I know not everyone can say, and I know where my next meal will come from – because of the kindness of friends, because of the lessons I've learned along the way, because the life I've lived has led me here, with all my mistakes behind me as a kind of foundation, a validation that the mistakes I'm bound to make in the future will probably not kill me, that no matter how low life can seem, it always seems to be cyclical and therefore always comes back up.

There's plenty to be concerned with out there, and plenty enough of it that will, essentially, sour your mood, block your creativity, *disturb your wa*. The most important things, I think, are to stay true to yourself, and also realize how your life impacts others. We're all pebbles making ripples in a pond, or something silly and sentimental like that, so we all affect, and are affected by, others.

Personally, when I die, I hope there are people who think enough of me, who were positively impacted by me or my actions or my philosophies in some way, that someone will want to put together some little tribute. I hope it's not soon, but I do hope I'm making some sort of difference.

And I hope the people who have inspired, supported, and befriended me in the past can be proud of the things I'm doing in the present and will do into the future. I hope I make more mistakes, because they indicate that I'm taking chances and being bold. I hope I do a few things right, too, and that I find my audience, speak to them, and tell them the things they need to hear.

WHIMSY

This past week, we survived April Fool's Day. This isn't always going to be the case. There's a strong history of bad and worse pranks being pulled every year. I've never enjoyed those where someone actually gets hurt or is put at risk. Many are simply the same thing a million other people did last year and the year before that and the year before that. At least I didn't notice many of my friends posting this year about their fresh pregnancies.

Seriously, if you learn on April First that you're pregnant and want to tell somebody – anybody – wait a day.

I think the best April Fool's prank I've ever seen is the spaghetti trees. This happened before I was born. I still remember seeing pictures of spaghetti trees, and I still run into people who think that's how spaghetti is grown. There may be some harm there, I don't know.

Tangentially, I'm also not a fan of movies or television comedies that rely on the stupidity of their characters for laughs. I stopped laughing at people stepping on rakes watching Looney Tunes cartoons when I was seven. Other examples are downright mean-spirited.

The truth is, I love a sense of whimsy, and I do – really, truly – have a sense of humor. So when April Fool's comes around, as it did just a few days ago, I prepare myself for the onslaught of amateurs. April Fool's is to funny like New Year's Eve is to serious drinking: amateur hour, and it shows.

I'm not saying the jokes *you* made weren't funny. I'm not saying the political satire didn't cut straight to the heart of matters. I'm not saying all stupid comedies are stupid. And I would never deride you for your tastes – what you think is funny and what I think is funny don't have to be the same thing.

But I'm not really about funny. Whimsy implies a sense of fun more than a sense of the funny. I'd even go further and say it often implies a sense of magic, and I've always been a fan of magic.

In part, whimsy is about not taking yourself too seriously. Even in my *DarkWalker* novels, horror adventures about a guy who walks through the dark untouched by vampires, ghosts, and ghouls, I try to have fun. That doesn't mean they're funny books. They're not. But a certain level of absurdity, I think, goes hand-in-hand with whimsy.

The Princess Bride is an extraordinary work of whimsy, and also a fantasy, and also a comedy. *Alice's Adventures in Wonderland* is a textbook example. Textbooks, especially *A Mathematical Introduction to Polygons: A Study of Angles and Lines*, probably aren't. However, the cookbook of the same name, *A Mathematical Introduction to Polygons: A Study of Angles and Lines*, could be enormously fun in the right hands.

I don't think April Fool's Day celebrates whimsy and foolishness the way it should. Instead of seeking to make fools out of each other, maybe we could celebrate foolishness. Host Monty Python or Steve Martin film fests, binge Netflix standup comedies, go out on adventures. I don't just mean the types of adventures where you absolutely mustn't forget your handkerchief or your towel, but the kinds I'm always telling you to go on: discovery. Only a fool thinks he can sail over the horizon of a flat earth, discover an entire continent already populated by people, and declare himself a hero.

If my definition of whimsy and foolishness seem a bit wibbly-wobbly and timey-whimey, it's because when I started watched Doctor Who in the mid-2000s, it was the whimsy, more than anything else, that kept me coming back.

If I sound like the victim of a terrible practical joke, all I can tell you is look at politics and politicians in my lifetime. If you think I'm against making jokes, I should tell you something funny but all my jokes are stolen from funnier people than I. Maybe you think I don't understand the nature of April Fool's. And maybe you're right. But I'd like to point out – I keep the spirit of the April Fool alive well past the First.

One aspect of whimsy is enthusiasm. To throw yourself whole-heartedly into a project, the book you're working on, or the music or the painting – to believe you can complete it, that sort of statement of belief and intention is the kind of enthusiasm I'm talking about. In a very real way, it's absurd, this thing we do, this incorporation of symbology to express our innermost fears and desires, to illustrate the world in all its glory and all its shame. We're not talking, always, about projects that can be handled in a day or a week. It's a long process from writing the first words of a book to publication, and that's followed, possibly, by the interviews and book reviews, the blog tours, signings, and conventions, where you basically step out into the world, state, "Look, I made a thing," and expect people to listen. It's the most foolhardy of expeditions, and perhaps the most noble, though of course you can find a million examples of ignobility to prove me wrong.

And of course I'm wrong. There's no way I can define who you are as an artist. There's no way I can dictate all the things you must and must not do to be worthy of the label *artist*, or any other label you wish to have. All I can do is encourage you, and illustrate what I think makes me an artist and how some of the things I incorporate into my own work might benefit you. The truth is, some of it won't.

InkStains, for instance, a story every day for a year, is absolutely ridiculous, impractical, impossible for some people because of the nature of your day jobs or families, or because of the way you approach your art. The way I use notepads, to take notes on a project not only before but as I write it, and the way I skip on outlines but have a destination in mind when I start a bigger project – these methods won't work for everyone. And they shouldn't.

We all approach our arts the way we do it. Someone outside of us might validate it by buying, consuming, reviewing, and recommending our work. Or they might point out all our flaws – not just the flaws of the work, but our individual flaws, the mistakes we've made, how we have not earned these titles we aspire to.

I can tell you this: a writer writes. A writer doesn't just talk about writing. Conversely: if you write, you are a writer, and if a great many people say that doesn't make you a writer, they're wrong. I'll say it again. If you write, you're a writer. That doesn't make you good or bad or provocative or influential or important or fun or whimsical. It's just a damn title. You don't have to fight for it. Titles don't mean anything, anyway.

I may have strayed off topic.

Getting Lost

I'm getting ready for a trip. Next week, I hit the road, and I'll be driving for most of three weeks. I'm doing this the old fashioned way: I'll pack what I can into the car and hope for the best. My budget is next to zero.

First stop: Nashville, where I'll get together with my mom and sister as my nephew performs his final undergraduate concert before running off to the Boston Conservatory to get his Masters in music. It's a good nine hour shot for me and whatever music I bring. I might have a few phone calls – hands free, of course – but this will be the longest solo drive I've done in a long time.

When I say old fashioned, I mean that. Every day I'm in Nasvhille, if I hand sell a book to someone, I get to eat dinner. Because that's where I am right now: I'm a writer struggling to make his bills every month, and most of those bills involve eating and a roof.

And when I say old fashioned, I mean I'll probably sleep in my car along the way, because there's no budget for a hotel, not until I get to Indianapolis where I'll be a Guest of Honor at Mo*Con. They describe this event as a bar con, in that there's not a whole lot of panels, there won't be a dealer's room or artist's gallery, there will just be guests.

After that, I'm off to York, Pennsylvania for The Horror Show with Brian Keene's annual telethon to benefit the Scares that Care charity. They help burn victims and cancer victims, and that weekend they'll need your money more than I do. I can skip a meal, it'll be okay. It all starts Friday, May 11 at noon, runs twenty-four hours, and we aim to raise over $20,000.

Then, somehow, I have to get home.

The problem with road trips, for me, has always been that I forget something. One thing. It only takes one. On my way to a wedding once in Ohio, everything that could go wrong did, including the fact that, though I'd remembered my suit, I had to find a new tie.

I'll be driving north on 65 and east on 70. These are not numbers I'm used to driving. I may get lost along the way.

It's important to get lost along the way. Sometimes, the destination is also important. I have six days to get from Nashville to Indianapolis, so there's time to get lost – as long as I'm at Mo*Con before it starts.

I hope to get lost in some interesting places and discover some interesting things. I'll bring my camera. The Nikon. The one with the bag and all those lenses. I don't know what I'll be shooting, but it's always best to be prepared.

Another time, another trip, maybe I'll do it on 35mm, but not this time.

Or maybe this time. See what happens when I say one little thing? I don't have money for 35mm film or developing – and to make it truly impossible, all my film cameras are in storage a thousand miles away.

When I prepared for this move to Virginia, part of that meant consolidating, putting things away, hiding my library, waiting for what comes next. I tried to plan for what I expected, but the real trick is taking care of the unexpected.

The unexpected comes out of nowhere. It comes from the left when you're looking right. It comes from above when you're looking down. It comes from inside when you're looking out. A lot of art is born of the unexpected. It comes, not just from the things we know and feel and believe, but from the sudden collision of unrelated ideas, of new ideas – they don't always have to be new to the world, but new to us, as artists. Then we can apply all the things we are, the filter of our self. That sounds very new age but it's not, it's just an acknowledgement than any art I make has to, inherently, come from or through me. My fingers. My mind. My eye. My vision.

You can't plan on the unexpected, but you can raise your awareness of it. You don't have to travel hundreds of miles to mysterious cities to find something unexpected. It can be right there in your house, inside you. The unexpected is a force of nature, and when you're consciously watching for it, when you're constantly looking, maybe it won't catch you unaware or by surprise, but it sure might find a way to infiltrate the expression of your art.

QUESTION: WHAT THREE BOOKS WOULD YOU TAKE TO A DESERTED ISLAND?

THE FIRST BOOK HAS TO BE *HOW TO SURVIVE ON A DESERTED ISLAND*. THE SECOND BOOK HAS TO BE *HOW TO ESCAPE A DESERTED ISLAND*. THE THIRD WOULD BE ONE OF THOSE BIG BLANK BOOKS, PEN OR PENCIL ATTACHED, SO I CAN CONTINUE WRITING EVEN WHILE I WAS THERE. THAT IS REALLY ALL THAT MATTERS. I WON'T NEED TO BE READING FICTION WHEN IN THE MIDDLE OF A LIFE OR DEATH SITUATION, I'LL NEED SOMETHING THAT WILL HELP ME SURVIVE THAT ISLAND UNTIL I CAN LEAVE. I DON'T HAVE A HIGH HOPE OF SURVIVING FOR A VERY LONG TIME WITHOUT THAT KIND OF AID.

ARTISTIC CHOICES

I rarely talk about photography on the podcast, in part because I'm no expert. I play. I dabble. I've been paid for shoots, I've sold prints, and I act professionally; but there's much I don't know, and my art, my primary and fundamental art, is prose.

But many concepts apply to all forms of art.

When I shoot, I have to pay attention to the subject of my shot, which may or may not be a model, and also the background and the foreground. I can impact these by selecting locations or by manufacturing them. I can adjust the amount of light that falls on the subject, or the direction of that light, even if sometimes I can only do it by choosing the time of day to shoot. I can change the amount of light that reaches the lens by adjusting the aperture and the shutter speed. I can use a different length lens to get closer to the subject, and I can use that same tool to change the background of the shot.

Ultimately, the light that hits the lens is what creates the photo. How that's manipulated, either in the camera at the time of shooting or in the darkroom or digital processing after the shoot, is the photograph. The image itself is a collection of lines and curves made visible only by the application of light and shadow.

Since I've moved to Virginia, I haven't been shooting much. I haven't gone out on many random shooting expeditions, I've not been working with any models, and I've not shot any events, concerts, or portraits. It's because I'm focusing most of my energies on writing, and other things most more closely associated with my writing. For some of my self-published books, that means cover design, layouts, publication, and distribution. It also means I'm focused on the business, talking to publishers and editors, selling my stories and books, arranging for appearances, signings and conventions and the like. It also means doing freelance proofreading and editorial work to generate a little extra income.

In reality, all these arts are connected, and they share concepts that at first glance aren't always obvious. When shooting, you think about what to include, and what to exclude, from the frame. You compose the shot. You eliminate the things you don't want to see – sometimes by stepping into the frame and removing something physically, sometimes by the amount of background you choose to see, sometimes by moving the camera closer or further from the subject. If you're shooting a model and there's a piece of trash, say an empty *Big Gulp* cup, you might take it out of the scene and throw it away. You might position yourself further from your model and use a longer lens to minimize the amount of the background that you capture. You might arrange to shoot with the light behind the model so she's in silhouette and without detail.

All of these choices, conscious choices, are often dictated by the needs of the shot. If you're shooting an ad for a watch manufacturer, that silhouette shot is likely to be out the question. Unless it isn't. Depends on the parameters of the shoot. But those parameters dictate the choices you make, and some of them won't even feel like choices at all.

The same is true in fiction. We have to choose what to show and what not to show based on the needs of the story. It's part of why stories don't always seem realistic. Why did the action hero never stop to go to the bathroom? Because it happened off screen, off stage, out of the scene, because nothing that happened in that bathroom moved the story forward. Unless you're Crocodile Dundee.

This is why I'm so fascinated with how other artists work, especially artists doing things outside of my own experiences. Creativity is, ultimately, universal, and while it may take some creativity to apply the methods of photography to the methods of sculpture – dammit, we're artists, we're supposed to be creative.

I've read books about conductors, about dancers, tight rope walkers, painters, photographers, writers, and filmmakers. I've explored other forms of art and other kinds of artists like a knight of Camelot in search of the Holy Grail. Because I believe in the interconnectedness of all arts. I believe the similarities that unite us are stronger than the differences.

Consider some form of art that is not your primary art, something you've maybe not done at all. I'm not suggesting you should try your hand at modeling in clay if you've never done it. But maybe watch some videos on how to do it. Read articles about particular artists in that field. Learn a little bit about what makes them tick, how they approach their work, the practical ways in which they've overcome the obstacles they face.

Then see how all of that might apply to you, to your art, and to your obstacles.

FORCED INKSTAINS STORIES

A listener asked if, while writing the InkStains, I couldn't come up with a premise one day and forced out a story I didn't like just to meet the quota?

The answer is yes. Obviously there are going to be days that are better than others, there are going to be times when you have an idea and you know going in what it's going to be. And there are other days you just sit there, open to a blank page, set your nib down to the page and just started moving your hand. When the stories didn't turn out good, they were still exercises in discipline. They may even have been exercises of some sort beyond just the discipline. But some of the stories just aren't as good as others. I definitely have favorites. Never tell them that, though. The stories shouldn't know I have favorites.

I think some worked better than others, but they weren't always the stories I had planned ahead of time. Some stories where I sat down and started writing with a blank slate and no direction, often influenced by my immediate physical surroundings, turned out to be the better stories. And some stories I'd thought about for days turned out not to be as good. Since the object of InkStains was to write a story every day, I didn't include a quality assessment. It didn't matter if the story was good or successful, because even from the failures you can learn.

What mattered most was that I was able to open up the well of my creativity and draw from it every day. I pushed through the lackluster performances. If something I wrote yesterday wasn't my favorite story, and for whatever reason I thought failed, I wrote something new today – and maybe that would be a good one.

Clouds Challenge

For this week's InkStains challenge, the sky's the limit. Whether you want to write, illustrate, paint, sculpt, cook, dance, sing, or anything else, look to the sky for inspiration. Not merely the sky, but the clouds.

I was in a plane recently. I looked down and saw a dragon in the clouds. Years ago, I saw Mount Hood poking out of the clouds. The other night, I saw Mars, all bright and red, peeking from behind a thin layer of clouds. Look to the cloud stuff, the spun sugar, cotton candy, whatever you want to call it — and use it for inspiration. Use what you see. Ask questions only the clouds — or whatever you see in the clouds — can answer.

These are creative exercises. Be bold and daring and original, avoid the clichés, skip the most obvious and boring things, ignore the first thing you see because that would be *too easy*. Push yourself. Make your creativity sweat. Tomorrow, do it again. And again after that, and on the fourth day, and the fifth. It's a five day InkStains challenge only because I love you, and I want to make you better than you are. I want you to see beyond the things you see. I want you to find inside yourself something you don't even know is there. If you need more than five days, go for seven, or nine, or thirteen. Take a day off in the middle and do it for a whole month, a month of cloud stuff, which doesn't have to include clouds at all.

WHEN I DID INKSTAINS STORIES WITH MONTHLY THEMES, I FOUND, IN THE FIRST WEEK OR TWO, I WROTE ONE OR TWO UNEXPECTED STORIES AS I WORKED THROUGH ALL THE MOST OBVIOUS ITERATIONS OF THE THEME. THIS IS THE SAME THING. WHEN YOU REACH THE SECOND HALF OF THE MONTH, WHEN YOU'VE USED UP ALL THOSE OBVIOUS AND EASY THINGS, YOU'LL HAVE NO CHOICE BUT TO SEE THINGS YOU NEVER IMAGINED SEEING. A DRAGON IN THE CLOUDS? THAT'S NOTHING! THAT'S EASY! THAT'S *BORING*! A DRAGON MADE OF SUGAR EMERGING FROM AN OLD CIRCUS COTTON CANDY MACHINE? NOT TERRIBLE. A FLIGHT OF DRAGONS MADE OF SUGAR EMERGING FROM OLD CIRCUS COTTON CANDY MACHINES FLAVORED IN YELLOW, GREEN, BLUE, AND RED? EVEN BETTER. PULL FROM YOUR OWN EXPERIENCES, FIND SOME UNIQUE ANSWERS, AND DON'T FORGET TO HAVE FUN WITH IT.

THIS IS *PLAY*.

MUSIC AND LISTENING

I recently spent most of three weeks on the road. I put together play lists for each of four legs of this journey onto my phone. From the phone, a device broadcasts the music on a low power FM band so I can listen through my car radio. If there's an actual station in the area that's at or near that band, I have to adjust the frequency to find something cleaner.

This was a terrible way to listen to music. Sure, I could sing along. On the interstate, that's exactly what I need. But I actually *like* music. I enjoying listening, and this was the lowest possible fidelity you could get. Too much electronicization, too much compression, too much FM radio interference, and too little resonance.

When I got home, I went back to my turntable – I wish I had a different one, I liked my Technics turntable from when I was a teenager – and I broke out Pink Floyd's *Dark Side of the Moon*. I turned down the lights, poured some bourbon, closed the doors, and pumped up the volume.

On occasions like this, I believe I can really hear the difference in the vinyl. Every note had depth and breadth and soul. In the car, the music was something I was listening to. In my darkened office, the music was something I experienced – not just with my ears but down to my bones. It was thorough and complete and delicious.

By the time they reached *Great Gig in the Sky*, I had forgotten all the potholes in Indianapolis and the crevasses of the Nashville roads and even the monsters lurking in the Pennsylvania woods. If I haven't told you, I think *Great Gig in the Sky* is one of the best recorded songs ever, and you should do yourself the favor of listening to it on vinyl. I mean actively listen, as a primary activity rather than while driving or cleaning or mowing the lawn or whatever other chores you're doing.

I listen to music a lot while I write, but I don't spend enough time just listening. I have a hundred vinyl records, give or take, including a lot of good stuff from my parents. I'm only aware of two records I've lost over time, and I've already replaced The Who's *Tommy*. I've got John Lee Hooker and Billy Joel and Yes and the Beastie Boys and Leonard Cohen and the Police. My tastes are more diverse than that, but I've only recently started buying vinyl again, so I simply don't have a huge chunk of what I've listened to in the past twenty years – Kate Bush, Tori Amos, Concrete Blonde, ZZ Ward. I was buying CDs. There's nothing wrong with CD's or downloads. But there's a difference, at least in how I approach it, when I'm listening to records.

As with anything else, I look at the whole package. The Roger Dean covers on all those Yes albums are so much more vibrant in full size. I remember the design elements on Pink Floyd's *The Wall* from when I was 10. I love good cover art, and even appreciate the special discs in other colors or with artwork on them. I love the posters some of those old albums used to include, and the liner notes, and the way all of that is laid out to work together to compliment the music.

A lot of that can be considered a kind of collaboration, wherein a variety of artists contribute to create a whole package without necessarily working directly together. And while the music is what's most important here, I cannot neglect the other, associated work – what you might call the artifacts of the album.

SAY YES TO OPPORTUNITIES

I never really considered moving to Spain. The country never made my list. Madrid never made my list. I have a list of places I would love to visit. I'd love to get back to Paris and maybe live there this time, since I've only ever been there for a couple of weeks. Prague is at the top of my list, and now that I'm going to be in Europe, I'll try to make that happen. [Author's note: circumstances prevented it.] I would love to return to Sydney and never leave. I lived in Sydney once before – for the same reason I'm going to Madrid.

Madrid is something of a surprise. I wasn't expecting it. Like when I moved to Sydney, it's because my partner accepted a position in an animation studio. We're storing everything we can now – throwing it into a box – and moving with whatever I can carry. I'll have a notepad, a fountain pen, my camera, and a change of underwear.

I will arrive with nothing else in Madrid, but I'll have a place to stay. Unlike when I was in Sydney, I will not be permitted to work a day job. The company that hired my partner in Sydney also supplied me with a work visa even though I didn't work for them. This company is a lot smaller.

But this is not a complaint. I look forward to having the time to really focus. I can see it now: in the morning, I can walk my partner to wherever she needs to go to get to work, probably a bus station, or maybe straight to the office. I'll stop at a café, have a breakfast of churros and chocolate, and scribble in my journal for an hour or two, maybe stories or essays about my impressions of Spain or Madrid or other adventures, then going back to the apartment and working for the rest of the day on book after book, novel after novel, project after project.

I do know I am lucky and fortunate to be given this opportunity. I didn't do anything to earn this. I'm just along for the ride.

Part of this, though, is the ability to say Yes to an opportunity. When Adventure knocks on your door and says, hey, why don't you come on over here with me, if you can say yes then you've got a little bit of what it takes to be a writer.

There are other types of adventures. Children, families, other careers, might prevent you from being able to travel to someplace like Madrid at the drop of a hat – but these are the adventures that make us who we are. We are the sum total of all of our experiences, all of our prejudices and biases, and nothing but experience will break down destructive prejudices into their most basic and fundamental components until there's nothing left. They serve no purpose. They do not help expand our knowledge of the human condition. They do not expand our knowledge of our own selves. And they do not help expand our creativity.

Getting out there, going on even those short journeys, taking advantage of opportunities that come along, or just trying something you've never tried before, is fundamentally important – I would say vital – to not just an artistic life, but life in general. Many of us spend too much time standing around the same place doing the same things, never stretching our wings, never even realizing we have wings to begin with. (Metaphorical wings, of course, not actual wings.)

Develop your metaphorical wings. Take advantage of these possibilities. I'm looking forward, more than anything else, to finding out what I don't even know, learning about things I hadn't even imagined were there to learn. I'll have to learn a new language. They may speak English at the studio my partner will be working at, but if I want to buy food I'll need to be able to converse and transact in Spanish – Spain's Spanish, as opposed to Puerto Rico's or Cuba's or Mexico's Spanish, all of which are just different enough to be their own things.

I'm embarking on a new adventure and entering what may officially be known as my Spanish Period. But this is not a quick move for me. It's already begun, and it won't end for another month or more. I have commitments to signings and conventions.

We took everything we own, everything in this small house – you'd be surprised how much can fit into a small house – loaded a rental truck, and took it down to Florida. We've already got a storage unit there, a full storage unit, and intend to stuff more into it. The things left in Virginia were primarily furniture we have no intention to keep; a few kitchen tools like pots, pans, forks, and plates, that I'll bring to storage later; and the things I expect to shove into a suitcase before getting on that plane to Spain.

The trip was uneventful, but it was long. It was a lot of miles, and my body hurts because it's old – it's probably older than I am – and there was a lot of stuff to be done in a short period of time. When I returned to Virginia, Max, the cat, greeted me at the door and hasn't left my side since. It's probably the longest he's ever been left alone, even if there was a cat sitter coming in every day.

I returned to a barren house. My desk was gone, the bed was gone, most the kitchen was gone, the rugs were all gone. Cat hair, in the form of tumbleweeds, drifted on the slightest breeze. The night I got back, I cleaned what I could – which has proven useless, as it re-accumulates every time I blink – watched a bunch of dull YouTube videos, and didn't accomplish much of anything.

That first night, I'll let slide. I needed to recover, to recoup, to re-familiarize myself with changed surroundings. But I have hard deadlines. *DarkWalker 4* is written, yes, but needs revisions, as well as layout and design work if I have any hope of hitting my Scares that Care release date. I have a day job to return to – I'm not sure when, next week's schedule isn't up yet – and I'll spent a lot of time this month at the movie theater. I had errands that needed running, including bringing fresh food into the house, because I like to sometimes eat.

MY REVISIONS PROCESS

I edit on paper. I print the manuscript, double spaced, so there's room to write between lines. I don't go immediately into revisions after writing. That's too quick, too close. It's all too fresh, and I need a bit of distance before I can go back.

I edit with a thick, vibrant blue pen, because I don't want to miss anything when later entering these changes into the computer. Blue contrasts nicely with the black ink of the printer. And a long time ago, red reminded me too much of high school. I decided early on that blue was my color. Anyway, blue penciling has a long history in editing, and it felt right.

The revision process is where I try to make the words right, where I fix the mistakes, remove the extraneous, and strengthen what's left. I'll make changes because of things that happen later in the manuscript that I didn't know about when I started, I'll fix typos and wrong words, I'll rearrange sentences, I'll sometimes bleed more blue onto that page than the black ink it was written with. This is normal.

And I do it in big chunks. I devote days at a time to it. I believe part of the editing process is making sure everything runs smoothly with everything else, and the best way to do that is to look at everything all at once. Though I can't really do that, I can at least condense the time. I take breaks between sections, just as I do when I'm writing, but generally they're short, meal breaks and the like.

It'll take several long days or weeks to get through an entire manuscript, even if I'm working at what might be described as breakneck speeds. But I can't go any quicker than the story allows. Sometimes, I'll get caught up on a thing and have to figure it out before going on. This isn't getting all the words down with the idea of fixing it later, this is the fixing, so when I run across a reference to Interstate 30 in Pennsylvania, and I know for a fact that's impossible, the road must be called something else, I stop and either question people who know or question the internet – which always knows and also always lies.

Also, I'm taking notes again – I know I've told you how much I do this – partly for things I need to remember later in this revision process, but partly because I have a *DarkWalker 5* and *6* to write later, and it wouldn't do to forget the loose ends that need to be tied, the questions that need to be answered, the characters we've seen only briefly who will be returning in all their glory.

All of this revision process is predicated on the fact that, as I write my first draft, I do few if any edits. This isn't the only way to work. I know people who edit yesterday's writings in the morning before starting today. I know people who sketch out their outlines and fill in details and more details until the outline becomes the novel. I know people who plan every chapter, every scene, every word. And I know people who set out in a particular direction and discard all concept of charts and maps. Generally, I know where I'm going with my first draft, but it's a process of discovery because I don't necessarily know how I'll get there or what will happen along the way.

The one thing I know about writing is that there's no single path, no one way that is the right way. There are rules, there are guidelines, there are times to chuck all that aside and go forward. There are stories of authors who have succeeded, and others who have failed, using every method you've ever imagined. It's all okay. It's all fine. In my experience, whatever the story needs, that's what I'll give it. If this is my method for revising *DarkWalker* novels, I may, in the future, on another project where everything is different, approach it in a different way. That's one thing no one's ever told you: you may have learned how to write this novel, but the next novel is going to be a whole new game.

LANGUAGE

I'm about to move to Spain. One of the many things I'll need to do is learn the language. I know a dozen words. They're probably all wrong. None of them are even phrases, so my ability to communicate will be limited to pointing and grunting and hoping the other person speaks at least some English.

But I've already, with the help of a friend in Orlando, determined the title of my Spanish memoir. I'll know how to say it when and if I come back to the United States: *Hombre Lobo Americano en Madrid.* An American Werewolf in Madrid. Because yes, I have hair. And yes, I've written stories with werewolves, if not any straight-forward werewolf stories. And it's fun. While I might not actually write a memoir of this nature at all, that didn't stop me from playing with the idea while on the road this past week.

Here's a sample entry:

> WE GOT TO BED EARLY LAST NIGHT, JUST AFTER MIDNIGHT. BUT I'D HAD AN EXTRAORDINARILY BUSY DAY OF WRITING, FIRST IN THE CAFÉ WITH MY FOUNTAIN PEN, THEN IN THE FLAT WHERE I FINISHED THE FIRST DRAFT OF MY NEXT NOVEL. UNFORTUNATELY, I FORGOT TO MAKE DINNER, SO TAPAS FOR EVERYONE!

You see what I did there? I projected. I imagined a scenario, a series of scenarios, that not only included me writing, living, and eating in Madrid, but completing whatever next novel I happened to be working on. Yes, I have a good idea of what I'll work on next, and yes I'll be doing a bit of research before I go. But I can't imagine *not* finishing projects anymore, so of course it's going to be done.

Also, I learned recently there's a statue of the fallen angel in Madrid, so I wrote this other possible entry in my memoir to come:

I MET THE FALLEN ANGEL TODAY IN THE PARK. THE CONVERSATION WAS A BIT ONE-SIDED, BUT I APOLOGIZED FOR MAN'S SHORT-SIGHTEDNESS. I FIGURED IT WAS A SAFE BET, FORGIVING THE DEVIL.

What will actually happen? I can guess, I can envision, or I can go and discover. I choose all these options, of course. I'm a writer. I work with *What if* all the time. I extrapolate. I devise scenarios in my head before they ever could occur. I have entire conversations with people real and imagined, possible and unlikely. I don't generally hold you to the promises you make in my imaginings, but I suspect one day, hopefully in a far distant future, when I lose control of my mind, I will.

Look into your own future. Imagine a scenario of some sort, likely or unlikely but at least not impossible, and explore it in even the slightest of ways. Here, I've started a memoir about a place I haven't been to, haven't seen, don't know much about – in a land where I don't even speak the language. None of that has stopped me, and none of that should stop you. Be creative, and incorporate the things you want to accomplish – like finishing that novel. Make it not just realistic, but a solid goal. This isn't strictly a creative writing exercise, but of course it is. It's not a new age affirmation, either. A lot of new age practitioners will tell you it's all about reinforcing the positive, laws of attraction, telling the universe what you want to bring about; but I think this is beyond that. You also have to prepare for the obstacles. You have to train yourself to continue to work, to struggle and strive, for what you want to accomplish, and it'll take more than envisioning a happy ending. It'll require all the sweat and focus you've got, and it will not always end the way you think it will. So you're also welcome to explore scenarios you don't want to see happen. Once it's established, you can maybe devise a plan to avoid that end.

Reimagining the possibilities is part of what gives you the strength to get through today. Today, you may have impossible obstacles, you may be caught in a rut, you might not know how to escape it – but if you remember that everything is temporary, that today doesn't always have to be tomorrow, that there's a way through whatever you're struggling with and whatever is overwhelming you – I think it helps to be able to envision a future day in another city conversing with statues.

SELF-CARE

This is the 21st century. We've learned a lot about genetics and robotics, about medicine and space travel and quantum physics, psychological sales strategies, and three dimensions in film. We have automobiles that move faster than we can control, we have weapons that will level cities and eradicate civilizations, and we have Chinese food in takeaway boxes we've never used correctly our entire lives.

All of these are products of our collective creativity, our ingenuity at work, individuals who saw something that could be better, stronger, faster, or fiercer, and did everything it took to make that happen.

We are absolutely incredible.

We're also terrible, especially in groups, especially when someone figures out how to manipulate those groups to further their own personal agendas.

I'm a cynic. But I'm also an optimist. I don't necessarily trust all individuals – especially not politicians, CEO's, or anyone whose primary motivation seems to be greed. It's not that I don't trust them to do what's best for *them* – I don't trust them to do what's best for all of us, for society in general.

We are social creatures. If something you do is good for you, but also good for other people – like the person who came up with ice cream, or the person who decided red lights mean stop and got that adopted by pretty much the whole world – we can accomplish some amazing things.

Sometimes, however, in order to do something good for other people, you've got to take care of yourself first. You have no foundation to help others if your life's in turmoil. The same is true with art – it's hard to write or sculpt or paint when you're facing eviction, repossession, heartbreak, and failure. So when you need time for yourself, it's okay – it's imperative – that you take it. No one is required to support the weight of the world. No one's shoulders can handle that alone.

But we are, remember, social animals. If you're facing hard times of any sort, if you're facing obstacles you cannot overcome, if the only future you see seems bleak and dark and broken – I can remind you it's only temporary, all things are temporary, nothing lasts forever, change is inevitable, and there's no obstacle you cannot overcome – but I know better than that. I know we can't always lift ourselves out of the maelstrom of malaise. Sometimes it's circumstances, sometimes it's external factors we have no control over, sometimes it's chemical imbalances that need professional attention. Sometimes, the best thing to do is to work on yourself, and sometimes that will involve reaching out.

You don't have to ask for help every time. Just talking to a friend, especially a friend you haven't spoken with in a long time, might be all you need. Sometimes, it takes more, it takes planning and plotting beyond your ability, and you have to ask for help. Sometimes, you have to reach beyond your own circle of friends, to organizations designed to help, to doctors if necessary, to attorneys, to pop psychologists, even to churches and community groups if that's what it takes.

I'm not going to tell you how best to care for yourself. Some days, it might be just a bottle of wine and a bubble bath. A walk through the woods with the mobile phone powered off. A concert or a magic show or a sporting event. We're all unique, we're all individuals within a vast society – a series of interconnected societies. We're all part of the same race that created chocolate. We – you and I and all of us together or alone – can do everything. Never forget that.

When you're working on yourself – knowing you'll never be done, we are always improving, individually and collectively – you may find art is only one of many outlets (or tools or meditations or forms) of self-care. Use your art if you can, or clear yourself so you can use your art. Personally, I always feel best when I can be pursuing my stories and ideas – I have so many ideas, I couldn't possibly explain them all. I always feel best when I've got an outlet for them. When I'm not working, when I'm not creating, that's when I lose sight of who I am, who I'm supposed to be, and how I'm supposed to be contributing to this society. It takes a lot to shake me that deeply. That, of course, is when I'll reach out and ask for help. Sometimes, I reach out and ask without asking. Overall, I've found we're a society filled with people who will give a minute or an ear or a shoulder or a piece of bread.

We've managed to survive, as a society, all the way till today despite many ups and downs, despite wars and diseases, despite despots and villains, despite adversity and catastrophe. We are amazing. You are amazing. You deserve to take a moment to breathe when you need it.

LIVING IN THE PRESENT

Do you live in the now, in the present, accepting what comes, adapting and adopting as necessary, finding joy and meaning in your current experiences and circumstances? Or does the past trap you like vines and ivy, pulling you deeper into what was, forcing you to wallow in things you cannot change, the past glories and failures that have led you to wherever you happen to be?

I try as much as I can to live in the present. I have no control over the past and I have little control over the future; but right now, presently, today, I find myself more and more living in the future. I'm moving overseas in the next few months. My home has been reduced to a couch and this computer screen and a miniscule stack of books – the other thousands being in storage with most my earthly belongings.

I'm finding I can do without many of them, at least in the short term. I don't even need a bed, right? I need a place to write and maybe some food and a tall glass of water – ice water, because it's summer and it's hot. I've got my pens, and I'm narrowing it down to the half dozen I'll bring to Spain – but I'm glad I'm not writing a series of InkStains stories right now because everything would be set in a Madrid I haven't even seen yet.

I am scribbling stories all the time, of course, just not in any sort of organized way, and I keep going back to tomorrow – the very near future. I keep going back to Spain, and how I'm going to get there. I've got a thousand miles of driving before I reach the airport – and what if instead of flying I booked passage on an ocean cruiser? And what if, instead of a cruiser of some sort, I just booked a room on a cargo ship?

That's the kind of thinking that leads to little scribblings like this:

THE CREW ON THIS SHIP WORKS ALL DAY AND DOESN'T SPARE A THOUGHT FOR ME, WHICH IS AS EXPECTED. AT MEALS, HALF OF THEM DON'T SPEAK ENGLISH, SO WE PLAY CARDS FOR BOTTLE CAPS AND COUNT THE DAYS.

Trust me, I'll use this. [Author's Note: I did. The end result is a story called "Bottle Cap Pop."] I love the image, playing cards for bottle caps – what kind of cards, what kind of bottle caps, why are we stuck on this ship in the first place? There's so much opportunity. That's a bit of

what the InkStains projects have always been about – opening the mind to possibilities and impossibilities.

Lately, my mind's been narrowing its focus.

Here's another scribbling from my pocket notebook:

> I WANDERED ANOTHER STREET TODAY AND GOT LOST AGAIN AND DISCOVERED AN OLD TAVERN WITH A CELLAR. IT WAS DARK DOWN THERE AND WELL HIDDEN, SO IT WAS JUST ME AND THE RATS AND A COLLECTION OF OLD BOTTLES OF BOURBON. SMOOTH STUFF. THEY NEVER EVEN KNEW I WAS THERE.

I was intending to talk about something else this week, but my focus has been shattered. It happens to all of us. We still work through it. For me, I'm afraid the only cure will be a breakfast of churros and chocolate on the other side of the ocean. Then I can get busy writing my memoirs, the real or real-ish things I see and do and discover in my travels. I have future projects to work on, future books, future sights to see, wine to drink, rivers to sail, horizons to reach. But if I don't take a moment to take care of what's in the here and now – if we as artists lose track of the fact that we're still alive and living even when it doesn't seem like we are – I'll never reach it.

Scares That Care

I want to tell you about Scares that Care Weekend.

I don't mean about the people they help with the money they raise, the cancer battlers and burn survivors, because you can go to their website and learn all about it. www.scaresthatcare.org will tell you everything about who they are and what they're trying to do, and www.scaresthatcareweekend.com will tell you about the weekend itself. (All of this is important, of course, and if you're not familiar with the organization, you should look into it. Sure, I have friends who are involved, but it's a good cause and well run and has helped more people than I can count.)

I'm just back from Scares that Care. I want to talk to you, as a writer and artist, about conventions in general, and I'm going to use Scares as my example because it's freshest in my head.

A little background: my first convention, sometime in the early 90s, was I-CON, at Stony Brook. It looks like they might not have had a convention this year, but that sounds like a sad story and I'm not here today to tell you a sad story.

I-CON was my first. I walked in and bought a day pass. I was young still, just out of college, living on Long Island, unpublished and unconnected to anyone in the industry. Nothing changed afterwards. I have very few memories of the con, except for the vendor room and all the Star Wars action figures, because I wasn't ready. I'm sure there were panels, but I don't know if I attended more than one. I didn't actually meet any authors and I didn't make any friends. I was still painfully shy, and it was a monumental effort just to go on my own.

My second convention was many years later, still in the 90s. Living in Orlando, Florida, I was still unpublished but by now actively trying to break into the industry, and I had a few friends who were also aspiring authors, and we had at least one honest to god true and published author friend, Owl Goingback. Chris Kosarich and I and Owl – and maybe others, I don't remember – drove up together – and I might be remembering this wrong, maybe Owl went on his own, it was over twenty years ago – to DragonCon in Atlanta. I was a new member of the Horror Writers Association. Acting HWA President, James Moore, got me into the green room because, although I wasn't published yet, I was earnest and had intentions.

This was the convention where I bumped into Clive Barker into a bar – literally, we backed into each other in a bar. We chatted for a bit. There's no reason he'd remember it. The next morning, at a talk of some sort, he referenced something I'd asked about – some stupid-seeming question guided primarily by my youth and ambition.

A few years later, February 1999, I scraped up enough cash and favors to get to the World Horror Convention in Atlanta.

That World Horror Con changed my life. I met some of my best friends in the industry that year, including Brian Keene, Mikey Hyuck, Mike Oliveri, and Geoff Cooper. I know we make for a motley crew; and at first glance, besides the writing, there seems to be no reason for us to be friends. There were other people, tons of other people, friends and colleagues who have stayed in my life ever since. My first professionally published story was released in an anthology that same weekend. I was excited and in my element, surrounded by like-minded people – and unlike the other conventions, I was ready this time. I connected with people who would impact my career in the future. I talked with authors and editors and publishers and artists, some of whom are gone – too many have died – some who have left the industry or moved on to other things.

For years after that, I attended every World Horror Convention until I moved to Australia and it became impractical and unaffordable.

I can't count anymore how many conventions I've been to.

This past weekend was my third Scares that Care Weekend. Instead of being surrounded by like-minded people, other writers and artists and editors and such, I was surrounded by friends and, yes, family, even if not by blood. I spent hours talking to some of the absolute best people in the world. I sold out all my books, again, making it three for three at Scares. The question I was most asked was, What's bringing you to Spain? I told a few people Iberia Airlines, but mostly I said I was following a girl.

I gave a reading Friday at midnight to a packed house, which was amazing, and I'm told I did a good job of it. I read my newest story, "Bottle Cap Pop," a weird, dark, absurd little piece I have no idea what to do with.

A friend gave me a silver dollar, an Eisenhower, that I can keep as a talisman connecting me to my home country when I travel Europe. I started thinking about how, if the country destroys itself while I'm gone, I'll become the Last American. He wanders Europe – you can tell him by the coin he carries. The Last American would be something of a mystery, a man without a name, a cross between Clint Eastwood and John Wayne and, well, me. The legends of the Last American would be varied and widespread, and the book would be told by a young girl, maybe 12 years old, repeating stories she's heard, all the things he's done wandering the wastelands of Europe. No, I don't know why they're wastelands. And no, he's not *literally* the Last American; there are enclaves of refugees, but that doesn't change the title. At the end of the book, he reaches the town or village where the girl lives. The Last American is an old man now. He still carries the coin, and maybe it's more than just a talisman, I don't really know. But it's not me, not John Urbancik at all, but Brian Keene.

I'm not sure how big an audience there is for that story. To be fair, though Brian and I have a different approach to a lot of things – he writes to elicit a sense of dread, I write to encourage a sense of awe – I think we have near-identical moral compasses. So the story makes sense on all sorts of levels. It would be less metafictional than that, probably, if I ever actually write it.

This came up solely because someone gave me a coin.

And that's what I'm aiming at here. That's what I'm trying to talk about. Yes, my best friends in the world were met at these conventions. Yes, they're great for reaching readers and connecting with colleagues and doing business and having fun. But they can also be incredibly inspiring. They can be invigorating, and they can be incredible. Yes, they can be overwhelming when it's your first time. There were plenty of people here this past weekend who had never been to a convention before, some of them writers whose names you are going to hear in the near future. But even when overwhelming, conventions can be a shot in the arm or a kick in the ass or whatever you need to move you to the next step.

They're not vital. You don't have to attend a convention to find success in these fields. I'm not trying to tell you you've got to go. But they provide so much more than they seem to at first glance. They help you develop a foundation of friends and inspiration. Sure, you might find yourself drinking until late in the morning, but you will also find a number of people who don't drink at all. And sure, you might not understand all the in-jokes and history shared between me and Brian and Jim Moore and the people we've known since forever. In twenty years, you'll be in our position, having built these memories and lifelong friendships, raising toasts to absent friends, lamenting the failures and missteps of the past, and looking forward to tomorrow's victories and adventures. Because that's what I did this weekend. What did you do?

PAPELERIAS

One thing I love about Madrid is the *papelerias* which seem to be everywhere. If you're not familiar with them, you can almost tell what they are from the name, especially when you know this is a city full of *fruiterias* and *cervecerias*. It's a shop, as best as I can tell, that specializes in paper, notepads, pencils, and pens. Perhaps a stationery store.

It's like someone asked what would John want in a shop, then made a whole city full of them.

They're all different. They have different approaches and styles. One shop on the walk to *Montcloa* seems very casual, with bright neon colors, aiming perhaps for the middle school crowd, while another near the Friday night pizza joint is targeted toward professional artists and craftsmen, as evidenced by the high end drafting tools in their windows. And there's one by my apartment (near the palace) that seems to have been especially outfitted for me.

They've got my favorite notepads – Leuchtturm1917, a German notepad I rarely saw in the US and was only able to get online, and only when they happened to have one or two color options in stock. Here, there's a wall display in a rainbow of colors, and the pads are lined, dotted, or blank.

They've got one of my favorite pens, Lamy, another German company, in styles I've never seen, in every color and nib size. While I've seen displays occupying maybe a square foot of space in some bookstores in the US, here they've got walls and spinning cases and, well, I've never seen so many in one place before.

They've even got my favorite bottles of ink, *Iroshizuku*, from Pilot.

I have to assume, therefore, that everything else in this store, all the other pens and pencils and notepads, the Rhodias and even the Moleskines, were designed with one very specific customer in mind: me.

I'm trying to restrain myself. I'd have to sell quite a few books to pay for one of these pens. Wish me luck.

BRAVE AND BOLD

On this show, I rarely focused on the negative aspects of the business, of politics, or life in general, because that's never been what this is about. It's never been what I'm about. Sure, I can be cynical, but I'm also an optimist – the combination hurts, trust me – but I always intended this show – and book – to be encouraging and helpful and hopeful. I have talked about obstacles and things that haven't gone my way – but in general, if you want news about the latest controversies, if you want gossip of the most salacious kind, I'm not your guy.

I'd much rather spend my time, and my breath – there are only so many of those left in this lifetime – telling you that yes, things can get better, you can get better, you can improve your skills and nurture your talents and become a better person – which is not a way of slyly hinting you're a bad person now. Maybe you are, how would I know? – but that's not what I'm saying.

I want you to go out and explore your creativity. I want you to push your boundaries and discover things – maybe things that have previously been discovered, sure, that doesn't matter, because they're new to you.

I want you to be bold in your choices, and courageous – and see what I did there, trying to not say to be brave and bold because that would make me think of Batman – I want you to be the best you can be.

Yes, some days will be better than others. Conversely, some days won't be as good as others. That's okay. Some days will be absolutely horrible, terrible, outrageous, and deeply troubling – I'm not talking about regular everyday things here, I mean the loss of friends and loved ones, the loss of jobs, unexpected illness and injury and accidents. The trick has never been to work through all that – to force yourself to do something you're not ready for. Art can be extraordinarily cathartic and play a very positive role in recovery, but there are times when it's impossible to focus.

Even then, I find myself scribbling on paper. My scribbles tend to form words. Sometimes, I grab a pile of sticky notes and write the same words over and over again, varying how I write them, using different calligraphic styles, changing up the ink colors, all sorts of stupid things because just the action of my hand moving a pen, just the sound of a pen scratching paper, just the look of fancy J's and X's and other letters, calms me. Doing this on a not-terrible but not-great day gave me the title *Echo*. Long before I ever had a story, long before I ever sold the novella to Eraserhead Press, I played with four letters in different handwritings until I found a style that worked for me, spoke to me, and demanded attention. I repeated those letters again and again on a sticky note that I then ripped free of its pad, crumpled, and tossed in the trash can.

Sometimes, I save those kinds of notes just so I don't forget. A big part of my brain believes good thoughts and ideas will stick with you whether you keep that note or not. But there's another part of my brain that, when I go through old notepads, sees something I wrote – like a phrase I scribbled while briefly in Nashville, the phrase *You will know her by her red violin* – and sometimes seeing it again later doesn't revive the initial thought but inspires something new.

MY MADRID WRITER'S CLUB

Last week, I walked through Madrid until I found a bar with celestial paintings on the ceiling. The bartender spoke no English, so I ordered *uno vino tinto* – a glass of red wine – and waited for someone else to arrive. It was my first time joining a group of writers in Spain – who write in English – so I knew no one and nothing and didn't know what would happen. One of the group's moderators gave a talk about setting, and then there was a writing session. Everyone opened their Mac laptops – seriously, half the group had these tiny quiet little machines – and started tapping away. I broke out my fountain pen and a very small notepad and wrote this:

HERE I SIT IN A BAR IN SPAIN ON SOME ROAD I'VE NEVER HEARD OF. THE WALLS ARE BLUE AND YELLOW AND ORANGE AND GREEN, THE WOOD TABLES ALMOST AS OLD AS I AM, THE CURTAINS AT THE STAGE STOLEN, AT LEAST CONCEPTUALLY, FROM OLD AMERICAN MOVIE PALACES. AND ALL I CAN THINK IS I'VE BEEN HERE BEFORE. NOT HERE, NOT PRECISELY, NEVER IN THIS PLACE, BUT I'VE BEEN IN A BAR JUST LIKE THIS, WITH THE SAME CELESTIAL ART IN THE CEILING, THE SAME STARS, THE SAME PEOPLE WITH MAYBE DIFFERENT ACCENTS. EVERYTHING THROWN TOGETHER WITH AN EQUAL DEGREE OF LOVE AND LACK OF BUDGET, AND ALL OF IT FOR THE SAME PURPOSE.

THE WOMAN AT THE BAR KEEPS THE WINE FLOWING AND I'M ABLE TO CONNECT, THROUGH THE LABYRINTH OF STAIRS AND CORNERS AND ALCOVES, TO THAT BAR BACK IN ORLANDO WHERE ONCE I MET A SINGER — A SONGSTRESS, A TORCH OF HER OWN, WHO MIGHT HAVE BEEN THE LOVE OF MY LIFE IF THE STARS HAD BEEN DIFFERENTLY ALIGNED. HERE, SHE'S A POET, SHE'S A LIGHT IN THE DARKNESS, SHE'S A SPY IN A FOREIGN LAND JUST LIKE ME, AND THERE'S NOT ENOUGH CIGARETTE SMOKE TO HIDE THE TRUTHS OF US. SO WE SMILE, WHAT MORE CAN WE DO, AND MAYBE, ONLY BRIEFLY, SHE TOUCHES MY HAND OR I TOUCH HERS, AND WE WHISPER WORDS THAT PRETEND TO BE PROMISES, AND WE SHARE THE BRIEFEST IMAGES OF DREAMS WE IMAGINE OR INVENT.

I'VE GOT MORE SCARS THAN THE TABLE, WHICH IS OKAY, IT MAKES ME AND THE BAR REAL, OR SOMETHING LIKE REAL, BUT I'M JUST A GHOST AND SHE'S LESS THAN A MEMORY, SO WHEN SHE OPENS HER MOUTH TO SING I'M NOT HERE IN MADRID AND I'M NOT IN ORLANDO, BUT IN BERLIN, BEFORE THE WALL, WHEN THE WORLD WAS BLACK AND WHITE AND THE CABARETS DANGEROUS BUT NOT DEADLY, AND I REALIZE IT REALLY IS LOVE, AFTER ALL, ALWAYS HAS BEEN, AND IT ALWAYS WILL.

The writing session was meant to focus on setting, and while the moderator suggested we work on our current projects, that wasn't appropriate for me at the moment. My work in progress is all setting and place and atmosphere – but on my laptop, which is neither small nor quiet, back home. I drew upon my memories, I drew from the place I was at and places I'd been and places I'd never been. I borrowed from actual people to make the people in the story. I borrowed from myself to create the narrator – but you should know better than to think it's purely autobiographical. I borrowed from myself but also other places, maybe even a little bit of Walter Mitty. I utilized many of the tools available to me, and I think, for a quick first draft handwritten in the corner of a dark bar after sharing a few glasses of wine with strangers, I didn't do too bad a job.

In a very real way, this little story, all our little stories – I wasn't the only one who wrote something quick and easy and complete – are InkStains.

Failing to Adventure
Like an Adventurer

I met a friend for Sunday lunch at a statue – you can do that in Madrid – and from there walked to another statue. He'd show me The Crystal Palace, and I'd show him the Fallen Angel, both in Retiro Park. We walked to the statue of the fallen angel, representing all the agony being cast out of Paradise, we ate, then we walked to the Crystal Palace – The *Palacio del Cristal*.

I should admit something. I can talk a lot about the things we, as artists, should do to live a more thoroughly artistic lifestyle. But that doesn't mean I enact all of this all the time. I can get lost in myself. I can forget. And lately, I've been forgetting something absolutely vital.

I do not know this city. I do not know this country. I don't know the history or culture or language, and I don't know what's around me. I had walked through Retiro one time before, to get to the Fallen Angel, but I had entered at a particular entrance, walked a straight path to my destination, and saw nothing else but trees and park and maybe some flowers.

That had been a mission. This time, it was a meandering. An exploration. A random wandering that happened to include specific destinations.

I've been locked in my apartment most the past few weeks working on one project or another, banging out words, scratching through other words, rearranging still more to make them pretty. I've been talking with publishers about things I can't tell you about yet, and I've been making good progress on a relatively unique book project I'm not yet ready to share – but what I haven't been doing is wandering aimlessly.

Wandering Aimlessly. It should be all in caps and italics. What I mean is, it can be difficult to seek inspiration. Sure, I once went to a necropolis on an inspirational research trip; but it was directed by a particular project. I mean the kind of inspiration that births wholly new projects or adds new dimension to current projects.

When I went out for lunch on Sunday, I had no idea I'd be seeing the *Palacio del Cristal*, and I had no idea it would impress me the way it did. Thoroughly and completely and to the bone. There was some sort of art exhibit there – glass art, even – but it wasn't the art that spoke to me, it was the architecture. It was the ironwork and the glass walls, and the way it all worked together. Photos barely begin to capture what it felt like and what it inspired inside me. I can't tell you exactly, I can only say it lit some sort of fire inside.

And it was only the beginning. Later, that same trip out, we saw a store called *Ágata de Fuego* – agate of fire. I imagine they sell, I don't know, rocks, right? But I also imagine much more than that, so I'll probably work on a short story called "Ágata de Fuego." How could I not?

There was something else in the streets, too: a door, barred and barricaded, with an assortment of graffiti and a beautifully rendered dragon. Again, there's a story there, a thousand and one stories in that single doorway, I'm sure of it.

That's how inspiration works – you don't seek specific things to inspire you so much as you open yourself up to be inspired, you allow yourself to see the things you haven't seen – or things you've always known with fresh eyes and vantage points. You basically discover the mysteries and magic already existing in your world.

That's what I've been failing to do recently – those random wanderings that allow us to stumble upon unexpected inspirations.

What will I do to correct this? Two things. First, in the morning, I'll go out – I'll leave my apartment with a notepad, as I'd originally intended, find a place to sit – maybe a café, maybe a park, I don't know – and scribble nonsensically for thirty or sixty minutes or something, whatever that day allows. The second thing I'll do is go exploring. I'll walk down roads I've never walked and I'll keep my eyes open, I'll listen as best I can – maybe it will even help me with the language – and I'll allow myself to find the big and the small inspirations that are there right now just waiting for me.

KEEP WRITING DESPITE FAILURES
AND OTHER TRICKS

For InkStains, it was important, a part of the discipline, to push through to the end even when stories had gone in a wrong direction. Many never succeeded as stories. They never came together. But the best of the stories – my personal favorites, at least – came from both those that were pre-planned and given time to gestate and develop, and those that started with me scratching out an opening line and finding some way to follow that first sentence.

There's a lot to be said for practice, for discipline, for pushing through to the end, and I think most writers have to write a number of terrible stories before we're capable of writing anything of worth. That number varies depending on the person, what they've studied, what they've done, and what they've read. I know people who have spent time and effort re-writing – I mean copying, word for word – the stories of other writers in order to get a sense of their rhythm, to understand how it feels to write those words and that story. It forces you think about story in different ways, especially if you do it by hand – I mean writing it out, rather than typing it. Copy and paste won't work here.

The best way to learn to write, or to learn any art, is to start doing it. Go full in and forget, at least at the beginning, about how this will end. Will you improve? Definitely. Will those first stories be worth the effort? Yes. Will they be worth selling? Probably not. But even writing a story that doesn't work, that fails, that leads nowhere and accomplishes nothing, teaches us.

Another great help to improving your skills is critique. If you have never been part of one, find a critique partner or a critique group. Examine other people's stories with a critical eye. Never be destructive; there's no point to that. Look for the things they're doing that weaken the story and the things that strengthen it. Learn from both. You'll most likely recognize the same things in your own writing, so you learn by critically examining what others have done. If you have people critiquing your own work, pointing out your flaws, it's perfectly acceptable to ignore their comments. I mean, if you've got five readers and they say five different things, you don't need to do any of those things to make the story better. But if five people comment on the same thing, even if they approach it differently, a bit more attention is warranted.

The trick, of course, is to write, to keep writing, to face your obstacles and continue writing anyway. The trick is to make the time – forget finding the time, because you never will – *make* the time to write or art. Another trick is to get out and live a little. Do things, see things, experience things you've never experienced before, because these are the things that feed the fiction, and these are the things you'll draw from as you write. The concept of "write what you know" never meant simply to write about real things that have happened to you. It means to take from real life, to write about real emotions and real reactions, to borrow from your own past, your hopes and fears, your dreams, the mistakes you've made and the triumphs you've had, and *use* them. Use them thoroughly and completely to tell your stories. Because no one else, no one, not here, not now, not ever, can write your stories.

CONCLUSIONS

FINALE

InkStains has been quite a project for me, and it's become a massive part of my life. It started in 2013, on the first of January, when I wrote the very first InkStains story. Technically, it started before that, when I played with ideas for the project by scribbling names on sticky notes at my day job after deciding I would write a story a day because I wasn't being true to myself.

By the end of that first year, as I neared my 353rd story – every day except one day off per month – I was looking forward to the break and ready to stop. By the end of the first week in 2014, I was ready to start again.

I didn't until the next January, 2015. I did a third set in 2017, as I started the InkStains podcast that would run 100 episodes.

That, truly, is my story. My InkStains story. Sure, I've gotten a bunch of the stories gathered in little books, and I've just compiled a lot of the podcast talks into this book. So the story isn't really done, and it's never completely gone. Even if the episodes have disappeared from the Internet, I'll never truly and completely go away. I'll haunt you. Like a ghost, I'll live in the back of your mind. I'll be there pushing you to be productive, to be creative, to be assertive, to be whoever it is you are.

Because that's the most important thing. I started writing InkStains because I felt like the world, the day job and schedules and calendars and my lack of success, was eroding my sense of self. After a heart attack, after I returned from a confrontation with death, I realized I was doing everything wrong.

Today, I'm writing fulltime but still seeking my success. I try to help when I can, and the podcast has been a part of that, but it reached the point where I've said everything I can, at least up till now and in this format and structure. The time I spend on this show every week should be spent on my writing – on saying the other things I need to say, on telling the stories I need to be telling.

The truth is, I have a lot of stories to tell.

They've been gathering inside of me. The pressure continues to build. There just aren't enough hours in a day to let them all loose. I'll do my best to release what I can.

I have some books contracted for release, but I'm still working toward a success I haven't yet achieved. I feel like I'm making all the right kinds of progress – and I hope this podcast and this book have given you some of the tools that will help you achieve your own successes.

The most important lesson I can give, the most important lesson I've ever learned, is to never forget who you are. This will of course mean something different to everyone, but I've always known who I am, and I've always wanted to live as that truest version of me. For a long time, I put it off and tried to be something and someone I'm not.

It says it right on my business cards: Writer. Photographer. Adventurer. Man. Writer is front and center, the very first thing, and there's a reason for that. The rest are just descriptors. Together, they've got cadence. Individually, the other adjectives fail to create a comprehensive picture of who I am. But *Writer.* You can say only that, and you have a good idea of who I am, as long as you skip the stereotypes. I'm not pounding coffees at a Starbucks and scribbling nonsense in my Moleskine while wearing black tee shirts and smoking cloves. I'm not talking about writing anywhere near as much as I'm actually *writing,* and apparently the stereotype doesn't write. If it takes me three years to write a novel, and another three or even five years to work through revisions, and another year or two to sell it just so I can wait another year for it to hit bookshelves and die a quiet death – that's just another stereotype, ain't it? I don't know anyone who actually does this – not anyone who's older than college age. I won't lie – I've scribbled in Moleskine notepads at coffee shops – but I've scribbled complete stories, went back and revised them, then did something with what I wrote.

When it's time to live your life – the time is *now,* stop waiting – the best things you can do are the things that make you happy, the things that bring you joy, the things that bring you fulfillment.

There's a lot tied to that. I know. There are other obligations. There's a whole world out there that demands your attention and your time and your energy, and you can't ignore it. But if you ignore the parts of you that are truest, you'll find yourself, like I did, facing death, with no answer to the question of why you failed to do the things you wanted most to do.

Those things might not be artistic in nature. That doesn't make them any less vital.

Not everyone who practices art, who plays with their artistic tendencies, intends to make a living with their art or even to show it to anyone. That's fine. You have no responsibility to anyone but yourself. Play with your words and your pigments on your own time, in private, in secret – if that's what you want, it's perfectly fine. The rest of the world may miss out on a brilliant talent – but trust me, there are plenty of brilliant talents out there making the effort to be heard, and many of them have their hearts set on a particular goal that may be vastly different from yours.

A friend of mine, a good friend, someone I've known for decades, has his first novel coming out in the relatively near future. He has no desire to be a novelist or write for a living. He has his day job, something he's good at, something he enjoys. The writing is a side thing, and for him, that's perfect.

For you, that may also be perfect.

Another lesson, I suppose, is to not lament missed opportunities. Sometimes a chance comes and goes, and you don't take it – for whatever reason, often good reasons, often reasons outside your control – and other times, opportunities are offered to others but not to you. That's fine. There will be other chances. The world won't come crashing to an end just because you couldn't do this one thing.

I mean, every year there's a Year's Best anthology of stories, and every year you don't make it – every year I don't make it – doesn't equate to failure. It's not a sign of anything. I'm willing to bet – real and actual money – there'll be another Year's Best next year, and the year after that, and the year after that. The misses don't prevent you from taking advantage of opportunities still to come.

The time you spend cursing your luck and cursing yourself and wishing you had done something – that's time you could devote to doing something else, finding those other opportunities and chances, and finding your personal successes. Don't get weighed down by the things behind you when you haven't got the slightest clue what might still lie ahead.

I keep saying lessons.

These aren't lessons. These were never lessons. These were discussions. Yes, they were one-sided discussions – it's just me saying things – but nothing I've said here has been meant to be a hard and fast rule. I'm not even sure they're meant to be guidelines. I've been sharing the things that have worked for me, the thoughts and ideas and methods that guide me, in the very real hope you'll also find some of them useful.

We all may be unique, but it's sometimes shocking to realize how much our individual experiences are, if not universal, at least widely shared.

I expect you to take some of my suggestions and toss them. I hope you'll find meaning, and even truth, or something like truth, in some of what I've said. I hope you'll find your own thoughts and ideas and methods, your own paths, to follow.

WHAT'S NEXT? YOU DECIDE

What's your future after you're done with this InkStained book? I want you to go out and make things. Make stories. Make paintings. Make music. Make movies and sculptures and food and dances and podcasts. Explore everything you're interested in until you find what really works, what speaks to you on so deep a level you simply can't ignore it.

Final Challenge

You've read the book. Now it's time for your InkStains Challenge. But this isn't going to be a three day or seven day or even a year long challenge. This is forever.

I challenge you to be the best person you can be. Not to merely strive for the best in your art, but strive for the best in your everyday life. Help other people when you can, ask for help when you need it, learn more than required, teach what you know, choose kindness when you're able but stand up for yourself and your loved ones and sometimes strangers. Do not follow blindly, do not lead poorly, and try, when you can, to be a light in the darkness.

Because the times we live in — the times we've always lived in — can be filled with darkness and struggle. So try to always assume the best of intentions in everyone, even when the people around you seem to have given up in defeat or disgust.

And, because this is a book about art, be the best artist you can be. Find your voice and use it, achieve the goals you set out for yourself, and work on the assumption that, no matter how hard it seems to be, no matter what odds have been stacked against you, you can find a path to your success. Remember your success and your path do not have to look like anyone else's. Beware of anyone who proclaims theirs is the one true way — because there's no such thing. Be true to yourself.

Remember: your art is not an exercise in futility. It is essential.

ACKNOWLEDGEMENTS

This book captures the heart of my InkStains podcast, which aired 100 episodes across 2017 and 2018 with the Project Entertainment Network. I had a lot of help along the way, especially from my listeners, my fans, and my friends. Project Entertainment Network's Armand and Shelley Rosamilia were a joy to work with, and although I've brought this podcast to an end, that doesn't mean you'll never hear from me again. It was Brian Keene who suggested I take the things I said on the podcast and put them into a book.

I couldn't have done any of this without Mary "Mery-et" Lescher. She supported me emotionally through all of the InkStains stories and podcasts, brought me to live in places like Spain and Australia, and has been with me throughout my entire writing career. She backed me one hundred percent, just as I always backed her one hundred percent. Once upon a time, she worked for Disney Feature Animation on films such as *Beauty and the Beast, The Lion King,* and *Mulan.* She also made her own art. We once combined our talents to put out *The Christmas Letters,* a collection of her holiday cards and my stories. After earning a Ph.D. in Art History from Florida State University, she transformed her dissertation on the history of the Walt Disney Feature Animation Studio in Orlando into a book, *The Little Studio That Could,* forthcoming from The University of Illinois Press. Cancer stole her from me, and from the world, in June 2019, as I was finishing pulling this book together. I hope I've done something here that would make her proud.

www.ingramcontent.com/pod-product-compliance
Lightning Source LLC
Chambersburg PA
CBHW020855180526
45163CB00007B/2512